HEALING
THE
BODY POLITIC

HEALING THE BODY POLITIC

Rediscovering Political Power

Erwin A. Jaffe

 PRAEGER

Westport, Connecticut
London

Library of Congress Cataloging-in-Publication Data

Jaffe, Erwin A.
  Healing the body politic : rediscovering political power / Erwin
A. Jaffe.
    p.   cm.
  Includes bibliographical references.
  ISBN 0-275-94361-5 (alk. paper)
  1. Power (Social sciences). 2. State, The.   I. Title.
JC330.J34 1993
303.3'3—dc20   92-20051

British Library Cataloguing in Publication Data is available.

Library of Congress Catalog Card Number: 92-20051
ISBN: 0-275-94361-5

First published in 1993

Praeger Publishers, 88 Post Road West, Westport, CT 06881
An imprint of Greenwood Publishing Group, Inc.

Printed in the United States of America

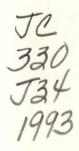

The paper used in this book complies with the Permanent
Paper Standard issued by the National Information Standards
Organization (Z39.48-1984).

10 9 8 7 6 5 4 3 2 1

For R. Peter Sylvester (1927–1986)—
"friend, most valued colleague, philosopher," mentor

Contents

Acknowledgments

I would prefer to believe—wouldn't we all?—that I see exclusively with my own eyes and think only original thoughts, but twenty-seven years of teaching have taught me otherwise. I am in debt to many others.

Two masters of political thought, Thomas Hobbes and Hannah Arendt, find themselves—unhappily, each would probably say—locked together on these pages. They are not present to object, so I am at liberty to weave together their work, and have done so. I have an especial regard for and owe much to Arendt's work, which is cited regularly and discussed at length in Appendix B.

Among the people I know or have known, there are many to thank. Gifted former students—I have been fortunate enough to encounter them everywhere—have been a constant source of inspiration. A few read parts of the manuscript, a difficult assignment in any event, but more so when one looks at the work of a former teacher. My particular thanks, accordingly, to Terry Savage of the University of New Hampshire, Manchester, for his thoughts and suggestions about Part One. Tim Finnegan was kind enough to read Part One. My thanks go to Jeffrey Stamps of the Networking Institute—and to his partner and wife, Jessica Lipnack—for sharing their view of contemporary organizational and communication models; to Peter L. Harris, who took time out of a hectic schedule to read a section and make suggestions; and to William A. Grimes, whose friendship—above and beyond his grasp of politics—is a source of strength for me.

Roby Harrington saw an early version of the first half of the manuscript and his thoughtful assessment persuaded me to reconsider and rework some of the material. Ed Millman did the same for a later version of Chapters 1 and 2. Linda Morley volunteered to examine Part One. David

Thomson shared thoughts with me about the content of the book. Karla E. Vogel of the University of New Hampshire, Manchester, has, with enthusiasm and cheerfulness, stepped in and helped me with the dreaded word processor. The staffs at the University of New Hampshire Library, both in Manchester and Durham, were most helpful. Joan E. Howard, a gifted reader and commentator, did a superb job of "scrubbing" the entire manuscript and made valuable suggestions in an upbeat, encouraging way. I am grateful to all of them.

Peter Savage, who died in 1982, first encouraged me to write and to submit to criticism. I have not forgotten his thoughtfulness, his excitement over the promise of a life in the academy, nor the rewarding but all-too-short times we had together as colleagues. The book is dedicated to R. Peter Sylvester. His Socratic "midwifery" drew out the best in faculty and students and he proved in deeds and words that the true teacher—and he was surely one of them—is first and foremost an ethicist. He is sorely missed by everyone who had the good fortune to work with and know him.

My extended family has contributed substantially to this book. I cherish the encouragement, constant support, and friendship of Sandra Gale Behrle. I thank my sister, Geraldine Applebaum, and my mother, Elsie Jaffe. My wife's mother and father, Amalie and Max Hirsch, her aunt and uncles, Else Nussbaum and Paul and Walter Hirsch, driven from home and polity by the Nazis, not only survived the agonies and losses but remained intact—they taught me lessons about being together available neither in books nor the academy. I—we—miss them. Finally, I cannot summon apt words for my wife, Marianne Hirsch Jaffe, she who reinforces, reads, reviews, "puts up with," and still believes. That the book exists at all, I owe entirely to her.

HEALING
THE
BODY POLITIC

Introductory Remarks

I speak positively about political life in this book. But I am aware of American impressions of politics, too many of them entirely reasonable.

— Politicians are not to be trusted.

— Voting is no guarantor of democracy.

— Corruption is society wide.

— Racism persists.

— Few of the governments of which they are aware—national, state, county, or local—function effectively.

— Violence is present in New Hampshire as well as New York City; in Iowa and Oregon as well as Milwaukee and Los Angeles.

— Action is rarely initiated to prevent potential ecological disasters or to respond when they occur.

— Revenue-raising systems provide insufficient funds for education or services for the elderly or impoverished, young or old, and the tax "system" is an un-coordinated maze of levies imposed differentially, variably, and unfairly by federal, state, and local governments.

— Some businessmen have walked a thin line between criminal and legal but indefensible conduct and have been encouraged or permitted to do so by friendly politicians, officials, and laws.

— Political parties speak for no principles but insist that to be in office, whatever the means used to get there, is preferable to being out.

— Unattended to problems fester nationwide, not only in inner cities, but in the national "infrastructure" and rural America.

— There are few occasions for public approval in spite of the wealth and good fortune of the American Republic and the constant reiteration of upbeat predictions by pundits, politicians, and professors.

In sum, the positive image of political life I present is counterpoised to ongoing negative experiences and attitudes. That is, the United States seems impotent with respect to domestic public or political affairs. Our much-praised private institutions, banks and automobile manufacturers among them, are not in much better shape than the country, and bailout scams have increased the public's cynicism. The larger manufacturing units in the steel industry are not well managed. Airlines, freed of what is said to be harmful government intervention, go bankrupt. The hospital and private medical system installs faceless bureaucratic systems to handle the most intimate and private of relations, while generating staggering and ever-increasing public as well as private expenses. Meanwhile, computers, which should be used to extend human intelligence—and sometimes are—have been applied willy-nilly to rote problems.

This book looks at what our political life has become and how it got this way, discusses the circumstances and beliefs that contribute to our lapses and failures, then speculates about the possibility of improving the situation. It is about politics but insists that the word does not refer to something dirty, despite the scandal-ridden version of politics that purports to serve us today. It attempts to explain why we believe that no political solution—given the present dominant view and conduct of politics—is likely to make things better, but also claims, with typical American optimism, that we can rediscover and then restore the virtues and values of political life.

My optimism is not rooted, however, in clever slogans or quick fixes, but in the conviction that what we have done can be undone. However, to understand political life, a complicated history and set of images—most unfamiliar to us and some the very opposite of what we have been taught to believe—have to be explored. I intend to do that, yielding neither to the temptation to popularize nor to hide behind academic obfuscation. Expect to find here, accordingly, serious discussions coupled with an effort to write in plain English.

PART ONE
POWER, POLITICAL LIFE, AND LANGUAGE

1

Initial Thoughts on Power

POLITICAL POWER'S FORGOTTEN MERIT

In politics, I am always, metaphorically speaking, with others; this requires, with respect to those others, awareness, consciousness, judgment, and "common sense" as well as calculations and guesses about their expectations and conduct. It also requires "power."

But many Americans—including journalists and scholars—equate power with control or domination or influence. They use sentences like these: "He is one of Washington's leading power brokers," that is, he knows which strings to pull; or "The United States is the most powerful nation on earth," in other words, dominates the world because of superior military and other forces. These sentences portray "power" as a person's or nation's dominance of peers, as something substantial and possibly quantifiable, whose possession diminishes others.

I do not wish—nor do I have the "power"—to eliminate these usages. They give an accurate but overly simple account of a word with complex meanings. I do ask the reader, however, to set aside the formula "power = control" and consider an earlier one: "power = the ability, capacity, or faculty to do, to act, to accomplish something." For example, the solitary writer's, composer's, or craftsman's "power" is a creative faculty that fills previously empty space. The idea of control is still present in this usage, but the thrust is different. Mozart's and Shakespeare's and Emily Dickinson's and W. E. B. DuBois' "power" consists in this: where before there was "nothing," now there is "something." This may be circular—Mozart's works of genius are explained by a faculty called "genius"—but it well states an often forgotten, positive connotation of

power, the human faculty without which there would be no music, painting, architecture, house building, society, constitutions, governments,
or everyday orderliness.

Consider power, however, as it appears *among* people rather than within
a single individual. Acting alone, I decide how to proceed with my play,
poem, letter, or symphony. Acting plurally, I take stock of others—or at
least attempt to do so—and power becomes joint, communal, collective,
plural; it depends on others, anticipates responses from them, and tailors
actions accordingly (though not always with precision). True, the solitary
composer or writer considers how the music or novel will "play"—how
it will be heard or read by others. But decisions about its shape and
qualities, though informed by these considerations, grow out of an individual's impulses, imagination, and inclinations as well as the work's
intended character. The writer's creativity is essentially individual,
whereas political power's central "business" is the presence, the needs,
the responses, and therefore the inevitable involvement of others. It controls yet simultaneously depends for support on those who are controlled.
That suggests a possibly unavoidable clumsiness in political life, which
from beginning to end is the by-product of "committees" rather than individuals, of the "many" rather than the "one." But clumsy or not, the
plural character of politics suggests that power cannot be approached as
if analogous to an individual's possessions. It is a phenomenon of
"togetherness."

This view of power—as a general, plural, or collective source of
achievement—has faded from our perceptions and discourse. We are
obsessed with "power over" things and with those who are said to exercise influence or control, those "in power" or "powerful," and their
opposites, the powerless. Plurally generated political power is rarely if
ever positively mentioned. Instead, we insist that power is something
to be shielded from or to "get hold of" and use to advantage in order
to do to others before they do unto us.

I would be insensitive and uninformed to pretend that the powerless
do not exist or to overlook abuses of political power—twentieth-century
history offers terrifying instances. But if power is seen exclusively as the
visitation upon others of what they would not choose for themselves,
its significance as the basis of action on behalf of rather than "over"
people—prime recent examples have occurred in the old Communist
bloc—is forgotten. Then we are at a loss to explain how or why people
can be pulled together into community or nationhood or how they come
to accept and even venerate documents, laws, or institutions. Nor can
the distinction between the legitimate and illegitimate exercise of control
be maintained. The thug and the policeman, the breaker and upholder
of the law, become indistinguishable, and neither government nor politics
any longer makes sense; they are not concerned exclusively with what

we are required to do, but also with what we wish and choose to do together. Governments undertake tasks that require joint activities and ongoing support. We note (and welcome or deplore) the arrival of a huge chain store in a nearby mall, sit in the resulting traffic jam, and curse the inadequacy of the highway. Convinced that the cause of the congestion, the store, is best managed privately and for profit, we ought not conclude that private highway networks are needed. Indeed, the idea is self-contradictory. Roads lead not only to the mall and new store but also to other businesses and, ultimately, home. A thoroughfare is public. It's not some corporation's or real estate dealer's, but "ours," a literal realization of the linking together I have called "power." In our system, private enterprise helps keep money and goods moving and people working but depends on public activity to hold things together—rules and regulations, a supply of money, the enforcement of some kind of order. If people believe that malls are exclusively private and forget that public expenditure and public access make them feasible, then the word "political" gives up its central or fundamental meaning. With it goes the understanding that there are rules of the game that make human enterprises possible and depend for their existence and workability on "power."

POWER AND VIOLENCE, DISTINGUISHABLE BUT OVERLAPPING

In political life, power and violence, separately or together, transform the world. Since they usually occur together, work in tandem, reinforce each other, and appear to foster similar responses (obedience and/or resistance), they are usually viewed as identical twins identically clothed. Look at them closely, however, and the resemblances diminish. Indeed, if they could exist in pure form, they would be opposites.[1] The existence of power suggests the presence of numbers and agreement; violence is "opposite" in that it *requires* neither support nor more than a single finger pressed against a revolver's trigger.

Political power, insofar as it originates in agreement, means that some person or agency has been *given* the right to make decisions for others whose acquiescence legitimizes the decision makers' actions. The agreement confers the right to rule or lay down rules, and these, in turn, produce regular, predictable conduct and stable relationships. Agreement creates power; power generates entitlement to rulership; rulership produces rules; rules encourage predictable conduct. However overwhelming the word sounds, as in "he had to contend with the powers that be," power provides for and enforces security. It is to collections of human beings what a security blanket is to a young child: to face legitimate rulers, comparatively speaking, is warm and comforting when compared to facing violence.

Violence substitutes submission for agreement, replaces empowerment with commands, and when widespread, warns the wise, or for that matter even the foolhardy, to be wary in the presence of others. It breeds chaos. A gun pointed at someone's head, the quintessential example of violence, produces immediate compliance but also forces the victim to consider reprisals. The order that guns "restore" (as in the phrase "troops were called in to restore order") seethes below the surface with the widespread urge to man the barricades again. The use of troops to threaten people with violence, if they do not immediately stop what they are doing, produces compliance, not agreement. Violence, therefore, begets counter-violence and disorder along with submission, while power initially reflects the desire for order, security, peace, calm, predictability, and reasonable expectations respecting others' conduct.

Why, then, are power and violence regarded as similar, connected, or identical? The answer requires consideration of the rhythm of human affairs, which is governed both by self-interest and public interest, even when individuals willingly work together on behalf of common goals. Once violence is superseded and rulers empowered, a new struggle follows, reminiscent of violence but different in that it takes place *within* a set of rules and mutually acceptable possibilities—a conflict over the questions, "who is or ought to be in charge?" "who will sit on the throne or in the legislature?" Once this struggle develops, power more closely resembles violence than it did initially.

Yet the difference between them is a political constant. When political power is operative, a "power struggle" takes place within ongoing rules of the game; those who agree to empowerment want the rules to operate but would rather be in control than be controlled. When violence is used, rules are ignored. Strength is substituted for them in the form of fists, weapons, tanks, explosives, and so on. Violence may be natural and necessary for predators who kill prey to survive, but for humans it is an option justified, not by an appeal to "nature" or "human nature," but to circumstances and situations. It is a response to a world that doesn't appear able to devise agreements, since they require a willingness to give and take, and fosters instead a single-minded concentration on self or cause, either of which is said to justify its usage. Power, since it opens the way to a degree of pacificity and represents the existence of a prior agreement to agree, does not require explanations and justifications; it is the by-product of give and take and presumably reflects an atmosphere in which everyone is to an extent willing to continue the dialogue. In contrast, the absence of the possibility of talk that resolves issues becomes an excuse for violence.

To reiterate: political power, whenever and by whomever exercised, means "empowerment," authorization to rule over, on behalf of, and in the name of empowering agents. It depends upon agreement and authorization. Violence also determines outcomes but ignores agreement or empowerment: it shapes events by employing superior or greater weaponry and strength. However, the two overlap. For example, once installed, those who seize rulership through violence seek and often secure support and therefore the semblance of empowerment.

Violence is often regarded today as equivalent to political action. Governments carry out raids that mirror the acts of terrorists. Assassination is seen as a means of disrupting or destroying not only individual victims but the nations they serve. An assortment of violent acts are described as "political": the forced movement of peoples; mass slaughter and genocide; the ostensibly "accidental" but actually planned (or at least acquiesced to) destruction of the lives of millions of forced migrants; the deliberate cover-up or generation of mass famines; the authorization of ostensibly unlawful actions by legally empowered officials; and the willful destruction of the environment in plain sight of but without serious resistance by governments. Many regimes and groups have been responsible for violence, including the Stalinists, the Nazis, the Chinese Communists, the Israeli government, the Union of South Africa, the Cambodian regime, the government of Iraq, and the governments of the United States of America and of El Salvador and Guatemala—in addition to individuals and corporations. The countless victims have included Jews, Christians, Muslims, Armenians, Turks, Kurds, Gypsies, Germans, Russians, Poles, African Americans, Native Americans, the people of Colombia, Guatemala, and other Latin-American nations, individuals of every description, and the earth itself. Violence against masses of persons, while described as "politics," does not differ from the gunning down of innocent children in a California fast-food restaurant, an escalating murder rate in the United States, or a willingness to look the other way in the presence of the homeless and rejected, a passive way of countenancing or even condoning the violence done to victims or to which they have succumbed.

These examples underscore the distinction I stress between power and violence. "Legitimate" governments or leaders do not bomb their own people, ignore their suffering, organize holocausts within their countries, fund terrorist activities, or point tank turrets toward citizens. Leaders who order an attack on their own people are not "powerful," if we use the word "power" precisely. They are desperate to retain control and willing to use violence to do so. During the twentieth century, however, the difference between the thug and the politician, between terrorists and the powerful, has been all but lost. An indubitable consequence is confusion over the distinction between orderly and disorderly conduct.

Conceived of abstractly or as pure, power—and by using the word "pure" I mean to refer here to the logical extension of the idea of power; "actual" power is always contextual—depends entirely upon cohesiveness, cooperation, acting together, and support, on the creation of an entity that represents the persisting togetherness of a community. Power's disappearance is signaled, its purity tainted, so to speak, when people pull apart—refuse to support what has been previously created, consented to, maintained. If that happens regularly or among large numbers of them, they are on the verge of empowering something "new" or opting for anarchy or total voluntarism, a situation in which they exercise selective vetoes, give and withdraw support for the rules and the regime regularly and at will. Power, in contrast, Thomas Hobbes (1588–1679) declared centuries ago, is "strengths united." When people "disunite," no longer acquiesce in an established, ongoing entity or agree that they are joined together, and when they regularly refuse to accept this or that act initiated by a previously legitimate regime, political power is evaporating. Rejection of the rules increases. Ties weaken among the constituents. The policeman, the governor, the president, the prime minister, and the city official no longer possess the legitimacy granted normally to holders of their positions. The supporting base of the regime weakens or has begun to crumble. To "see" this process, try the streets of many U.S. cities at night and more than occasionally in daylight, the subways of New York City at bad moments, or the nation's suburban sprawl, all of which feature free-for-alls and a persistent unwillingness to pay attention to rules. Or recall the recent disintegration of regimes in central and eastern Europe. Insistence that the rules apply to everyone except me is the hallmark of power's absence or impending disappearance. Violence is then substituted for civility, unless the population is unusually sophisticated and able to develop orderly procedures without any agreement to agree, that is, mature enough to understand the demands of authentic anarchy.

Furthermore, the idea that power is an entity, a fixed, material substance like a piece of property or a machine gun that can be purchased or grabbed, as in the phrase "in power," narrows it to mean an instrument of domination or control *per se*, treats the term as if it represents nothing more than a greater capacity to do harm, and thereby—by ignoring support and empowerment—converts it into a synonym for violence. It is certainly accurate to say that the Bolsheviks seized control of the Russian government, held it at first tenuously, and enforced their rulership by a mixture of progressive efforts, terror, murder, threats, and old-fashioned patriotism. But as recent events have proven, their empowerment was always in question, and the system they developed mixed a pinch of popular actions with a massive dose of repression. This regime, like so many other twentieth-century governments, all but eliminated politics. When political power *exists*, the policeman speaks for and the thief acts against the law. When political power *exits*, policemen become vigilantes and cannot be distinguished from gangsters. If Robin Hood is a popular hero and the sheriff the people's enemy, political power has been displaced or altered. If neither is empowered, then neither acts legitimately and both engage in violence when they take action against anyone, since the right to police others no longer exists. If Robin Hood, supported by the community, now polices the community, then the sheriff has become an outlaw. The entanglement, the seeming inversion, is that in our terms the popular figure is in effect rightfully in charge though he is an outlaw in the eyes of the monarch and officialdom. He becomes an incongruity, a "prince of thieves." A further complication is that the apparent King is actually a pretender; he has seized the throne and thereby done violence to the legitimacy of the Crown. Violence in this instance has overcome power. In the story of Robin Hood, of course, the "bad" and illegitimate ruler is replaced, the rightful monarch returns to "power," the "good" robber is recognized as an officer of the King, and the image of legitimate government and proper rulership is restored by a reversal of circumstances. And to reinforce the sense of legitimacy, the hero turns out to be the son of a nobleman. All along he had "really" been a leader who by inheritance deserved support!

Sometimes, perhaps often, legitimately empowered rulers use offices to oppress, destroy, or rob the people who empowered them. In our terms, they ignore the agreement that installed them, violate the conditions imposed on officeholders, and thereby substitute violence for power. Indeed, I have just described what must be the widely held perception of many African Americans, who never seem to be in position to participate fully and therefore live in an order established and consecrated by others. Once slaves, they now are citizens who to a large degree neither make nor alter the rules nor shape the society. For many of them, that situation makes the distinction between violence and power ambiguous. But if they see little virtue in power and cannot distinguish it from violence for obvious reasons, many other Americans also express ambiguity about those who are "in power" and apparently believe that they too have little or nothing to say in establishment of the rules. While there are undoubtedly many sources of this attitude, a primary factor is the weakening of connectedness, community, or polity. Political power undergirds what we choose to do together, and if people cannot recognize its value—if it has in fact lost its reason for being—the polity diminishes accordingly and violence threatens to become a primary vehicle for expression.

THE THREE ASPECTS OF POLITICAL POWER

What happens before power is actualized? There is something that necessarily precedes its appearance or actualization—an awareness, recognition, moment of consciousness—that makes people (a group, a tribe, those who find themselves in the same place) recognize the need to come and join together, to work out arrangements whereby living together in relative peace becomes a matter of routine. That awareness, though it precedes the actualization of what is usually called power, the right to rule, or even the empowerment I have discussed, is as much a part of "power" as anything that happens afterward. Once aware of the need or desirability of joining together, humans have the capacity or ability to associate and socialize, not as ants or bees do—guided by genetic codes—but as an invention or artifice that chooses to override or ignore "nature's" commands. For example, equality is in fact unnatural: our eyes, ears, and brains tell us we are different from, rather than equal to, one another. It is easy to find someone smarter, more athletic, or quicker of wit. Our political will or judgment, however, tells us that everyone must be treated as equals, that since the agreement to live together peacefully is artificed and requires constant maintenance, the parties to it are, in an elemental, though arbitrary way, equivalent to one another. The idea of equality, in other words, is artifice, a contrived way of building a world. Political power shapes and reshapes that human world in accordance with judgments about what is needed or desirable.

I refer to this anticipatory sense or feeling, an awareness or recognition, as the moment of initiation, that moment, time, or occasion when political power is about to come into being and become actual after having been merely a potential inherent in the presence of many human beings. This moment of initiation is important because it "starts up" power and, as I hope to show, also turns out to be necessary to preserve it. Unless recognition of the need to be joined together persists, and the potential or "potency" to join together is constantly re-actualized, political power cannot operate or function. Even after a government exists, this awareness is vital. Should it vanish, away will go the realization that power and its medium, politics, are necessary and/or valuable. And without that realization, questions will repeatedly be heard: "why should I pay attention to the rules?" "what's in it for me?"

To reiterate: Before it is actualized, power requires plural and mutual recognition that it is needed and desirable. It requires the same thing, now called support, after it has established a government, a leader, a church elder, a witch doctor—after the "politicking" has been formalized. Awareness of the need for power is before the fact and is its necessary condition (using the word "power" in the context of numbers of people rather than as a possession of individuals). Support must be ongoing after the fact; it maintains already-established political institutions. It is the later version of that earlier awareness or recognition. What leads to power's actualization and is necessary to its survival—the potential that is present beforehand and the support that afterward maintains effectiveness—are part of what might be called "the power manifold."

Obviously, where there is a "before" and an "after," there must be an "in between," which I call the foundational aspect of power. It, too, is complicated. Its existence is testified to when people have come together and efforts are then made to create an ongoing structure, framework, or constitution. This foundational aspect establishes and firms up the procedures that will govern political life.

I suspect that we have ignored the "before" (initiation) and the "in between" (foundation) at considerable cost. We are primarily aware of the third aspect of power, the politicking that takes place after governments and rules are in place, as everyone struggles to get what they need and want. This is the stuff of talk about power brokers and powerful nations. It is largely concerned with the exchange of support for favors, reduces political questions to a single issue, gratification, and thereby shunts aside consideration or understanding of common or society-wide problems.

Political power is far more complicated than this. Unless humans choose to risk constant contact without rules for order, they "come together" and generate power, the first aspect of which includes mutual recognition of the need and a preliminary agreement to agree (*initiation*). The relationships that follow are a distinguishable aspect of the power manifold. A framework of rules and institutions, formal or informal, written or unwritten, is constructed. Its purpose is to stay together and bring order and as much pacificity as possible to individuals' relations with one another by providing a kind of social glue (*foundation building*).

Established, operating rules, agencies, laws, and rules of the game are a third aspect of the power manifold. They follow initiation and foundation building. But these rulers and political institutions are no longer, strictly speaking, mere agents of those who came together and created power. They take on an official life of their own and now rule or govern those who empowered or continue to support them. This aspect of power—the actual operations of agencies of control and command and all the efforts to control them—is *politicking*. Yet it requires continuous reaffirmation in the form of *support*, which is today's version of yesterday's initiation.

Paradoxically, rulers are the mirror image of what we initially called power—the coming together of people to carry out and take responsibility for mutually desirable activities, for everybody's business. The powers that be are not mere agents of the empowerers or reflectors of that moment when joint action was initiated, as we first said. Political power, initiated and formalized by people working together, becomes the means to control its initiators, founders, supporters, and paymasters. This tension between support and command is a permanent fixture in power relationships and politics.

This makes for inordinate complexity, particularly when democracy, a system of governance that presumably responds to, rather than merely commands, the population, is what we desire. Complexity, however, does not mean "beyond comprehension," and I will later discuss the amalgams and tensions between command and support. Furthermore, important questions must be asked: Can we rediscover power, particularly those two aspects, initiation and foundation building, that give it a fuller and more congenial meaning and simultaneously curb domestic violence? Can or should we reinvigorate politics, the medium through which power is manifest? I believe the answer to these questions is yes. But an answer must be explicated. To that task I now turn, beginning with a discussion of the ambiguities that necessarily accompany political talk.

NOTE

1. For the discussion of power, violence, and politics in Chapter 1 and throughout this book, I am indebted to the work of Hannah Arendt (1906–1975). This chapter relies on her *On Violence*, first printed in book form by Harcourt, Brace and World in 1970. No one who reads this chapter and what follows and who knows her other writings will fail to recognize her influence; obviously, I cannot say whether she would have accepted my interpretation.

2

Politics and Ambiguity

Politics and ambiguity are bedfellows whose affinity for one another is at least as old as the argument between Thrasymachus and Socrates in Plato's *Republic* over whether the ruler or the ruled is advantaged by his position.[1] Wherever there is politics, ambiguous feelings—recognition of the need for it coupled with suspicion of what the need leads to—are inevitable because the sources of that ambiguity are built in:

— Political entities are not concrete or "real" in the same way that apples and automobiles are.

— Political relations are never fixed or precise. In politics, delegates or representatives stand in for others, but the exact meaning of representation can never be certain. Relations between leaders and followers or civil servants and the public they presumably serve are similarly imprecise.

— Political talk, except when it refers to exact numbers, as in elections, resorts to images, symbols, similes, and metaphors that often mean different things to different people.

— Political institutions are human constructs and therefore neither "natural" nor permanent. They change, and the changes produce disagreements, anger, tension, and a constant return to the thought that "I have to protect my own skin" and not worry about "the general interest."

CONCRETE AND NOT-SO-CONCRETE THINGS

We have concrete visual images for fingers, mountains, and automobiles but not for political entities. The United States of America, the State of Arizona, and the Kingdom of Jordan can be located on maps. Their wealth, physical characteristics, and codes of law can be described. We can speak of Arizona the place, but the moment we refer to "the people and State of Arizona," we aren't talking about a land mass. Its 3,385,000 people (1987 estimate) are a bewilderingly variable collection of living, thinking, doing creatures. Although Arizona exists, "it" is less concrete than either the people or the land that constitute it. So, too, are other political entities. They are abstractions, political "spaces" we treat as if they were concrete. We can talk about but not literally touch them. To use a fancy word, they are reifications.

So when we talk politics, our language often is necessarily non-literal. Note the Preamble to the Constitution of 1787: "We the People of the United States, in Order to form a more perfect Union, establish Justice, ensure domestic Tranquillity, provide for the common defence, promote the general Welfare, and secure the Blessings of Liberty to ourselves and our Posterity, do ordain and establish this Constitution for the United States of America." "The People" obviously didn't write, ordain, or establish the document; the drafters, now called Founding Fathers, did. Words like "the people" or "the United States of America" are figurative, not literal. We treat them as concrete—as we speak of corporations as persons—but they are not. To claim that four million people scattered along the Atlantic seaboard in the 1780s established a constitution is to sweep together into a single unit strangers whose awareness of one another was minimal. That's reification. It's also typical political ambiguity.

POLITICAL RELATIONS ARE NEVER PRECISE

The Constitution's framers *represented* their states and the people who lived in them. They were delegates sent by state governments to act on the states' behalf. But the delegates ignored instructions by replacing rather than fixing the Articles of Confederation and thereby violated the older document's rule governing changes, which required that *all* states ratify amendments; the Constitution declared itself "adopted" if nine of the existing thirteen states ratified it. So much for representing the existing "sovereign" states. Representation involves gaps between those who are represented and those who represent. Delegates often act on their own. There is not, nor can there be, a one-to-one or "perfect" relationship between the representative and those who are being represented.

Furthermore, since politics requires a person who, or entity that, stands for or represents others, there are bound to be differences of opinion about how well that "representing" is carried out or why it ought to be allowed. Attempts to adjust to or work out these differences are commonplace. But political talk often tries to cover up ambiguities—what is remote is said to be close, what is impersonal is portrayed as a person and, on occasion, an object of passion. These claims are always debatable. My skin is close, but what is said to affect me or to be good for me because it is in the "public interest" may seem less precious to me.

Similar ambiguities affect relations between leaders and followers. We can personify and locate heads of state, presidents, governors, congressmen, and members of parliament. But the exact relationship between titleholders or leaders and constituents is unclear. Does a leader tell followers what they should do, think, or hope or strive for? Or do followers shape the views and attitudes of leaders? Does the leader speak for all the people in the community or nation? The answers vary in each place and at different times. In the Soviet Union, not too long ago, the words of the general secretary of the Communist Party were "the law" and his disapproval a source of terror. Events have since proved how quickly such things may change. The relationship between officeholder, whether elected or appointed leader or civil servant, and the represented population is volatile, changeable, and ambiguous.

We don't necessarily follow leaders into every breach, approve of their every action, or remain convinced that what they do is for our benefit or the nation's. The likelihood of conflict between what is "good for all" and "good for me," already referred to, is a constant. When ordered to do so, I accepted induction into the United States Army. But it was not clear that my best interests were well served by giving up two years of my life to be dragged out of bed every morning, run ragged, and forced to wash dishes or peel potatoes; to exercise, march, and shoot rifles and mortars; or to be exposed to live gunfire in practice or possibly wounded in action and given a "purple heart" or killed and celebrated in a service during which someone says, "he gave his life for the good of his country, and that was a great and noble sacrifice." I might reply, were I still able, that this is moving talk, but frankly I would have preferred to be around to enjoy my youth and to give or listen to an oration rather than be the subject of one. To serve or represent one's country is, except when faced with an indisputably just occasion for war, a good example of how a political entity can engender ambiguous feelings in citizens—recognition of the propriety of service and a simultaneous desire not to be summoned.

An example of leadership in the United States is the House of Representatives, a body of persons who stand in for the people who elected them. But that "standing in" process is not clear-cut. Delegates elected by a plurality of voters best represent those who voted for rather than against them; once in office they are presumed to represent a district, which includes opponents, supporters, and the largest single group of all in the United States, non-voters. When a congresswoman speaks, supposedly the voice is not exclusively hers but her constituency's. Yet she is expected to manifest the wit and wisdom of a leader rather than the commonplace thoughts of the "average" citizen. In addition, *de facto* (as a matter of fact) and *de jure* (as a matter of law or right), an elected congressman has the right to speak for the district—until the next election. But wishing to stay in office or "move up," he must maintain support and be wary of offending voters.

Similarly, the U.S. president supposedly represents the entire nation. A sheriff represents a county's law, a judge "justice," an attorney her client. Were these roles perfectly played, the titleholders would be entirely representative and in effect disappear as persons. But this requires an effort equivalent to what Plato demands of his philosopher-kings, who never are self-seeking and who serve, not others, but "the good." Plato, however, was never able to persuade anyone—apparently not even himself, since his later works make lesser demands on leadership—that such selflessness is likely.

Sometimes we accuse leaders of "abuse of power," which suggests that there is an authorized usage of office or position on behalf of whoever or whatever can give that right. The individual who presents a subpoena to appear in court or the postman who brings a notice of jury service exemplify that authorization. The recipient of the notice is thereby brought into the direct presence of "authority" and "legitimacy." (See section on authority and legitimacy in Chapter 5.)

TRYING TO COMPENSATE FOR AMBIGUITY

Political language and references attempt to work around or clarify ambiguities by resorting to figurative talk—imagery, similes, metaphors, and symbols. We say that a leader is like the head of a family, using a simile for an image we understand. Head of family means person in charge; therefore, a head of government is in charge. But "like" and "the same as" are not equivalents, and there is always the possibility that a simile will create still more confusion. Think about it—is the head of any of our governments in any sense "like" a family head? Or we use metaphor, transferring a figure of speech in which an attribute or quality not literally applicable is assigned to an object. This opens up but also troubles the imagination. If we say, "all flesh is grass" or "you cannot step into the same river twice," meaning in both instances that life, like the grass and the river, like nature itself, is in constant flux, we may have uttered a truth, but we are not speaking precisely. Yet metaphors, like similes, are an inevitable part of political talk.

Plato likened leadership to weaving—pulling diverse strands into a coherent cloth—or to the true work of physicians whose proper concern is the well-being of patients, thus implying that the leader is physician to the populace. Leaders have been referred to as "lion-hearted." The late emperor of Ethiopia, Haile Selassie, was "the lion of Judah." The first president of the United States of America, George Washington, is "the father of his country." But this kind of talk can be perplexing. How does one "father" a country? What does one mean by the phrase "a thousand points of light?" Political talk is weighted down with such metaphors, similes, and symbols.

A typical symbol is a national flag, a mere piece of cloth on which a symbol or representation is printed or embroidered in specified colors. Replicated by the dozens, hundreds, thousands, they are displayed, hung, or waved. The United States flag, "the Stars and Stripes" or "Old Glory," consists of thirteen red and white stripes running horizontally across the width of the cloth "representing" the original states and a blue canton in the upper left corner containing fifty stars, each "representing" a "State" in the Union. The flag is used at ceremonies, flies over football stadiums and baseball fields during games, is carried in parades, flown in front of houses, and draped on coffins during burial ceremonies. The United States has a "Flag Day" (14 June), and the flag's treatment and handling are prescribed in sets of rules [Public Law 94-344]—it should be flown thus and so, hoisted briskly, taken down at a particular time of day, never desecrated. And it has given rise to song: "You're a grand old flag, you're a high flying flag; And forever, in peace, may you wave. You're the emblem of the land I love, the home of the free and the brave. Ev'ry heart beats true under Red, White and Blue . . . "; "Oh, say can you see by the dawn's early light/What so proudly we hailed at the twilight's last gleaming?" Americans are not the only people to respond to these symbols. Russians cheered wildly when the Soviet Union's red flag with the hammer and sickle was ripped down and replaced by the older Russian tricolor, and the actual dissolution of the Soviet Union was confirmed by the substitution of the Russian for the Soviet flag.

These pieces of cloth symbolize the nation and stimulate emotions. The flag stands for the country, and alleged improper treatment of it has occasioned more than one fuss in the United States. In the 1930s and 1940s there was agitation about the refusal of Jehovah's Witnesses to salute the flag, leading ultimately to a Supreme Court decision that the Bill of Rights protects religious resistance to the worship of idols. More recently, flag burning as a form of protest caused another flap. The intense feelings of those who would burn the flag or of their opponents, who would punish the flag burners, demonstrate the symbol's importance. Flags "represent" the nation. They purport to give concreteness to or reify the nation or polity by creating a symbol that "embodies" the abstraction.

Of course, symbols, metaphors, and similes are not exclusively political. To refer to someone as an ass or a fox is to speak in similes. But in politics that kind of talk is more than an attempt to be colorful. It reflects built-in ambiguities. The term "Founding Fathers" makes the Constitution's writers authoritative. The notion of a statesman as a master weaver does the same. Cliches—the leader as shepherd or as captain of the ship of state—portray leadership and politics similarly. The polity exists and has captains because the community at large needs to be guided, taken care of, made safe—those conditions constitute the public interest. But such talk is not always persuasive. Who is capable of abandoning self-interest? And where are the physicians whose sole concern is the well-being of the patient?

POLITICAL INSTITUTIONS ARE ARTIFICED AND ALTERABLE

Institutions (the state, the nation, the church, the family, the corporate and financial structure) are not found in nature. They are fabricated—given life by human creators. They are also intangible objects, unlike persons or the sun. But however intangible, they often outlive their creators and thereby remind us of the work of artists.

Perhaps a comparison of "politics" and "drama" will illustrate the artificed and alterable character of political life. Plays, films, and political institutions are authored by humans and often live on after their originators die. They involve "representation." In drama, actors impersonate the characters, interpret the lines, and thereby give meaning to the original texts. Two productions of Shakespeare's *Henry V*—the film directed by Sir Laurence Olivier twenty-five years ago and that in 1989 by Kenneth Branagh—represent the original very differently, though each follows the text impeccably. In ancient classical theater, the distinction between actual events and staged presentations was reinforced by the actor's mask (*persona* in Latin, from the Greek *prosopon*). Masks, not the "real" faces behind them, are seen by the audience; they are characters impersonated in the drama. In modern theater, the same effect is achieved without masks by the professional actor whose skill includes the ability to disappear "into" the character played. Actors in performance become, insofar as possible and for a time, indistinguishable from the fictional beings portrayed. Their skills mask their persons and personalities.

What has this to do with politics? Simply this: citizens, political leaders and officials, representatives and senators, bureaucrats and soldiers, are like the *persona* of ancient theater and the actors of today. They take on roles though they remain themselves and as individuals are, at least initially, quite distinguishable from the roles they play. As members of organizations, human beings become, in a manner of speaking, characters or role players. In sum, it is easy to believe that "all the world's a stage" and that actors, business persons, and politicians are similar or even identical because they stand in for someone other than themselves—a character in a play, a corporation's stockholders or management, or a district's population.

Given the current importance of mass media, it is more than ever tempting to treat politics as if it were entirely an entertainment. The temptation is heightened by talk of images, image building, photo opportunities, and staged events. When a president's voice quivers or tears glisten in his eyes, we wonder whether he is moved by the issue at hand or simply a good actor or a total phony, especially since political leaders, like actors, are now coached to appear informed, sensitive, gentle, tough-minded, vulnerable, responsive, determined, athletic—to be or not to be as the occasion presumably warrants. And like other performers, they earn ratings. This theatrical element, the result both of extended media coverage and awareness of its importance, reinforces politicians' belief that they are on stage even when they permit or encourage interviews at their private homes or when citizens insist that politicians' private lives ought to be exposed in public. Small wonder contemporary Americans have come to see representation as related to acting and entertainment—and to judge accordingly. Small wonder, too, that traditional American suspicions of politicians have increased. Since actors, after all, are never themselves, we ask, "just who are they?"

But long before the advent of television, "double lives"—and the ambiguities inherent in officeholding—were evident in politics. The phrase used at the death of a monarch, "The Queen (or King) is dead; long live the Queen (or King)," distinguishes title from person. The *office* or *role* of queen and king is immortal like the body politic, realm, or Sovereign; the living person holding the title is a mere mortal and in time expires. Similarly, the old English notion of "the King's peace" refers to the maintenance of civil order, to a general state of affairs rather than to the personal life of a monarch. If I disturb that order and rob travelers on the highway, I offend and harm the victims, but also the realm itself, that abstraction called England, whose good order and peace, secured by a Sovereign, is shattered by my conduct. My prosecution and punishment is in the hands of the Crown, which exists to maintain peace and to guarantee everyone's safety not only within but also outside of the home. The traditional understanding of criminality is that the victim's destruction, loss, or injury, obviously important and in need of sympathy or revenge, is comparatively inconsequential when weighed against the damage to the community at large. For when attacks are left unpunished, civil society as such dies, and, in time, no one is safe.

However, we increasingly have difficulty distinguishing between "the community's peace" and an individual's or group's sense of the correct order of things. Take as an example contemporary emphasis on the feelings and views of family members seeking revenge for the murder or abuse of a loved one. Widely reported by the media, these personal responses, understandable as they are, weaken understanding of the basis for and character of criminal prosecutions—of how the State, an abstraction requiring a personal representative to become concrete, acts on everyone's behalf in such instances. They therefore diminish appreciation of the symbolic element in politics, since literal focus on the victim, family, and criminal underestimates other citizens' admittedly emblematic but unquestionably equal stake in the community's (or King's) peace. The mother who says, "I will not rest until the criminal who attacked and killed my daughter is executed," cries out for revenge, which she and many others equate with justice. But in political life the many persons who together make up the community have the greater stake in bringing to justice those who violate its order. "The King's peace" or "general welfare," typically figurative examples of political rhetoric, attempts to make concrete the safety and security of an abstraction, the nation or community, by protecting real, existent humans. The shift from abstraction to concreteness depends on realization that every person has an *identical* interest or need: If anyone may be attacked, so may I. The ancient saying, "*salus populi suprema lex est*" (Cicero), "the safety or welfare of the people is the supreme law," well expresses that idea.

Role playing is not confined to office and title holders. When a citizen votes, though each acts separately—marks the ballot secretly—he or she momentarily behaves as a character in a scenario written by the civil code, law, or constitution, since the process of voting is as scripted as the lines in a play. Voters represent the political community because they perform a function deemed by some societies as vital. They also appear in public and act publicly by going to the polls, while hidden from view and acting privately—individual preferences remain unknown to the public. That is why a secret ballot that offers a single candidate or option is a contradiction in terms. Its secrecy is farcical, since it presents exclusively an already-ruling point of view and provides no opportunity for individual preference. Completed single-option ballots are equivalent to blanks. They duplicate one another, and sameness renders them antipathetic to the secret ballot—unless the voters choose to return them unmarked. Single-option ballots, regularly employed in the past in the Soviet Union and used by the Nazis to conduct a plebiscite in Austria after Hitler had seized that country in 1938, cannot be described as secret, whatever any government declares. In contrast, the secret ballot masks individual votes and the overall results—massed arrays in which individual values or votes are summarized—hide individual choices in a tally.

Politics always generates these representational activities with multiple and often ambiguous meanings. They have occurred in many forms: the Greek idea that true government serves the general interest (to govern is to serve; to be ruled is to be advantaged); the later belief that a king is God's emissary on earth (the ruler serves God, therefore the population at large); and the contemporary belief that voting is a blend of participation, rulership, and obedience.

THE MEANING OF POLITICS' AMBIGUITIES

Politics and its study, political science, have borrowed language from other areas. Among the ancients, rulers were described as weavers, pilots who steer the ship of state safely past the rocks, physicians who work solely for the health of the patients. Theatrical terms have been echoed in political talk—its dependence on dialogue, use of representation, and even pageantry. But in spite of contemporary television's capacity to bring events to us "live," political life is or ought to be readily separable from the impersonations and created scenarios of dramatists. Governments and corporations may concoct fictions and indulge in playacting, but their impact on our lives is far more direct than any movie's. Politics may be entertaining, but is never mere entertainment; when it fails, the blood on stage is real.

Furthermore, all members of a community are in or affected by politics whether they realize it or not. They regularly deal with and are dealt with by individuals who represent them. But they are both audience—watching, applauding, hissing, sitting in judgment—and participants in what is being watched. Similar double meanings affect every phase of politics: A president of the United States speaks for and in the name of the people of the United States but is also the proxy for a political party—a part of the population. Congressmen represent and are elected by the voters in districts. The representative represents, is someone's agent, is not herself, strictly speaking. The same principle is true of states and governments—they stand for or reflect an agreement or inherited, habitual practices that constitute the basis for their existence and yet they rule over their supposed constituents. In each instance, the ambiguity is built in.

In politics, ongoing tension between my interest and "ours" is normal. Political entities always reflect the needs and concerns of more than one person—and that is true even in dictatorships. By attending to "general" affairs, politics bridges the gaps or fills in the spaces among people and produces a community or state, a single entity with a particular name. But since that entity stands for something other than itself, the pretense of singularity gives way to the fact of plurality, and the ambiguities already mentioned pile up—and there are more. Kings have been portrayed as God's divinely chosen agents as well as embodiments of the will of the people. Presidents and prime ministers claim to speak on behalf of large numbers of people. Communist leaders once declared that they were executors of historical mandates derived from the writings of Marx, Engels, Lenin, Stalin, and Mao. But whatever they claim, leaders have also been agents for political parties, special interests, close friends, family, or themselves.

Governments and political communities, then, are "everybody's." I suspect that most people intuit this, whatever they are told or taught.

Americans may say that they have little regard for politics or politicians, condemn presidents and congressmen for mismanagement, or call for the end of politics. But they recognize, I believe, that politics ought to be better, that handling the public business makes special demands on officeholders, that political organizations exist to reflect widely distributed needs and interests, to be selfless, mere *personae* behind which stand the concerns of a larger population. And the law provides for similar political restraints among financiers and brokers. Leaders, in sum, are expected to meet special standards; disgust with and anger at them reflects these intuitions. This remains true despite the detritus of twentieth-century politicking—bloody, futile wars; killing fields; totalitarian monstrosities (whose day may at last be at an end) bent on dehumanizing humanity; bureaucrats who think they are the masters rather than the servants of citizens; "power brokers" and manipulators who bilk the public realm; and gangs who regard themselves as outside the law. Political life does not and probably cannot survive when supervened by these selfish, narrow, or monstrous purposes. It depends upon commitment to the general needs of a public and is supposed to be the property of all, the plaything of no single individual. That many Americans say they no longer believe this possible is an ominous sign.

Perhaps the depth and seriousness of our doubts is novel. But what is not new is that the idea of representation always runs into the urge to establish and maintain individual identity. No system of representation can ever fully resolve this tension, which eases but never entirely disappears, even when confronted by widespread understanding of general or community-wide purposes.

NOTE

1. Thrasymachus contends that justice is always defined by rulers in accordance with their interests. Socrates' lengthy reply—for all practical purposes much of *Republic*'s text—boils down to an analogue: as the doctor's real interest is the health of the patient, so the ruler's real interest is the well-being of the city. Thrasymachus sees the ruler as advantaged by his position; Socrates sees the polity or city as the beneficiary of rulership.

3

Some Thoughts about Connections

TWO VIEWS OF CONNECTEDNESS

Thomas Hobbes (1588–1679) and Hannah Arendt (1906–1975), political thinkers separated by three hundred years and by astonishing changes in human affairs and thought, employ very different premises. Hobbes portrays men as atoms or particles, discrete, isolated, impelled to move toward and away from objects of desire and fear. Since the same objects of desire act as magnets to different persons, and since as a result they are always in short supply, humans clash, compete, become mutually destructive. Furthermore, they can never be satiated: a man without desires, Hobbes says, is dead; he is no longer moving. In life, there is no end to desiring. Trapped in a world that does not offer enough to go around and in which, even if supplies increase, desires perpetually escalate, humans are doomed to war with one another until they learn to reason and conclude that they must achieve peace and can do so by contracting with one another. The alternative is to live permanently under the gun. The polity, then, is an artifice that exists because of human selfishness, never-ending shortage, and the impossibility of fully satisfying anyone. When men finally learn to ratiocinate or reason, they agree to exchange unbridled liberty to do as they will for rules and order presided over by a Sovereign. A commonwealth has been founded; permanent war, chaos, and universal paranoia are thereby avoided.

Arendt sees humans as born into a plural world. Their existence is shaped by plurality, the presence of human clusters; they are not, as Hobbes had maintained, individuals driven into contract by the harsh realities of unregulated liberty. Although each is genetically unique, uniqueness as a condition depends on plurality: humans are "selves," individuated and made complete only in the presence and through the recognition of others. Arendt maintains that my individuality depends on others in whose presence it can be confirmed; they recognize that I am an individual who appears before them, that I am someone other than and distinct from each of them. The polity, which joins together people, is a "space of appearance," to use her phrase. That is, political entities— brought into being by the generation of power, by actualization of what is only a potential in single, disconnected individuals—are spaces in which, since I join with others, I can be seen or make myself visible because others are present to see me. Connectedness is elemental in the human condition or manifold, while genetically assured individuality, ironically, can be realized only when I am joined to others.

Although both see human connectedness as complex, Hobbes thinks reasoning brings it about; Arendt believes that plurality—the given presence of many human beings—means that being connected to one another is inherent in the human condition, while individuality, though genetically guaranteed, is in effect plurality's by-product. Genetic (natural) uniqueness is the necessary but insufficient condition for individuality, which is, in the context of human plurality, an aspect of the artificed space of appearance. Both writers wonderfully portray the tension between individual and group, but in this respect neither entirely speaks a language that provides imagery we can fully grasp—in Hobbes' case we also have trouble believing in a process that depends on everyone reasoning his way into contractual agreement, and so the problem must be looked at in a slightly different way.

Both are correct to claim that human beings learn to live with one another within a framework of rules, but to understand how that might work in our time requires examination of what actually connects, separates, and reconnects us and then, again, pulls us apart. But we do not live as Hobbes portrays us in Chapter 13 of *Leviathan*, hypothetically minus the capacity to speak and reason. Although there are days when it seems otherwise, we do not simply grunt at one another and exist as isolated, mutually hostile particles at constant war with one another. Neither, as Arendt suggests, are we necessarily conscious of our individuality as a reflection of a plural humanity. Let us therefore try to understand the problem of connectedness and self-centeredness by using familiar images. That done, we ought to be at a point where the relation between "connectedness" and "politics" can be better understood.

BEING CONNECTED, SEPARATED, AND RECONNECTED

We are formed by the union of two human beings. Our existence begins in the comfort, warmth, and safety of another's body. During gestation, we are connected to and dependent for nourishment on our mothers. Following birth, interdependence keeps us tied to others, and as we grow older we are reminded regularly that no person is an island, that we have obligations to one another, that we must be good neighbors, have pride in our communities, respect the flag, love and serve our country, ask not what our country can do for us, but what we can do for our country, recognize common ties to all of humanity, and accept responsibility for and help those unfortunates who have insufficient food to feed their children here or in distant, seemingly exotic parts of the planet.

But our bodies and minds speak to us individually in a different language. Neither my broken bone nor my toothache is shareable literally. I can talk about my pains, physical or emotional, but no one else truly feels them. Conversely, there is no certainty that I care to or will spend my time thinking of the needs of others when my needs—and as Hobbes warned, my desires—constantly tug at me, urging me to take care of "number one" first.

So the sense of human connectedness and separation weakens and strengthens alternately. The infant is ejected from the womb, pushed out into the world. But, despite the severed cord, he or she remains connected to the mother. The child is not liberated or independent because untied: human infants are dependents in need of shelter and nurture. They cannot navigate by themselves; their vision is poor, senses weakly developed, and neurological and skeletal development incomplete (although the encoding that shapes maturation is present). Furthermore, presuming that they are to be more than mere eating, sleeping, digesting machines, the young must be taught by those who protect them, including lessons in how to speak the common language. Crying and fussing at first suffice as signals, but they give way to talk and dialogue.

In short, though the initial connection between the newborn and others appears to break dramatically, humans reconnect. Severing the cord cuts off direct nourishment but not the need for nurturing or connectedness. At life's earliest stages, bonds consist primarily of protective and feeding systems for the young as well as efforts to teach language and acceptable conduct. But once learned, shared language and behavior patterns become as natural as the pumping of the heart or the grinding of the digestive system. The potential and equipment for language are physiological and anatomical. Language development, however, depends upon a social context; the particularities of language are rooted in our connections and placement within the humanly constructed world.

The infant's shift from making sounds to imitation of overheard language patterns suggests that by understanding when spoken to and by learning to speak in response, the child has been *reconnected* to other humans. The new link is less literal but no less real: humans share not blood but the sinews of a complex lingual system, an organized sequence of sounds with consistent, coherent meanings. And there are other languages that develop as aspects of the presence of others. We learn mathematical languages, which have been artificed in their entirety, products of an ancient but ongoing dialogue. Music speaks to us within a framework of its own cues and "talk." We are moved by and respond to Mozart and the Beatles, and these responses to rhythm, melody, harmony, and counterpoint are another construct of as well as testimonial to our connectedness. Even now Mozart instructs us in how a single voice, singer's or instrument's, can stand out from, yet interweave with, other voices, usually an orchestra's, but also instrumental and vocal combinations of many kinds. These are lessons in connectedness and individuation that cannot be fully expressed in spoken and written languages but are fully understood by those who have learned a particular version of the general musical language. An orchestra or band is precisely a combination of individually identifiable performers and voices who come together and whose performance blends. And so music, wherever it has appeared, whatever its development, whether a single individual chanting or a chorus memorializing the dead, is a language that reminds us of our connections to one another. As much as we wish to live up to our individual potential and gift and come to grips with our own identity, there is little doubt that these connections are as much a part of life as what we see in the looking glass.

There are other connections arguably critical to human well-being, not the least of which is the founding and ongoing operation of a linking entity other than sexual partner and family—be it a small nomadic tribe, a self-sufficient village of farmers and woodworkers removed from contact with the outer world, a sprawling empire, the principalities of medieval Italy, a contemporary metropolis, or a corporation. These conglomerations, each with a different history and etiology, share the ecological or spatial realities of the earth: that many beings exist on the planet; that humans are clustered together; that their survival requires usage of population-supporting soil; that they come to employ principles of work differentiation and division of labor that lead to the blending together of disparate tasks, each undertaken by someone who becomes a specialist. They produce institutional structures that become the primary means to continue joint undertakings while welcoming, at least under ideal conditions, diversity, individuality, and even the possibility of self-esteem. Languages, of course, provide important glue, making it possible for spatial groupings to function together—without a common language, the ability to communicate with neighbors is bound to be curtailed. When humans recognize the need to group together, to build a foundation for a community, they have discovered and initiated politics.

Those who believe this to be so argue accordingly that political life is among the primary foundational and operational aspects of human activity. Without politics, they suggest, without the coming together of individuals, no foundations can be laid for orderly individual lives; nor, given the presence of others, would peaceful daily existence be conceivable. It is not even crucial that these joining-together processes specifically lead to the establishment of formal governments. The point, rather, is that the regularities requisite to living together are necessary, however or wherever they are said to exist and whether rulership is or is not deposited in something called "a government."

Political connectedness is an arranged and artificed effort to initiate ways to cope with the presence of many humans on earth, following which there usually is an additional effort, namely, to live up to convictions about what it takes to be civilized. Humans, like it or not, share territory, concerns, and problems. Necessity may be the initial author, but ingenuity and creativity soon follow and help people invent a variety of ways to live together. Human civilization, accordingly, goes well beyond protection of turf, as it should, since, after all, even supposedly less civil animals spray boundaries to warn interlopers that they invade at peril.

In politics, therefore, we move from mere turf management to the complex phenomena of initiation and foundation, the initial coming together of people into some arrangement that produces "governance." As we learn to understand these initiating and foundation-laying events—though they can never be reconstructed in a firm chronology—we realize their significance for beginning and maintaining everyday political operations and activities in every society, not excluding the United States with its existent federal system and many governments, national, state, local, multi-state, and so on. Again, these operations are not spontaneous but require premeditation and continuation of the support originally associated with the founding, since that is always in danger of evaporating—as the Communist Party of the Soviet Union has discovered—even though governmental or political institutions are in place.

To sum up: nature makes young humans dependent but also endows them with independence and singularity, first by guaranteeing genetic uniqueness and later by providing a capacity for separateness that is a sign of maturation. Human connectedness persists, however, although it can become something of a struggle, since we cannot live in isolation nor are we, like bees and ants, interchangeable parts or functionaries of some larger, intricate structure engineered by nature. In human terms, the family, the tribe, the nation, are neither parallel to nor reminiscent of beehives and anthills.

PULLING APART: INDIVIDUALISM AND GROUP IDENTITY

American society, committed to the individual, revels in ignorance of the connections among humans. The sense of joining together has always been weakened in this large country by events and ideas that stress moving on to new territories and accomplishments. Today it is not uncommon for families to scatter among many states or settle on the two coasts. Further, we portray "success" as individual, irrespective of the advantages or disadvantages of birth, education, and access to position. In the United States, however, two different and apparently opposite ways of segmenting and responding to the populace compound the difficulty of maintaining the sense of connectedness and limit appreciation of the commonweal or public space. I call these "The Gospel of Individuality" and "The Gospel of Reified Groups."

The Gospel of Individuality

The American gospel of individuality preaches that each human being is an isolate perpetually in conflict with others. The physical spaciousness of the new republic and its reputation as a place of unlimited opportunity have contributed to this doctrine and to the disinclination to acknowledge connectedness. Our stories emphasize individuals who climb from poverty and obscurity to wealth and prominence. We regard institutions—family, friends, schools—as of lesser importance than individual achievement. We speak arrogantly of the New World, as if no human lived here until its "discovery" by Europeans. Authorities in various nations (Spain, Holland, England, Portugal, France) savored the possible enlargement of their respective domains and acted accordingly. Over time, however, events overtook them. Awareness of this "new" space, seen as virgin territory unoccupied except for a scattered handful of "natives," spread across Europe, drawing groups, then wave after wave of immigrants. Distance, novelty, and the presence of seemingly unlimited space altered the habits they brought with them. Meanwhile, among philosophers, the notion of new space in the world gave impetus to speculations about a time when the earth was in a more pristine condition and land widely available. They saw pre-civil humanity as paranoid and mutually antagonistic (Hobbes); mellow, innocent, and free of all social ties (Jean Jacques Rousseau, 1712–1778); or temporarily peaceful in the pursuit of property and its usages (John Locke, 1632–1704). In each instance, they existed naturally, without elaborate political institutions; that is, the discovery and the idea of new space in the world stimulated, as did the newly emerged market system, a belief that men as individuals, not men in polities, were central to human development and achievement.

For the new Americans the dominant theme, in time even in the religiously based Puritan commonwealth, was that any hardworking individual who knew how to seize upon opportunity, if need be by "moving on" toward the seemingly never-ending frontier, could reach heaven on earth. In the process, the idea of nation was reduced to and equated with mere turf, and turf redefined as "nature waiting to be used." Heaven, soon enough, was redefined as accumulation of wealth.

The Gospel of Reified Groups

Somewhat ironically, once the claim that individual effort ensures success proved to be a half-truth (as giant structures, particularly corporations, new monopolies, and governments achieved control of the economy), when individuals failed as a result of forces that overwhelmed them, when ethnic and racial mixtures generated new tensions, Americans began to emphasize the presence of different groups who, while not living in totally isolated pockets, carried with them distinguishing marks of one kind or another. In particular, these distinctive traits held true for members of groups relegated to secondary roles and greater-than-average impoverishment. Nativists declared that being visibly, that is, racially or culturally, different, these groups were ill-equipped to deal with American life; in time, the singled-out groups took up a similar cry, called attention to their specialness, and changed it from a mark of inferiority to a badge of distinction, pride, and honor—and also a means for capturing control of city hall. Individuality, to an extent, became an offshoot of group membership.

Another source of group identification was the forced settlement and enslavement of Africans during the colonial period and early days of the American Republic, which introduced into the population a visibly identifiable racial group who from the beginning had no rights. They were said to be inferior, therefore possessed neither of equal standing as members of the human race nor of the celebrated "rights of man." As a result, they had no entitlement to political community with whites.

The view that African Americans are "other than human" has been reiterated again and again in American writings. Thomas Jefferson asserted their inferiority, and he and James Madison, admitting that slavery was unjust, thought the problems posed by freed slaves could be solved only by shipping blacks to Africa, a startling notion given that a majority by that time had been born on this continent. In succeeding years, southern writers defended slavery by insisting that blacks were inferior—childlike, barbaric, sexually aggressive, and dangerous—and therefore had to be kept under the tutelage of kind masters. The infamous *Dred Scott* decision (1857), just prior to the Civil War, allowed that blacks could not be members of the founding political community and therefore, *de jure*, as a matter of right and law, were not beneficiaries of any ongoing, permanent constitutional protection. The Supreme Court declared that they were "not intended to be included" as citizens by the Founding Fathers but were "a subordinate and inferior class of beings, who . . . had no rights or privileges but such as those who held the power and the government might choose to grant them."[1]

The continuing arrival of divergent ethnic and religious groups further heightened American awareness of group differences, particularly as immigrants' descendants were increasingly labeled as Irish or Italian Americans, and so on. They were pressured by outsiders to assimilate and later by their grandchildren to preserve pre-migration heritages or histories. The ethnic-religious identities of Jewish immigrants, made palpable by distinctive religious, lingual, and cultural patterns, had the same effect. More recently, previously unnoticed groupings (unnoticed in the sense that their "identity" had become either a badge of inferior position in the society or an object of ridicule) have become visible as groups struggling to authenticate their equal standing in the community— women and gays, for example.

These separations have become so routine that they have entered the language, further compounding the problem of sorting out individuality from group identity and both from political connectedness. The truth is that there is no such thing, insofar as one attempts to describe character, personality traits, potential for achievement, or the possibility of political connectedness as a "black" (or white or yellow or red) person. There are individuals with identifiable characteristics, skin coloration, gender, cultural heritage. But the adjective "black" does not describe a set of human qualities any more than do "white," "yellow," or "red." They refer to indelible surfaces and particular histories, not significant qualities related to capacity, faculties, potential, morality, or sheer humanness. Of course, there is a deeply rooted lingual tradition that reinforces allegations of difference, for example, the association of darkness, blackness, and black with "danger," "inferiority," and "evil." It is equally impossible to speak with clear meaning of "gay" or "straight" persons. One can describe individual acts as heterosexual or homosexual; but the characterization properly refers to the acts themselves not to the entire gamut of characteristics that make up a person. One can refer to a black or white person who did X or Y, but no sense can be made of the leap from that observation into talk that characterizes an act as derived from "black" or "white" or inborn or genetic behavioral qualities. Neither is there anything but the most restricted precision in the sentence, "she is a Catholic." It cannot describe human characteristics comprehensively other than suggesting practices that a given individual is more or less likely to engage in, approve of, or support. Whatever the act, writing or performing a piece of music, painting a wall, or refusing to study, use of the adjectives "black," "white," "female," "Baptist," or "gay" to describe its author is senseless talk such as Thomas Hobbes often referred to, to wit, "round square"—unless it is the expressed purpose of the author to emphasize or depict the circumstances of people who are described or who describe themselves in those terms. While differences among human beings are "real" enough to permit us to group and label, the labels provide no reliable indicator of individual behavior. This manner of speaking, of referring incessantly to groups, relished by advocates and opponents of these groups alike, conflates surface labels with deep meanings. But we are habituated to and use this kind of language.

Additional groupings, many of them conjured in the halls of academe and corporate board rooms have caught the American eye, now focused on categories of people identified by "market research" that isolates those likely to buy this or that product, watch this or that television program, read this or that magazine or newspaper. Preoccupation with the marketing of goods and salesmanship, inevitable given economic pressures for ever-upward movement on sales charts, increases the tendency to separate the population into groups, each of which is subjected to differentiated sales pitches. These may be understandable and useful concerns in a business context, but from a political perspective they deemphasize or ignore connections other than a shared desire to consume and reinforce the practice, perhaps inevitable in a large society heavily engaged in buying and selling, of segmenting the population into industrial workers, farmers, white-collar workers, those in service jobs, public employees, teachers, and so on, each becoming a sub-class with special characteristics, needs, identities. This is not to deny workaday differentiations, but to suggest that their misuse further encourages lack of concern with the commonweal. An instructive example was the fuss during the 1988 presidential election over endorsements of presidential candidates by organized police unions and benevolent associations. Everyone seems to have agreed that the police have a special interest in law, order, and public safety, when in fact one of the central ideas of politics is that these are of the essence of *res publica*. If police associations are correct to claim this area as a special interest—and given the situation in many U.S. cities there is reason to fear that they are—then the implication is clear that the public at large is not concerned with questions of public safety unless and until they are involved as individuals or special sub-groups (for example, minorities plagued by public-safety lapses). That is disastrous for the sense of connectedness. It also means increasing indifference to the breakdown of civility.

The political system further exaggerates separate identities. Although earlier Americans, Madison among them, warned against the evils of faction, the system of governance has evolved into a playing field for lobbyists, favor seekers, and favor dispensers. Group pressure is now the most effective way to secure favorable legislation, or executive action, or to shape American society, except insofar as "elites" control society. Life in the United States is increasingly seen as getting "our" piece of the action or as akin to a well-stocked pigs' trough waiting to be assaulted, the largest share going to the best placed, or organized, the wealthiest, or loudest. The spectacle of a group free-for-all unencumbered by concern for the general or public interest has drawn comment but not the fire or contempt it deserves, for it has reduced politics and other institutions to little more than exercises in bidding for control and benefits.

This free-for-all is heightened by federalism, which has evolved into a governmental tower of babel. Overlapping jurisdictions and taxes as well as differentiated school systems may indeed induce loyalty to individual states and towns, but of far greater consequence is the way in which the attachments of Americans to multiple groups and different levels of governance repeatedly turn out to be little more than reflections of self-interest. Affinities for separate jurisdictions, to nation, group, and one another, compete in a milieu that often makes these seem inconsequential when compared to personal accumulation of wealth.

Americans, in sum, live in a world that places many pressures on their sense of connectedness. Groups differentiated by race, sex, wealth, intelligence, education, occupation, and state residency or by commercially invented categories (tendency of skin to respond quickly to the sun, dryness of hair, etc.) hold center stage. The not surprising result is a near obsession with group identities, in startling contrast to the rhetorical celebration of individualism and individual effort.

THE IMPORTANCE OF CONNECTIONS, OF BEING TOGETHER

The portrait of individuals either as disconnected competitors or group members exaggerates and distorts our situation. Humans are not isolates. Their civilizations are historical and evolving, not fixed in or by nature, and they bring different talents to tasks that evolve differentially. Since these tasks form patterns, humans, though singular, are not perpetually struggling with one another. They are joint tenants, the earth being an ark made not for two of each kind, but for many. Human claims of specialness, that is, that they are different from nature's other creatures in the scheme of things, have significance only in a context that incorporates (1) self-consciousness about existence, (2) awareness of self and others in that existence, and (3) belief that there are rules of the human game that apply to the world at large. To be civilized refers to conduct in the presence of others who are similar to but not the same as oneself.

This situation requires a complicated balancing act. While human beings have little choice but to deal with one another as a practical everyday matter, I do not have to give up concern with the question of whether any action is good for me and for mine, that is, my family, my friends, my immediate circle of interest. But as a matter of logic as well as experience "me and mine" is a phrase that makes sense only within a larger arrangement that necessarily includes others who are not "me or mine" but who are disposed to make and honor similar claims. In other words, the concept "mine" requires a parallel notion, "other than mine." Human beings are members of a set and that set—self, me, mine, others, theirs—is operative only with acknowledgment of the presence of others, not merely their existence but their equivalent claims to what is "theirs." When others agree that this piece of property belongs to me and not to the population at large, it is possible for me to preserve title to what I declare to be "mine." My claims achieve standing within a context of similar and generally enforceable rights to make such claims. If my claims are to stand up, yours must as well. This requires reciprocity: agreements, procedures, and structures to organize claims coherently. And reciprocity among strangers is precisely the occasion that makes the terms "power" and "polity" significant. I have rights only insofar as you also have them. I am free only in a context in which you too can claim to be and are similarly free. To have that happen, we are compelled to artifice and to initiate, to do something that acknowledges the linkages among *my* rights, *your* rights, and *our* rights.

This means, to borrow a phrase from Michael Ignatieff, acceptance of "the needs of strangers,"[2] although that is easier to say than to accomplish, and to the extent we think kind thoughts or in slogans—one bestselling writer maintains that a universal or worldwide cookies-and-milk break at three o'clock will bring us to a blissful harmony—we are being naive or just plain silly. Politics brings people together not because they are brothers and sisters in movements, in churches, in ethnic groups, members of some elite, political gamesmen who learn to feast at the public trough, or lovers of humanity and the common humanity of the entire species, but because we share, above and beyond respect for each other's claims or a "common humanity," something with all others, strangers as well as those who are proximate or known personally to us. Beyond that, politics is also supposed to deliver something we need and value.

OUR AMBIVALENCE TOWARD CONNECTEDNESS

We are, however, understandably and justifiably wary of phrases like "common humanity" and "the needs of strangers." Although our lives are filled with evidence of interdependence—the market system, education, insurance, street security, protection of rights—we ask when "common humanity" ever put food on the table. And the answer, that food arrives there after transactions involving others, is correct but difficult to make palpable, particularly when American prejudices and practices stress individuality and individual decision making as the keys to "the pursuit of happiness."

The tension between self-concern and joining together with others can never be fully resolved. We can, however, recognize both the importance of the individual and the commonweal, and take the unusual step, not always approved of by the logician, of recognizing that we live in a world in which these two, though they clash, are equivalently important. It is easy enough to recognize personal needs and the desire to be seen as individuals by others; the harder task is to appreciate what makes connectedness important to the search for individual fulfillment and identity.

We come into the world with marked differences in tribal, lingual, and even statistical arrays (we are tall, short, or neither; slight, average, or large of bone). We also have one single and undeniable similarity, that as humans we are more like one another than akin to eagles. But there is a second similarity, that we share the earth with one another and with others, and it is commonplace that this is true for every human being, whether or not he or she chooses to pretend otherwise. New global realities make it easier to talk this way: a Russian nuclear accident affects people around the globe; the setting off of nuclear devices in the Nevada desert broadcasts radioactivity everywhere; careless abuse of the waters of the Atlantic or Pacific, of the rain forests of South America, or of the entire planet produces a measurable and, at this time, widely reported effect on every creature on earth. This makes the notion "common humanity" tangible. But to be meaningful the term must suggest more than shared disasters—it refers to mutuality, to the granting of respect and trust to all persons, including strangers we will never know. To quote Ignatieff again, "common humanity" means that "beneath difference there is identity,"[3] most critically, acknowledgment of identity. When respect and trust are given, people in effect say to one another, "I know that you and I as members of the human race are by definition equal in standing, therefore in no sense the playthings, nor the objects of pity or of manipulation by, others." But once we speak that way, when we say that "'common humanity' requires all humans to respect all other humans," we have to admit that such talk refers as much to hopes and ideals as to any extant reality.

While shared global problems confirm our common humanity, many contemporary attitudes do the opposite. Excessive materialism and attachment to possessions weakens the sense of belonging to common humanity because it creates greater, still more artificial differences between us. Acquisitiveness also makes for combat, against which these days only an appreciation of the new global character of markets seems to be a barrier. But what of "have-nots" who benefit very little from this global marketplace? They and the "haves," in addition to being increasingly separated by poverty and wealth, also are bound to increasingly misunderstand one another. Over time most of the impoverished become alien to those of us who are more fortunate, barely recognizable as fellow humans, and so we must appear to them. To speak, therefore, of being connected to impoverished Africans or Asians (let us not forget Americans) may be to push human empathy beyond realistic limits. Many of us are disconnected from other humans who cannot know the things that have come to matter to us, just as we cannot fully comprehend the quality of their lives.

Furthermore, although I share the common condition of being human with every person on the planet, I also share particular places—New York City; Manchester, New Hampshire; New Brunswick, New Jersey; Modesto, California; the United States of America—with segments of that humanity. In those places and in many tribes, nations, empires, and cities, caring for "the needs of strangers" has never been, and probably never can be, fully realized. Assertion of shared humanness and problems with others, therefore, does not mean that humans automatically come together to deal with things that matter in common, that are *res publica*. It can mean, however, that we are alert to the needs of strangers as well as our own. Lectures need not inform us that we have feelings about how things we see look from behind the protective barrier of our own unique skins. But we do need reminders about the many others who populate and equally belong on this single planet so that perhaps we will look with fresh and "connected" eyes.

We have little choice but to deal with one another globally as well as in neighborhoods and regions. We have specific commonalities—race, gender, place of habitat. We have humanly artificed ties—religion, language, ethnicity, nation, occupation. And we are broadly linked together by "common humanity," however much our practices and institutions obscure this connection. Let me admit, however, that these ideas often seem farfetched. The sense of community, of being bound together in communities like Philadelphia, Pennsylvania, or Ann Arbor, Michigan, has weakened. When we talk, therefore, about joining together, our focus does not have to be global. The neighborhood or cities, states, and nations are arenas also in want of a renewed grasp of connectedness.

In sum, humans are the founders and maintainers of institutions, called here political, that deal with connections that are the givens of existence. I have not spoken either to the initiation or operations of polities and governments or discussed how, even with governments in place, the sense of being bound together in polities can attenuate and weaken to the point of disappearing altogether or how in other instances governments become so entangled with the "private" realm that together they, as well as politicians and leaders of what we call the private sector, can rob individuals of their rights to found, to assent, to consent. All of these require scrutiny if we are to revive political life or discover something else to keep us connected.

NOTES

1. *Dred Scott v. Sandford*, 19 Howard 393 (1857).
2. Michael Ignatieff, *The Needs of Strangers* (New York: Viking Penguin "Elizabeth Sifton Books," 1986). See Chapter 1, "The Natural and the Social," pp. 25–52, and Chapter 4, "The Market and the Republic," pp. 105–31.
3. Ibid., p. 28.

4

Life without Politics

A SEVENTEENTH-CENTURY VERSION

The previous chapter discussed what connects us and pulls us apart and claims that retaining or restoring connectedness—therefore political life—is important. I'm not convinced, however, that solid enough reasons have been given to support that claim. It is easy to see that having been freed from the parental nest, individuals need company, sexual partners, and "family" or some equivalent. So families or "partnerships" and communities are explicable. And these involve politics of a sort, as do other institutions like a church and the economy. But do the power struggles that affect all institutions prove that we need or ought to have politics or government *per se* or political as well as familial, religious, and economic entities? We have a way to go before that becomes clear.

We've noted the celebration of individuality and the tendency to identify individuals on the basis of their group connections, both increasingly used to deny the significance of political activity. Suppose we extend that discussion and consider what life would be like if politics, at least in its present format, were altogether eliminated. The work of Thomas Hobbes, one of the first modern political philosophers, is particularly instructive in this respect. He tried to use "privation"—being deprived of something we commonly have or possess—as a primary tool for analysis and concluded that any object can be studied by treating it (1) *as if* it can be broken down into constituent elements and then rebuilt part by part, (2) *as if* one or more of its normal or usual components or qualities had been removed, or (3) *as if* some quality or element had been added. Hobbes didn't give his technique a name. I call it *reconstruction*.

Suppose we wish to explain and understand the dynamics of human behavior making use of his procedure. Hobbes initially isolates the basic elements in that behavior, then "reassembles" them to see how they function in consort with one another—an exercise, he believed, in logic. Reassembly depends on a grasp of each part's operations and understanding of the relationships among the parts and between the parts and the whole. For example, watches or other "automata" are triggered into motion by the proper fitting together of springs and wheels; and humans, by a set of organs that have specific functions—a circulatory system, a brain, nerves to receive and send messages, and a controlling pump, the heart, which by pumping faster or slower mechanically responds to nerve signals that have been translated into desires and fears. He believed the same principles applicable to analysis of human behavior, which mechanically reacts, he claimed, to the push and pull of desires and fears. Human beings, in other words, were stimulus-response machines or pendulums.

He writes in *De Cive*, "For as in a watch, or some such small engine, the matter, figure, and motion of the wheels cannot well be known, except it be taken insunder and viewed in parts; so to make a more curious search into the rights of states and duties of subjects, it is necessary, I say not to take them insunder, but yet *that they be so considered as if they were dissolved.*"[1] That is, hypothesize the "absence" of a basic part or element: "Reconstruct" human beings hypothetically by eliminating or "dissolving" one or more typical or fundamental qualities in their makeup or nature. For example, although all animals communicate, some in sophisticated ways, we know of none as yet whose communication and language system are as complex as humans'. Hobbes suggests that by considering humans as if they could not speak but were otherwise unchanged, we expose the true significance of speech and language.[2] Since he regards speech as the basis of reasoning, its loss means that humans can neither communicate well nor reason at all. Hobbes thereby *reconstructs by subtraction*, that is, analyzes an object as if some part or element has been removed.

All of this seems farfetched, but consider that contemporary help for individuals who lose the power of speech depends on assessing carefully the consequences of that loss to them. Those who have not suffered a stroke leading to motor and/or speech deprivation must somehow understand the impact of the loss if they wish to comprehend the attitudes and behavior of the victim. They simulate the victim's condition intellectually, but they also imagine in themselves not only how it "feels" but also the consequent frustrations and emotions. In that empathetic state, they are better able to deal with patients. They "reconstruct" their own persons, subtracting good health, replacing it with a hypothetical stroke.

Hobbes also "adds" qualities or conditions to human circumstances. For example, in the construct that he calls "the natural condition of mankind" in Chapter 13 of *Leviathan*, he adds perpetual shortage to life's "natural" conditions, basing that addition on men's "similarity of desires," which produces shortages. Also, by defining liberty as a mechanical phenomenon, an "absence of impediments"—I am at liberty when no boundary, river, or person is in my way—he treats human behavior as analogous to the motions of physical objects. This is *reconstruction by addition.*

Presumably, Hobbes believes that a grasp of how something has been put together and may be taken apart or how it reacts when something "new" or previously unnoticed is added or taken into account is equivalent to understanding. He does this when he equates desires with inner motions toward and away from objects—swiftly moving, deeply felt, unmeasurable thoughts whizzing through the brain that urge us toward desired and impel us away from feared objects. These, he says, are motions made in less time than it takes to measure them. They can be observed physically because of *exterior* reactions—a shudder, a look of fear or lust in the eyes—but for Hobbes the unseen internal motions are primary and are followed by external emotions. He thereby "reconstructs" humans by adding hypothetically to their makeup an automatic, built-in, mechanical, push-pull system reminiscent of gravitational and anti-gravitational forces. In neither case, however, does Hobbes believe he is actually adding anything. Both the inner motions and the internal push-pull system, he insists, are real. But they can neither be measured like a ball in flight nor directly observed like tears. In his time no electronic or scanning gear existed to "read" electronic flashes in the brain or along nerve paths.

These reconstructions are not experiments, but mind and logic games. Hobbes believed that human affairs would always present special problems for experimenters; indeed, that experiments were manipulative and dangerous. But at the heart of his technique is the comment that the value or utility of civil and moral philosophy is demonstrated "not so much by the commodities we have by knowing these sciences, as by the calamities we receive by not knowing them,"[3] which is to say that if we consider the world *as if moral and civil philosophy are unknowns or absent,* we will learn their true worth and realize the calamity "we receive" by not being able to distinguish right from wrong or maintain a semblance of civic order.[4]

The most celebrated of Hobbes' reconstructions is his hypothetical consideration of humans in pre-civilized existence, referred to by later writers as "the state of nature."[5] This is not a description or anthropology of "primitives," but a logical discussion of desiring human beings stripped of the power of speech and therefore of the capacity to reason. Hobbes concludes that these less-than-whole humans inevitably make war on one another; their lives are, to quote his celebrated words, "solitary, poor, nasty, brutish and short." Humans who cannot speak cannot reason.

Humans who cannot reason will not discover the fundamental law that commands them to seek peace. Humans who do not seek peace, but remain driven primarily by desires, clash with one another and make each other fearful and miserable.

Similarly, Hobbes maintains that if you wish to study ethics, consider humans *as if they had no faculty or ability to distinguish right from wrong.* If life could be imagined without that distinction, might not the value of moral conduct finally be understood? His point, of course, is that what we normally take for granted may be vital not only to survival but also to what we regard as "humanness." Eliminate the capacity to distinguish right from wrong, and no human can operate under rules. Humans would as likely do each other harm as behave ethically and live brutishly in the grip of what he describes as a war of each man against every other man.[6] Furthermore, life under these conditions is chaotic. People believe they are doing what is "right," but others either are or feel injured. Every "neighbor" becomes an object of fear. Since no one knows what is unjust or just, and since there is no operative law or system of justice to regularize conduct, even the desire not to do harm is futile. Predictability disappears and the human world becomes unsteady, unstable, unreliable. Neither decency nor felony can be identified. Haunted by fear, men and women are governed by a "justifiable" paranoia. Neither their collective nor their individual lives have direction, since no one can possibly be impelled toward a mutually accepted goal unless he or she *agrees* to identify it as good or desirable. The word "decency" would have no more meaning than the term "square circle"; one cannot, after all, be good, correct, upright, honorable, responsible, and well behaved without having standards of decency, goodness, and so on to aim at.[7]

In sum, if right and wrong are unknown, undiscoverable, or impossible to achieve, human beings will perpetually feel unsafe, uncertain, and distrustful. Had such a condition ever existed or were it to come to pass, civilization and society would be impossible. Hobbes argues that to the extent that humans retain any tendency to revert to the war of each person against every other person, they make society unlikely and their individual lives unsafe. If they fail to master the art of mutual, clear communication, they cannot be safe because they cannot govern or control themselves; everyone is at liberty to do as he or she wills, since no person is bound by mutually understood rules. Some go about their business, while others decide to engage in random attacks on strangers.

A PRESENT-DAY VERSION

Suppose we borrow Hobbes' method and portray our world as if politics and politicians were to disappear, vanish, be banished. Here is the United States of America "reconstructed."

The good politicians, the greats of our history—George Washington, Thomas Jefferson, Abraham Lincoln—might still be remembered for their deeds and words, while the lesser figures would be forgotten. How come? With no political arena devoted to the preservation of the traditions of our past, we would have no occasion to recall any but the greatest of past heroes. Furthermore, some people already believe that politicians are parasites who add little to our existence except needless expenditures. Politicians, this view holds, start wars and tax us endlessly—at birth, at death, on payday, at the gas pump, in restaurants, at the supermarket counter, at the theater. In hypothesizing the end of politics and politicians, we would be speculating about the loss of little that is currently regarded as valuable.

Before exulting, however, we ought to take a closer look. What calamities, if any, would the disappearance of politicians and politics bring? What changes in society would take place without politics and its paraphernalia?

In the United States, the president, our leading politician, the chief of state and chief executive, disappears. One hundred senators, two representing each state in the Union, and 435 members of the House of Representatives also disappear. The Supreme Court of the United States no longer exists—it is part of the political system. Nor can judges for any federal court be appointed—no presidential nomination, no senatorial confirmation, no official to swear them into office, no Congress to legislate as to their jurisdiction in appeals. For that matter, the entire federal system of courts is gone.

Agencies of the federal government cannot exist without combined congressional and presidential policy guidelines, appointments, and funding. Likewise, the Treasury, State, and Defense Departments, the attorney general and Justice Department, the Federal Bureau of Investigation, and the Immigration and Naturalization Service. No longer will an Agriculture Department act as agent for and regulator of American farmers. Business and labor can no longer count on the Commerce and Labor Departments. Given the size of our national government, the list of vanished agencies would fill volumes. There would be no U.S. Army, Navy, Air Force, Marines, or Coast Guard, with their overlapping jurisdictions, rockets and air arms; also no missile sites, no storehouse of nuclear weapons, no vault of gold in Fort Knox, no warehouses of butter or cheese, no national petroleum reserve, no agency to regulate the stock market, no national insurance scheme to insure individual savings deposits at banks or "bail out" banking institutions currently in difficulty, no medicare payments, no social security trust fund, no hospital construction to speak of, no subsidies for airport construction, no federal taxes, no federally financed flood control projects, no agency to stimulate rural electrification, no forest rangers, no agency to regulate airway safety, no Environmental

Protection Agency, no Veterans Administration, no Housing and Urban Development Agency, no federal highway system, and no money and no Federal Reserve Board to control its supply and stabilize or stimulate the economy. There is, in short, no Constitution of the United States and therefore nothing that is a by-product of that instrument's existence. The estimated 3.1 million employees of the federal government are looking for jobs.

Politicians in, and therefore the governments of, the fifty states likewise will disappear. No governors, legislatures, state courts, judges, municipal governments, highway departments, drivers' licenses, highway building or maintenance; no snow removal in New Hampshire or the California mountains; and no police, state, county, or municipal. No fire departments. No laws or agents of the law or highway patrols. Indeed, no highways, since they are built publicly and authorized by politicians. Nor are there state universities, or colleges, or any state or local schools. Gone also are governmentally mandated inoculations against infectious diseases.

What, then, does it mean, using Hobbes' word, to "dissolve" all aspects of politics from everyday affairs? Minimally, activities undertaken now by governments on behalf of the population at large will no longer be present. What distinguishes those activities from what most people do daily? Clearly, they reflect *res publica*, everybody's business or concerns, activities in which everyone presumably has a joint stake and which have been dealt with by general non-private agencies because it was thought wise, proper, or convenient to do so. These tie us together or require jointly sponsored "public" activity. They include the joint need for security, rules of conduct that bind us—and not simply on the highway—and the need for a uniform and reasonably stable system of money. Eliminate the Constitution and government, but these needs will not disappear. They have to be met, unless someone can envision a contemporary society, linked together as extensively as ours is, in which there are as many currencies as there are states or cities. And these public activities serve a different "need," namely, that the United States of America is a shared space within which everyone's safety, health, well-being, and public interest, at least ideally, are protected. If we wiped away the *sense* of jointness as well as the *activities* that result, we would be saying that people can share space without awareness or active organization of what they share, without symbols of that sharing or operating institutions to act on behalf of joint needs. Moreover, if these are abandoned, we have to wonder whether anything would be left of what we call our individuality and privacy. Do these words mean anything unless they are distinguished from their apparent opposites, collectivity and publicness? My feeling and guess is that distinctions such as "private" and "individual" only have meaning in a context—privacy can only be significant where there is something that is non-private; individuality can only be meaningful in a context in which we are also tied to others.

Eliminate politics; we will still be unique and separate, which are genetic facts of human life irrespective of how many institutions disappear or appear. But eliminate all associations that could be described as political and we lose the arena that "guarantees" our privacy and individuality, which exist under present conditions because the thin wall that shelters individuality and the private from the outer world also faces outward toward public space. For the outer world to survive, the connected exterior walls must survive along with their interior sides.

The problems of retaining privacy, continuing to attend to public affairs and eliminating unnecessary government cannot be resolved by turning back to Thomas Hobbes. He provided us with a clue as to how we might study a mechanical entity that breaks into discrete and apparently interconnected parts, so that each can be understood along with the whole. He helps us evaluate what lies in store when we subtract or sever a vital part from some apparent whole, when we eliminate the human faculty of speech but still leave alive beings we call "humans." Were we inclined to agree that human mentality is constructed as Hobbes suggests, we might follow him further, but contemporary thought views the world differently. Human nature is not fixed. Human languages evolve and continuously reconstruct our perceptions of the world. Human purposes change accordingly. Part of the wonder, the joy, and the difficulty of the human condition is the presence of others who, not being identical to us, inevitably influence or color what we do, think, and consider. Their presence and their astonishing variability make contingency a certain part of our lives.

Furthermore, if, as Hobbes contends, we are forced to be connected to one another and ultimately to be peaceful because of wars arising from competition over desirable objects in short supply, our awareness of the difference between needs and desires alone makes Hobbes' scenario too simple. Human self-awareness produces changes in our impressions of the world and therefore what we consider "necessary" or "desirable," and this suggests that we look again at the words "power" and "violence."

NOTES

1. Thomas Hobbes, *English Works* (Molesworth edition), vol. 2, *Philosophical Rudiments Concerning Government and Society*, p. xiv (emphasis added).

2. See *English Works* (Molesworth edition), vol. 3, *Leviathan*, Ch. 13, paragraph 2, pp. 11-111, in which Hobbes speaks of considering humans' mental faculties "setting aside the arts grounded upon words."

3. *English Works* (Molesworth edition), vol. 1, *De Corpore*, Part 1, Ch. 1, no. 7, pp. 9–10.

4. Hobbes, in sum, reconstructs human behavior by isolating what he believes are the most general and universal characteristics of all humans. These, in his view, are

   a. that all humans have desires;

   b. that humans tend to desire either the same or similar objects, thus generating a shortage of desired objects;

   c. that humans communicate and speak with one another and derive all their understandings and meanings from language or lingual signs;

   d. that the faculty of speech makes reasoning possible and changes brute beings into creatures who reason and have passions, thus humans;

   e. that the most fundamental laws of reason command humans to find ways to remain at peace with one another, in other words, to overcome the inevitable conflict that arises because they desire the same or similar objects.

5. *English Works* (Molesworth edition), vol. 3, *Leviathan*, Ch. 13, pp. 110–16.

6. He has done something questionable, namely, laid out sequences or processes, though he denies it, that are the result of "universals" built into every human being. They all speak. They all reason. They all are impelled by desires and consequent passions. Each one who learns to reason discovers the same, so-called natural law that urges them to seek peace if they can have it, otherwise, to defend themselves. In other words, because of their desires all human beings are potential aggressors though capable of understanding the need to abandon aggressiveness. This approach to so-called human nature assumes a regularity which understates the contingent, developing, "accidental" character of humans and human affairs and leaves little room for individual nuances.

7. This assumes that standards exist as self-evident truisms, divinely revealed commandments or the by-product of logical and scientific reasoning. Few now feel as certain as Hobbes that such standards exist, or, if they exist, are that easy to discover or make operative, that is, to impose on conduct.

5

Composition of Political Life: Power, Violence, Legitimacy, and Authority

COMPOSING A POLITY

The need to be connected to others eventuates in a collective act, the establishment of political life. But how difficult it is to reconstruct the "case history" of the processes that bring people together into a polity. By comparison, an individual's bonding pattern, which is complex, is child's play to figure out.

Political life, politics, the polity, treating the three as synonyms, are the handiwork of a "crowd," and the means they use to make the process possible has here been called "power." But power has, as previously indicated, at least three distinguishable aspects—*initiation, foundation building,* and *politicking* (see Chapter 1).

Initiation, or the "moment" of recognition and beginning, is that "instant" when human beings become aware that their situation compels them to acknowledge and deal with each other's presence in a peaceful way. It depends upon understanding that the earth's space is occupied by many humans, most of whom are outside one's immediate circle; and that the presence of others requires ongoing and comparatively stable, not *ad hoc*, responses. Neither the need nor the desire for political connections and the actions that follow resemble "nature's" assignment of tasks to insect collectives or prides of lions. There are few genetic instructions—reproduction is an exception—resembling those that drive the behavior in hives, anthills, nests, and so on, or that pre-assign tasks to individuals as members of the species. Some claim that humans and other animals are similar, and I have no wish to argue with them. To avoid debate, I suggest simply that humans become aware that they are free to shape their affairs and world, thereby at once becoming both conscious and capable of transforming the conditions under which they live. They are then in position to initiate political life.

There is no way, however, to point to an initiating moment, to an initial opening up of "public" consciousness. It is a matter of conjecture. Something akin to it probably occurs when groups spring up unexpectedly—the recent appearance in public of those who overhauled communist systems comes to mind. The happy looks on the faces of people on the streets of Budapest, Hungary, and Bratislava, Czechoslovakia, during early 1990 provide a clue to what had happened, but little hard evidence. Something similar surely happened when assorted "Puritans" conceived of starting over in a "New Zion" of their own design in the New World. Likewise, in mid-eighteenth-century America one colonist after another must have shared a similar thought, the possibility of initiating a new nation by cutting the ties to England. But we have no record—how could we?—of anything like this occurring at the beginning of history. We have neither reports nor texts about such a time, certainly nothing that clarifies what it means to pass from the view that "we" merely refers to physical plurality to the sense that it refers to a need to act in relation to one another, to "do something" about the stubborn, permanent, proximate presence of others. We do have an American Declaration of Independence (1776) and see how it gropes for a "natural" explanation of what the rebels were doing: "When in the Course of human Events, it becomes necessary for one People . . . to assume . . . the separate and equal Station to which the Laws of Nature and Nature's God entitle them, a decent respect for the Opinions of Mankind require they should declare the causes which impel them. . . . We hold these Truths to be self-evident, that all Men are created equal, that they are endowed by their creator with certain unalienable rights." Self-evident Truths? Endowment of rights by the creator? Laws of Nature? More accurately perhaps, but less inspirationally, Jefferson might have written, though happily he didn't: "We hold that men living in the presence of so many of their own kind become aware that they must make political arrangements; that having also recognized the impossibility and oppressiveness of the present system, they hereby choose to set up their own commonwealth or commonwealths." Not a sentence to inspire patriotic fervor, but it would have given us a testimonial to an outbreak of awareness, followed by a first step toward foundation building. As it is, only public exchanges of views and private letters indicate growing recognition of the disadvantages of accepting rulership by a kingdom three thousand miles and many months away, and, later, of the difficulties to be faced by thirteen distinct and separated political entities. Beyond that, we can only guess at the span of the initiating moment and, since we are born into already-existent polities and learn—or once did—to accept them, we are unlikely to experience the initiating moment except on special and extremely dramatic occasions.[1]

We are therefore unlikely ever to be in a position to study the moment of recognition. The settlement of the American hemisphere is an obvious occasion for it, but the colonizers did not begin from scratch. Some were agents, others opponents of then-existent regimes. What they did was informed by past history as well as by opinions about existent polities. Initiation *precedes* all of that, and therefore we can only know, in a strictly political context, analogues such as the more or less spontaneous appearance of movements, uprisings, rebellions, or revolutions. But spontaneity, always limited by rules, mores, and institutional patterns, has itself been altered by the ubiquitous presence of television, which brings us "live" assassinations, murders, attempted coups, ethnic uprisings, combat, and efforts to install democracy in totalitarian regimes. Yet such moments of recognition must occur; how else to explain the resistance in the Soviet Union after seventy years of monolithic rule?

Foundation building is the effort to develop, install, and maintain a framework or rules of the game that presumably will govern a new or radically altered polity. Here we have many historical examples, among them the founding years of the American polity: Revolution, roughly 1760–1783; Independence, Confederation, and framing and adoption of the Constitution, 1783–1791; addition of the Bill of Rights and installation of the First Governments of the United States, 1791–1800; and Stabilization of the New Political System, 1800–1830. These seven decades witnessed the initial interpretations of federal and state constitutional authority, the claim (in *Marbury v. Madison*, 1803) and reluctant acceptance (confirmed in 1857 by the *Dred Scott* decision) of the Supreme Court's exercise of "judicial review"; the shaping of relations among the branches of government; the first exercise of control over foreign policy and diplomacy by the president; definition of the role of the Senate in treaty making; the adoption of national fiscal policies attuned to the commercial classes; the appearance and development of the world's first political parties; and the beginnings of the transition from a republican to a democratic system of governance. An apparently similar sequence in France, following the Revolution of 1789, produced very different results, and the new political system failed to stabilize, although "France" has survived as an abstraction transcending the more ephemeral monarchies, dictatorships, and republics that succeeded one another as governing frameworks. The Russian and Bolshevik Revolutions of the early twentieth century and the disintegration of the Soviet Union are additional examples.

Power, foundationally speaking, refers both to the initial appearance *and* later maintenance both of a body politic and of rules that govern its ongoing existence and operations. The use of these terms—foundational, body politic, rules—should not be construed as a suggestion that instruments of government or constitutions, in written or unwritten formats as in the United States and England, are necessary for political life to flourish. The initial and ongoing acceptance of some kind of framework and rules, not written documents as such, testifies to the framework's existence and significance.

This means that whatever is regarded as necessary—magistrates to preside, elders to construe traditions, legislators to promulgate laws, or kings and queens to reign—is put in place and begins to operate. This is the third or operational aspect of power, *politicking*, the polity conducting business, the most familiar element in political life. This third aspect of power includes all the processes for making and enforcing decisions that are what we usually discuss when we talk about politics.

There is no real dispute between those who in defining power emphasize consent or support and the scholars who claim that power is present when any X influences, dominates, or controls Y, making Y do what he, she, or it would otherwise not choose to do. This view, which equates power with control and blurs the distinction between the policeman and the highwayman, is an evaluation of politicking. Operationally speaking, the policeman and the gunman are "look alikes," since both ultimately "get results" through the potentially lethal consequences of refusing their commands. If one asks, "how does political power operate?" the answer focuses on domination, since it is undoubtedly true that once political life is operative, the questions that can be counted on to reappear are, "who is in charge?" and "what are they up to?" The result is a struggle over rulership—the Crown, the realm, the office, the largest number of seats in parliament, whatever. On the contrary, questions like "what is the origin of political power?" and "what guarantees its continuance?" focus on the beginnings and foundations of political life, the construction of a framework and instruments of governance, and the support that sustains politics. Accordingly, answers to these questions stress the joining together of people rather than the controls exercised over them after they join together and politicking begins.

The astonishing effort to dismantle Soviet "totalitarianism" and the decision of the Hungarian Communist Party to abandon its name and program and the emergence of a multi-party system in that country are evidence that independence can survive repression. Even "totalitarian" governments, though they terrorize, require support from citizens; otherwise, they cannot carry out schemes to terrify people. Power, in its initiating and foundational aspects, originates in and depends upon cooperation; in its operational aspect it depends upon support, unless it controls the means of violence, which in modern societies usually means the military.

The foundational/operational distinction may be further understood by conceiving of the polity as analagous to a house. In examining houses, we note their styles, decoration, exterior sizes, and interior dimensions and spaces, the desirability of views from their windows, exposures, the heating and air conditioning systems, and so on. These are operating characteristics—how the house functions as living space, shelter, or place of comfort and warmth. But we also examine houses from the point of view of what supports them physically, how they were framed, what had to be done before they were sub-divided into rooms, what designs were adopted to take advantage of the "best" possible views, and what makes them commodious, pleasant, and attractive. Questions like "how solid is the foundation?" "how reliable is the heating system?" and "how sturdy are the windows and doors?" look to basic construction (foundation) and the likelihood that it will be supported in the future. We are then considering both the house's fundamental constitution and the instruments that have been incorporated in it to ensure continuing habitability. We are examining it foundationally but also considering ongoing support.

That distinction is pertinent to discussions of political life. We consider initiation and the establishment of foundations or instruments of governance and their continuance or disappearance—what must happen *before* politics and political institutions appear and political power is operative and *after* governments exist and attempt to maintain support. But analysis may also focus on the actual operations of government: How are decisions made? How is support generated within the context of operating governmental institutions? This kind of assessment, common to political science and journalism, emphasizes ongoing politicking and resulting policies, while study of initiation and foundations emphasizes the origins, survival, and disappearance of politics. Of course, a difference in emphasis produces disparate impressions and views. Those who believe, as I do, that power depends on harmony and cooperation see a rise in violence and terror as closely related to the disintegration or absence of a community's or nation's cohesion. We see post-establishment support as similar to initiation, which depends on an agreement to agree. Those who stress power's operational aspect emphasize what gets done and how and regard influence as the key to politics. They are primarily concerned with the domination of some and the subordination of others, with who is in charge, how control is challenged; support to them is largely a matter of exchange of favors, or a *quid pro quo*.

I see no conflict between these two points of view when they are both given weight and due consideration, although I am convinced that an obsession with operations degenerates into the belief that every problem can be solved by buying off the discontented. By that route, politics becomes exclusively a bazaar in which buyers and sellers bid and counter-bid, trade and haggle. The likely outcome of long periods devoted to these transactions is that everyone becomes corrupted by the notion that policy is only to be judged by the question, "what's in it for me?" Conversely, obsession with "the general good" and maintaining general support can produce a tendency to speak in vague generalities about freedom and values, while ignoring the pressing daily needs of large numbers of people.

A more balanced view recognizes that where there is politicking, domination and control are present, but that insofar as an order or rules of the game exist and survive, cooperation and support (coming and remaining together) are vital to political power. Otherwise, political life may appear to be alive and well because existent governments still bark out orders but becomes increasingly irrelevant as violence increases. *The three aspects of power are all necessary to the continuing health of the polity.*

To reiterate: Serious problems follow when we confine our political attention to operations, to how things are done, to techniques, to "how to" questions. How does a bill become a law? How does someone win election to office? How do candidates appeal to different and mutually hostile ethnic groups? The answers must take the form of simple statements of means: employ the approach or tactic appropriate to your purposes. They do not fully comprehend the prior and ongoing agreements that justify, legitimize, sanctify, and authorize the employment of those techniques. Before one decides how to build a bridge over the bay, authorization is needed; specific policies depend upon a pre-existing and still-supported foundation, framework, or instrument. To understand politics, we must include both the establishment of the instruments used to make this authorization, the initiational/foundational aspects of power, and the politicking that affects, shapes, determines the character and timing of, and finally makes the decision. Furthermore, community unwillingness to support installed and presumably authorized governments, particularly when they invoke the power to tax or ask for sacrifices, indicates not merely operational but also initiational and foundational breakdowns. Increasingly, and not only in central and eastern Europe, such refusals challenge the very basis of government and begin, perhaps, to reverse the moment of recognition we discussed earlier. They open up the possibility that a different kind of recognition, valid or no, has appeared, one that says we need no government because everything done politically can be done "privately."

A similar focus on operations is visible in the stress on economic or social relations as the primary concern of political systems, although there is little doubt that contemporary economies and polities have become increasingly intertwined both in totalitarian and democratic societies. By economic and/or social relations I mean the trading off of something for another something, of resources for finished products, of finished products for money, and so on. These are organized ways of meeting social and economic needs by using exchange systems or markets. Society, the arena in which these exchanges take place, develops structures, relationships, and techniques to meet human needs and goals—survival; distribution of goods; worship of God; education of the young through institutions (family, tribe, school, university); and in "developed" societies, a reasonable standard of living. Politics is similar operationally to other exchange relationships in that every political system seeks to achieve certain concrete goals, above and beyond order and rules of the game. These involve allocation of resources and resemble economic exchanges at one level—questions about how to educate young people can be answered partially by a technical answer relating to resource allocation: raise taxes, build enough schools, strengthen universities to train good teachers, hire enough teachers, and tap your resources, even if it hurts. But support, a willingness to do, is necessary. Before exchanges can be made, there have to be preliminary agreements that provide the foundation for and stabilize exchange relationships and ensure that sanctions will be applied if the rules of the game are broken. There is a strong linkage between this politicking and the economic system: differential access to governments occurs because well-placed units or individuals have more capacity to influence policies that those less well placed. But there must first be an underlying framework and rules. There also has to be some willingness to admit that sacrifice for the general good may take precedence over self-interest. Those agreements are part of what I have called the foundational aspect of power; the actual allocations and the process by which they are made constitute "politicking."

It is also difficult to understand the possible relationship between political and moral issues, particularly since they are so often regarded as entirely separate. Politically speaking, doing the right thing tends to mean injuring the fewest people, a prudential, not a moral, response. However, there is another way of examining the possible tie between politics and morality, namely, by seeing the linkage in the light of power's foundational aspect: Before people can choose or reject "right conduct," there must be a setting within which right conduct is possible. A duty or obligation cannot exist outside of a context of established relationships or rules that take into account the presence of others. In other words, it must be possible to be moral before morality becomes a general possibility. How this possibility comes to be is by no means self-evident.

Among the requirements are the presence of others and the establishment of some kind of framework for dealing with them.[2] My conduct may seem to conform to a moral code or be called moral when I am in total isolation, perhaps living in a cave. But whatever I do in that circumstance can always be reduced to self-interest and doesn't necessarily involve duty or obligation. Morality is meaningful only within the given plurality of the human universe, where choices may be imposed on me between my "duty" or obligation according to some moral code and what

I perceive as self-interest. By looking at morality this way, we can see the differences as well as the connection between morality and politics: If morality is a reference to the conduct of human beings as they deal with one another in terms of "responsibilities" and "duties" and thus "right conduct," politics involves the prior arrangements that make it possible in the first instance to deal regularly and in an orderly manner with one another. Those arrangements become feasible through what is here called the foundational aspect of power. Those not covered by the rules—excluded entirely from the game or who reject it—cannot be or do not consider themselves to be bound either to prudent or moral choices as they occur within the boundaries set up by such rules. This reminds us that politicking can never ignore the other aspects of power. Where connections among people are limited or non-existent, there are neither "awareness" nor foundations jointly put in place and rules cannot be made generally applicable. Where people choose to "drop out," a similar though not identical situation prevails. Violence rather than the exercise of power then becomes the means of control. And violence is always answered by violence.

Political power's creation makes possible legitimated, authorized action in the name of some community or gathering of human beings. Without the initiating instant, the coming together that leads to construction of foundations and consequent rules and modes of politicking, we are handicapped in any effort to proceed with ventures such as the exchange system or the economy because the rules of the game associated with everyday operations must in some way be preceded by an agreement to be bound by rules generally or, at the least, to accept the presence of institutions empowered to enforce rules. We will also be unable to engage in other than self-interested activities, since given the tension between self-concern and responsibilities toward others, rules require a framework within which joint and general concerns are institutionalized, rulership is empowered, and legitimate enforcement of decisions can be undertaken on behalf of the community. Before we look at "legitimacy" and "authority," two key terms that help explain empowerment, we will further examine power and violence and the relation between them.

FURTHER THOUGHTS ON POWER AND VIOLENCE

Picture two different scenarios. The first, drawn from a celebrated movie (*2001*), portrays two groups of quasi-humans sharing the fresh water in a pool. An individual discovers that he can make weapons of the dried-out bones that are lying about. He uses the weapon to win leadership over the group and then he and his subjects drive the other group away. In this tale, violence establishes community, political power, and leadership, although there are distinctive groups or tribes on each side of the pool.

In the script I am using, human beings who are clustered together in a place (town) know, as do all animals, that fresh water is vital to them, and they also realize that maintaining a joint water supply is desirable and efficient. They create a supply system that provides water to each tap or outlet: my spigot or faucet and the town square's are tied to the collective supply and therefore to one another. While water appears to link people together, it is power from first to last that connects supply to user and user to user. First, there is the impetus to join together that establishes an agreement to agree. Second, agencies are established and rules promulgated—the foundations through which power is implemented. Third, policy making and management, and the contests and politicking that accompany them, continue as long as the arrangement or agreement survives.

At times, these two tales seem to be more similar than at first appears to be the case. Those who become leaders, who hold office, are "in power"; they are the designated or empowered officials. But there is ambiguity in this. They "run things," and therefore they rule their original masters, that is, control the citizens on whom they simultaneously rely for support. Thus the ultimate ambiguity of political life: that which owes its existence to the joining together of people comes to rule them. The example used here illustrates a further ambiguity. Not only do the designated rulers rule, but those who are ruled are ostensible partners in the decision making: the user of the water must abide by regulations but with others is co-founder of the agency that governs him. He is a supplier as well as consumer of the water.

Initiating moments, when humans choose to come together, are singular in that the entity they create is not akin to a tapestry as in Plato's famous analogy in *Statesman*, where he casts rulers in the role of weavers who string and hold together the threads that make up the *polis* or city-state. The polity is more fragile than a tapestry and needs ongoing support to survive. But the analogy is antipathetic to politics, which is neither fixed or final like a completed weaving nor the product of a master politician's craftsmanship. A *polis*, state, nation, or community is in effect re-founded every day, every year, every generation. Weaving ties together finished or "dead" threads into a colorful, new cloth; politics ties together living people into an ever-evolving establishment. Time and atmosphere erode a weaving, but in political life humans choose to remain together or pull apart or the ties, not reinvigorated, weaken, shred, snap. With them goes the support the polity requires even though its creations—agencies, institutions, constitutions, governments—persist, attempt to carry out their assignments, and struggle to stay "in power." But support absent, they are powerless. Like trapeze artists without a bar to grab hold of, they are doomed to crash.

Here is a possible scenario for powerlessness, one with which we are becoming increasingly familiar. For one reason or another, support and empowerment begin to disappear—"the people" no longer care about the government or think of it as theirs. Leaders become frantic because for all practical purposes they are standing on a platform without a foundation. Difficulties multiply: misunderstandings about the legitimacy of policies; consequent inability to carry out policies or tentativeness about their desirability or enforceability; finally, misapplication as well as outright rejection of the policies. Disorder sets in. As the agreed-upon rules are disputed and rejected, violence becomes increasingly important to compel people to do what supporters do when power, in its initiating and foundational aspects, remains present. Or, weapons in hand, people employ violence as a "justified" means of dealing with an increasingly uncertain and insecure situation. They begin to behave in a manner reminiscent of what Thomas Hobbes and John Locke respectively described as "the natural condition of mankind" or "the state of war." Or leaders make foreign difficulties appear to be domestic threats—in Aristotle's phrase, they "bring distant dangers near."

Power and Violence Occur Together

Obviously, the tale of the jointly established water supply, of pure power, errs on the side of peacefulness and cooperation. There is no such thing as "pure power" embodied in a totally empowered leadership that speaks univocally in the name of the citizens or population or whose actions never occasion disagreement. Recognizing this, Plato in the *Republic* changes the meaning of empowerment by rearing and educating philosopher-rulers who "know" the "truth" embedded, he says, in eternal, fixed, "real" Ideas. They rule on the basis of this knowledge; therefore "truth" replaces empowerment in political life. Political power becomes the offspring of a mystical alliance between irrevocable truths and those few who can comprehend them. Leaders are shielded from the body politic and its inevitable turbulence and dissensions. Support does not flow upward but is manufactured by propaganda and myths. This is not power but manipulation and domination by an elite. Plato's rulers are free of member- or citizen-generated power rooted in agreement and support, even though they may be restrained by the eternal verities of which he speaks.

Plato recognized the improbability of the rulers he invented, as did his student, Aristotle. True political power, in Aristotle's view, requires rulers devoted to all citizens' interests and is perverted when group or individual self-interest controls politics; it is present only when exercised on behalf of all citizens. And it is both "natural" and changeable—in the sense that an acorn naturally grows into a tree and therefore is fixed in nature, yet constantly evolving—in this respect resembling a geyser rather than a humanly constructed fountain. But natural imagery confuses talk about political life. Power, unlike a geyser, "gushes" because people *choose* to join their strengths together; it is akin to a fountain. It does not actualize in the absence of human desire, consent, and construction.

"Pure" violence is no more likely than "pure" power. A society in which human relations are entirely governed by violence—more accurately, a hell governed by "pure violence"—is as logically and practically inconceivable as one in which "pure power" or total agreement exists. A totally violent society would reduce life to a nightmare, of the kind we have occasionally witnessed when maddened killers spray bystanders with bullets or demented governments slaughter their own population or when violence is legitimized in warfare—which I treat here as an interruption of the normal play of political power.

In truth, power and violence occur together, and in different situations have variable weight and importance.[3] But cooperativeness is less noticeable than disorder. Our capacity to understand the degree to which power—as described here—is an ever-present potential among human beings has been weakened by our awareness of pathologies and of dangers lurking at home and abroad. Since billions of rule-confirming acts are performed throughout the world everyday, their sheer volume and commonplace character obscures consciousness of them. Who notices thousands of law-abiding, peaceable individuals when one of their number goes berserk? What draws attention are the comparative handful of anti-social, dangerous, or pathological acts, the violence in the streets, in families, and around the globe, that induce reactions ranging from fear to demands for revenge—particularly when conditions foster clustering of those activities in relatively confined spaces. There is no "news" in expected, correct, or rule-governed conduct. Violence, therefore, is a major preoccupation of the media; newsworthy means disorderly, except for heroics during emergencies or on the battlefield. Civil conduct, likewise, is less noticeable than acts of violence, just as to a human being most body organs' "behaviors" become palpable only when they malfunction. The problem with this obsession with violence, however, is not merely that it distorts, but that it induces sense battering and memory lapse in that we forget that civil conduct, which is rooted in power and community, is indeed all around us even if barely noticed when present. The virtues of power may be most obvious only after they vanish.

Murder and rape may be the most riveting indices of violence, but violence takes many forms. Fraud does violence to the rules of the game. Political chicanery makes government the understandable object of derision. Environmental pillage violates the inheritance of future generations. And the presence of violence terrifies even those who have been lucky enough not to observe or be victimized by it directly. Above all, violence forces us away from our fellows and makes us turn inward, thereby increasing the sense of disconnectedness, which in turn diminishes acceptance of or support for the commonweal. People, perhaps out of necessity, become obsessed with self-serving particularities, with their own well-being—thus their indifference to the larger community grows. The more this happens, the less one can speak comfortably of a political system or culture that holds us together and the greater the likelihood, since dialogue and involvement have less significance, that violence will increasingly be substituted for power. It is as if the nation is being attacked by a virus that wipes away all memory of the virtues and usefulness, not to mention productivity, of political power and its offspring, public systems, except as feeding stations for special interests. But perhaps a new dialogue will emerge that sooner or later will teach the nation to speak again of the "we" even as each of its citizens struggles to preserve the "me."

Violence's Irony, Its Demand for Justification

The discussion thus far has concentrated upon the *similar effects* of power and violence, that they result in action, and their *dissimilar sources*, that power originates in the agreement to agree, whereas violence originates in the attempt to force compliance or submission by means of weaponry or superior strength. But there are other differences between them. In response to violent acts, many advocate "an eye for an eye, a tooth for a tooth." If someone holds hostages, terrorizes a population, or maims or murders others, some say, "let's do him (them) in," and they call for immediate use of military force, "surgical strikes," assassinations, or nuclear bombs. Others appear pleased when told that U.S. airplanes have bombed a city in Libya or when the president draws "a line in the sand" against Iraqi aggression. And if parents are asked, "what would you do to someone who killed or maimed your child?" most say, "maim and kill him." Similarly, asked whether it is "right" to overthrow and kill a tyrant or invade a small country and capture a leader to put him on trial in the United States for alleged crimes, the majority appear to believe that such actions are desirable or good or just, a simple matter of giving him his due.

There must be, therefore, a standard that justifies violence. If so, it functions this way: someone murders or rapes a loved one of mine—that is an unjustified act—but if I kill the offender, my violence is justified. Furthermore, the belief is widespread that certain crimes can be answered only by violence, that is, by execution of the perpetrator(s). In other words, violence as such is not "forbidden" or "immoral," other than to those who espouse non-violence under every circumstance. But how to make sense of the standards that apply to the so-called positive uses of violence?

The problem, I believe, is to fathom the notion of "good" or "acceptable" violence: To make an omelet requires breaking eggs; lumber requires destruction of trees. Both appear to be justifiable, acceptable, and therefore "good" human acts. "To shoot at and kill the enemy" when a soldier is so ordered is similar. In each instance, the justification makes violence acceptable either because the end or purpose is necessary or generally approved of (the omelet, the house built from lumber) or legitimating reasons have been invoked (soldiers firing weapons, airplanes dropping bombs, missiles launched carrying frightful warheads). But the logic of these examples is dangerous. If an overwhelming majority of citizens voted for the immediate execution of every individual whose nose exceeds a prescribed length, mere agreement would hardly justify the ensuing mayhem.

Sorting this problem out is not simple. We accept "desirable" violence (egg > omelet; tree > lumber). But "justification" is often given for far more controversial actions. We ask questions and get answers that satisfy only a handful:

"Why did you blow up the plane?" "To strike a blow for our cause."

"Why did you order the bombing of Tripoli?" "To teach those who support terrorists a lesson."

"Why did you use poison gas against your own people?" "Because they were
rebelling against legitimate authority and had to be stopped."

These answers may satisfy advocates, but few others; and we can do better:

"Why did you shoot the intruder?" "To repulse or drive off an assault on my
property, my family, myself."

"Why did you blow up the reservoir?" "To hasten the revolution against a 'bad'
regime."

"Why did you launch the mortar?" "To carry out the commanding officer's
orders."

These responses are somewhat more reasonable, but they make clear that justification of violence must be approached gingerly. Unlike political power, which depends on willingness to work together toward mutual-ly acceptable goals, violence depends on the presence of one or more humans prepared to use anything that comes to hand to achieve particular goals or purposes. And that requires thoughtfulness, calculation, and judgment about its appropriateness; not merely a description of tech-niques, but also explanation and justification of the decision to use it.

There is irony in this. Violence, which seems mindless and arbitrary, is, on the contrary, tightly linked to a purpose and to thinking about that purpose—even when it is the result of rage. The irony tells us a great deal about why people come to rely on it. But neither the judgments nor the justifications bring universal applause. When the contemporary ter-rorist says that a bomb planted on a plane will bring about victory in his long-term struggle for justice, his colleagues may be satisfied, but others are puzzled, angry, and driven to answer violence with violence. But they, too, must "think" about it. Furthermore, it is evident that political power, however suddenly it appears or disintegrates, involves a concern for long-term activities. Violence, in contrast, looks for—but of course doesn't always achieve—quick and drastic change. The point is that however limited may be contemporary respect for politics, its intent, a direct outgrowth of the appearance and maintenance of power, is to resolve general problems peacefully. Violence, on the other hand, may seek solutions but can only create quandaries when applied to consequential questions. We can understand the joint effort to maintain a water supply or clean the streets but find it difficult to accept any claims for the "advantages" of violence, be it street actions to change the system or the death of 250 randomly present people on an airplane. It is difficult for non-perpetrators to see how such deeds will culminate in the freedom of oppressed people. Violence, particularly random violence, whatever its advocates claim, wins few overt supporters from the larger majority of people because it isn't delivered directly against the alleged authors of the injustices. Though mystically potent or "powerful" to its users, it frightens others and remains inimical and repulsive to those who might turn out to be, merely through the fickleness of fate, the next victims.

Violence is a destructive act or series of acts that change the makeup, structure, character, or shape of something in order to achieve goals or fulfill aspirations. It resembles but is unlike a natural force: the wind may erode Lincoln's nose on the Mount Rushmore monument, but planting an explosive there is a purposive act, and an example of violence.

Why, if violence entails thoughtfulness and is so commonplace, do we as thinking people understand so little about it? Perhaps because it is an unwelcome intruder whose continuation violates our sense of the proper order of things and undermines our wish to see human events follow a course that "makes sense," that is shaped by nature, God, good schooling, parental lessons, philosophy, historical "forces," and slow evolution. We want these patterns to imitate the slow and predictable movement and rotation of the planets. Interruptions do them violence. Accordingly, violence has often been regarded as an interference with the ongoing processes of "history," of the routine imposed by forces supposedly in control of human development.

During the industrial revolution, it became obvious that these "interruptions" might be put to use—they could cure or ameliorate inherited but unjust or inefficient patterns and structures. Violence might midwife revolutions and bring positive changes to life. If events followed patterns and if civilization's patterns were destructive for a majority of humans, they could be altered by violence. Otherwise, change is simply an echo of nature's millenial evolutionary processes. Moreover, as modern technology improved the tools of violence, the temptation to resort to violence grew stronger. The more some argued that human life paralleled natural developmental laws and must therefore proceed at "nature's" pace, the greater became the tendency of those who saw society as rife with injustice to argue that the cycle must be broken. Violence increasingly was seen as a desirable antidote and an opportunity for heroics, for cleansing society or the earth of whatever was deemed undesirable or unworthy of further existence. That mind-set was wonderfully beneficial in respect to the conquest of disease and ignorance but ravaged humanity when it hit on the idea of wholesale elimination of "undesirable" humans. In the latter part of the twentieth century, it seemed like the worst of all possible solutions to human problems, but it thrived because political power was in decline, as was meaningful dialogue.[4]

AUTHORITY AND LEGITIMACY

Authority

The term "authority" now refers to a number of distinguishable phenomena. To say someone is "an authority" means she is expert in a certain area. The expertise manifests itself in superior, more appropriate, possibly wiser judgments than those of any non-expert. Expertise respecting one's health or car is widely understood but has contradictory implications: (1) The qualities that make someone an expert are distinct and separable from the person who comes to possess them. (2) Expertise, although not the same as the person who possesses it, is understood to reside "in" a person who in turn makes use of it. (3) Acknowledgment by others, the non-experts, establishes the expert's or authority's reputation.

But "authority" that depends on the attitudes of non-experts is no longer, strictly speaking, authoritative. An incongruity—"residing in" one person, yet requiring someone else's acknowledgment—makes modern authority ambiguous: the non-experts apparently need some form of expertise to identify experts. Perhaps this explains why authority either becomes suspect or disappears altogether in a democratic era. If subject to affirmation by others, authority becomes as variable as anything else that requires continuous approval. If my mechanic's expertise fails at some point, his "authority" is shaken, although it would be hard to say that he suddenly knows less than before. A physician who misdiagnoses a serious intestinal disorder is said not to know what she is talking about. Her expertise, certainly her license, remains intact, but her authority is now in question. There is, in sum, something odd here—"authority" that depends on the attitudes of those who are not authorities is no longer, in the older sense of the word, authority. In contemporary politics, authority, once linked to hard and fixed standards, has come to depend on acknowledgment and approval ratings. It is said to be in the eye of the beholder as much as in the brain and hands of the holder.

A second contemporary view of authority ties it to the words "author" and "authorship." An author creates or begins something and therefore is, logically speaking, prior to and "higher than" his or her creation. This resembles the traditional idea that authority refers to the presence of a natural force or a higher being or human who stands above everyday human activity. God, the creator of the universe, is both prior to and higher than His/Her creation. Rome's founders were greater than succeeding leaders: Founding the "eternal city," unlike most human activities, is everlasting. Romans are born and die; Rome lasts "forever."

The term "authority" once linked rulership to something transcendent, fixed, and unaffected by the daily ups and downs of political life. It referred to position and station. For example, in the United States, we speak of "the Founding Fathers," attaching a degree of respect or reverence not only to them but to what they authored, namely, a new Constitution that was to serve, some came to believe, as the foundation of governance for all time. Similarly, though rarely today, monarchs claim to rule by "divine right"; they had "royal" blood, which is to say that they were entitled to hold and exercise rulership through their permanent genetic linkage with God, a linkage not dependent on the opinion of others. The coronation ceremony provides a wonderful opportunity to use the pomp of ceremony and the house of God to reinforce the claim. The king or queen is anointed in a church, God's shrine, preferably a large cathedral. A high priest places the crown on the monarch's head. The ceremony carries an unequivocal message: rulership and God are tied together; rulers are ordained by God, and their authority, therefore, is exercised with His blessing or on His behalf. This older view separated authority from the herd or commoners and reinforced hierarchy by making the monarch a subject of God. The structure of authority could readily be grasped by anyone. God is its source and creator; the king its bearer; the people its subject. The source of authority, empowerment or the right to rule, is therefore above human affairs.

In contemporary talk, however, the term "higher authority" customarily means those who literally hold top positions in a chain of command or rulership, a president or commander in chief or prime minister, who are said to be "in power." Or it refers to creativity. As God created the universe, so men create works that have a life of their own—buildings, literature, music, paintings. The separation between everyday earthly business and immortal entities is therefore maintained and echoes earlier interpretations in which the king was said to be God's designated spokesman for the nation's politics, as the pope is God's designated spokesman in the everyday affairs of the Roman Catholic Church. The light that shines on kings and popes is not placed there by the people but is said to come from God, whose priests anointed the monarch and thereby confirmed his or her right to rule, as long as such claims were taken seriously. The people in turn presumably had the good sense to be awed by God's concern with earthly matters. The belief that divine right places royalty above other humans, however, has all but vanished along with faith in the Deity's direct interventions. An earlier version of the same thesis may be found in Plato's "Theory of Ideas," which claims that the "Idea of the Good" is both higher than and the author of all other Ideas, in effect author of all truths and, when grasped, governor both of the universe and human affairs, and therefore akin to God. Belief in eternal, fixed truths usually produced controversy, yet surprisingly, Plato's portrait of a universe governed by them worked its way into Christianity as well as politics, philosophy, and superstition and to this day remains one of the most potent myths ever devised by a human being.

In some places, though heavily embroidered, the idea of a higher sanction for rulership is still meaningful. In England, the queen is not considered above other mere mortals but is "above" politics. She defers unfailingly to the majority party and government and thereby retains an identity unaffected by the everyday ups and downs of politics. The queen symbolizes the realm, a long-lived and presumably God-ordained entity, although the intervention of the media in the daily lives of the royal family and the consequent appearance of publicity seekers within it has weakened the overall sense of authority that the British combined with their approval of democracy, displaying their customary and refreshing disdain for logic in their political affairs.

In the United States, the Constitution of 1787 has taken on some of the color of traditional authority. Kept under glass for visitors to look at, the original signed copy is by implication eternal and immutable, other than by amendment, a very rare occurrence in U.S. history. In contrast, everyday legislation is ephemeral and gives way if found to be "unconstitutional," in conflict with the verities of the document. The opening passage's choice of words—"We the People . . . do ordain and establish this Constitution for the United States"—graphically illustrates the attempt to create and sustain the traditional sense of authority, this from writers many of whom had participated in an uprising against English authorities. The word "ordain," usually used in the certification of priests, sets the tone. Being ordained, the Constitution is endowed with an apparently perpetual authority that transcends everyday politicking, the ongoing bickering over policy among citizens and politicians. The notion of judicial review, grafted onto the document by a wily Supreme Court, reshapes this idea. It hands over guardianship of the Constitution to the Court, which is thereby free to say that the document changes even though it is "permanent." The fundamental meanings some profess to find in the document are beyond alteration unless by Supreme Court intervention (or, more rarely, by amendment); they are timeless and fixed, like Plato's Ideas. This attempt to capture the foundational aspect of power in writing and fix it for all time is a singular aspect of U.S. political ingenuity.

Reluctance to amend the Constitution of 1787 has been both a mechanically induced and intellectual preference of U.S. political life. The amending procedure is clumsy and formidable as the recent struggle over the Equal Rights Amendment once again demonstrated. The recent reluctance of Congress to endorse an amendment overturning the Supreme Court's flag-burning decision affirms the conviction that the document should be left largely intact unless change is absolutely necessary. The preferred American procedure is presidential and congressional action or policy making followed by Supreme Court acceptance or rejection in specific legal applications; thus the Constitution remains largely fixed in wording but lives on and evolves through such politicking. Breakdowns in the system, which have occurred occasionally, in time produce considerable impatience and irritation, since its ingenious design slows change and makes governments reactive rather than active. The Constitution has become the equivalent of the older notion of a higher authority; laws passed by Congress and signed by the executive are measured against what are said to be the views of the authors, the Founding Fathers.

The traditional view of authority, that it derives from a source above mortal human beings and their mundane affairs, entails the notion of hierarchy. Recognition of "higher" entities and beings rationalizes the appearance of hierarchy within as well as above the human community and lends credibility to the principle of rulership in human affairs. Rulership, when supported by traditional notions of authority, means obedience that runs upward from the bottom to the top. Authority therefore was once binding and arbitrary. In the Roman family, for example, the father's authority at one time extended to the point where he could order the execution of his sons. Obviously, we would be hard pressed to find advocates of that kind of empowerment. Authority, in any event, remains a term that accounts for empowerment by tracing its origin to something higher than everyday agreement or statutory law.

Legitimacy

Legitimacy is the employment of a previously agreed-upon right to control behavior; it is present when past agreements appear to settle questions like "who has the right to make decisions?" Typical is the agreement that elections will be decided on the principle of majority rule. Legitimacy means that there are rules of the game in place—what institutions of government will become operative, how governors are chosen, what limits government, who is entitled to make policy decisions, how disputes are resolved, and so on. It therefore preserves the foundations and longevity of the operational institutions of government and is a major factor in the ability to transform political power into an operational fact of life.

The hallmark of legitimacy's absence is the habit of changing the rules of the game while the game is being played out, in this instance, after the ballots are counted. Where legitimacy exists, winning candidates take office irrespective of the disappointments of current officeholders; vice-presidents succeed to office on the death or resignation of a president; the legitimate heir to a throne is given title when the monarch dies; the decisions of the Supreme Court are accepted by presidents and congressmen who do not agree with them. As time passes, legitimacy reinforces and stabilizes the rules governing empowerment. Without firm prior agreement to accept results, elections may take place, but they often prove to be irrelevant. In Latin American politics, winners do not always take office because legitimacy is not operative. Recent events in Panama highlight the significance of legitimacy, including refusal to install an elected president, a U.S. invasion, the secret swearing in of that legitimately elected president, capture of the Panamanian "dictator," General Noriega, his virtual abduction to the United States, and his trial in a U.S. court on charges having to do with drug trafficking. The entire sequence is well outside the boundaries of legitimacy.

When a new U.S. president is sworn in, his title and office are legitimated. He does not necessarily get popularity. He does not get automatic authority—the conviction that he is as wise as the Founding Fathers, as expert in matters relating to the Union as Abraham Lincoln, or as all-seeing as God. He receives acknowledgment of empowerment. The system has established procedures for empowerment understood and still endorsed by the population at large, the courts, Congress, and the military. This prior and ongoing agreement is as crucial to acceptance of a president as the statutory and constitutional texts that provide for it.

Confusion with respect to empowerment can be fatal to governmental stability. So can the appearance that an official no longer legitimately holds office. A president may discover that the populace as well as the Congress question his entitlement to rule. Recently, in the case of President Richard M. Nixon, impeachment and conviction, which would have removed him from office, became a real possibility because the president appeared to have exceeded or abused the empowerment granted when he took office. If a president encourages violations of the law, then the issue of legitimacy surfaces because of his oath to uphold the Constitution and therefore the law. By encouraging or ordering violations of the law, he undermines legitimacy and thereby threatens his own entitlement as well as that of successors. To permit that to continue unchecked would be to begin a process of deterioration that would culminate in the disappearance of political power, since legitimacy is a primary means of maintaining an atmosphere in which rules rather than *ad hoc* whims are the more or less fixed boundaries that contain and permit actions.

The case of Nixon's predecessor, Lyndon B. Johnson, looks similar. Empowered following the assassination of John F. Kennedy, he successfully utilized the emotionally charged atmosphere to push through an extensive legislative program. He was then overwhelmingly elected president in his own right. But his collapse did not result exclusively from issues of legitimate usage of his office, as did Nixon's, since the U.S. system, like most others, allows the president remarkable latitude in the conduct of foreign affairs and the prosecution of military engagements. One military intervention after another by U.S. forces in foreign nations—Grenada, Lebanon, Panama, Nicaragua, El Salvador, Vietnam, Korea, and the Persian Gulf and Kuwait—has been accepted and applauded by the American public and Congress since World War II. Rather, his reputation was destroyed by failures in the Vietnam War and his authority shaken in precisely the modern style earlier described. His policy judgment was challenged—was he in fact expert enough ("wise" or "cunning" or "knowledgeable") to remain president?

In the United States, empowerment is linked both to legitimacy and authority, which are facilitators of the operational facet of power. Authority and legitimacy are both enshrined in the Constitution. In addition, on an everyday basis, "Great" U.S. presidents are those whose authority (expertise) grew—Lincoln comes to mind—and whose legitimacy was in no way damaged by loss of trust, though obviously in a major dispute such as the Civil War, one region of the country no longer accepted the national Union and seceded. Lincoln, in response, cited his oath of office and its command to preserve the Constitution as establishing the legitimacy of the provocations he engineered that produced a war between the Confederacy and the Union. Since that time, the Supreme Court has interpreted the Constitution as meaning that the Union is indissoluble, even though Texas, Alabama, and others were violently forced to return, a sequence we might recall as we watch the dissolution of the Union of Soviet Socialist Republics, which has a constitutional procedure for dissolution. Of course, courts in the United States and elsewhere resort to legal fictions. That the Confederate States seceded, or that a war ensued, has nothing to do with courts. Nor could the resulting conflict any longer be resolved by dialogue. Instead, a bloody war, a devastating exercise in the uses of violence, ensued. Nonetheless, after the Union victory the Supreme Court "found" that the secession was "unconstitutional."

TOWARD A DEFINITION OF POLITICS

We have taken a look at the elements that compose political life and may threaten its dissolution. These provide us with a working definition of political life.

The initiation and foundation of a polity depends upon recognition and acceptance of human beings' connections to one another, even to strangers, who, though not acquaintances, family, or friends, come to belong together, usually in a place called nation or city or community or republic, which is then responsible for the care of everybody's things or affairs (*res publica*). A polity is a plurally shared public arena, singularly concerned with the joint occupants of that space, who, living in the presence of others, share problems with them, but who are not necessarily known to or intimates of one another. There is politicking in every institution—in the family (a circle of individuals tied together by bloodlines) or in churches, with reference to beliefs respecting God (who is apart from and above human beings) and practices (services and church organization)—but it is exclusively operational, a struggle to exert pressure, influence, or win control within those institutional structures. The "composition of politics" is a broader term that refers to and describes how and in what formats people draw together to resolve common problems in larger than familial, tribal, or friendship circles. "Political power" is what human beings generate when they operate together to get things done as choosing, selecting, evolving, transforming beings. Politics, in this broad meaning, refers to a population at large, who, whatever their other differences, develop and maintain political life and a public arena within which rules of the game ostensibly bind all participants or players.

Political power exists when individuals actualize the potential that exists in numbers, when they choose to act together, and remains present insofar as they continue to support what has been established or founded in consequence of the initial coming together. Power is not "the property" of an individual or an individual quality or characteristic. The policeman who says "stop in the name of the law" speaks on behalf of those who have empowered him, thus the difference between those who speak for the law and the burglar who violates it. Obviously, our experience also relates political power to particular territories, places, or spaces, which may be a matter of accident rather than choice.[5] No better illustration of the need for a place or space for the polity can be found than contemporary Palestinians, who assert that their homeland has been taken from them, and Israelis, who prior to the establishment of Israel, were recognizable as members of a cultural-religious group but were without the territorial status usually required to confirm the presence of political power. Both exemplify a cultural connectedness that clearly ties them together. But due to historical circumstances, neither's claims had given them the opportunity to empower a government of their own in a territory that was indisputably theirs. Before Israel's founding in 1948, and most particularly in the 1930s, Jews driven out of traditional European citizenships and declared stateless were entirely in the hands of others. They had spent the previous centuries living in states that adopted mercurial attitudes toward their presence or citizenship; the Holocaust hardened the resolve of many of them to build a state. It is an irony, a most bitter one for Palestinian Arabs—and presumably a frustrating one for thoughtful Israelis—that the Jewish state founded by a people who lived for centuries without a political entity of their own has reduced others to statelessness, involving the Israelis in an endless struggle that partially turns around the issue that had plagued their ancestors. It is a further source of bitterness that Israeli refusal to recognize the official existence of those who claim to represent Palestine echoes the problems that statelessness imposed on Jews prior to 1948.

Political life is rooted in (1) the potential that human beings have to relate their selfish, individual needs to general, shared (though not necessarily unselfish) needs; (2) the fact that human beings both occupy the earth at large and are clustered in specific portions of it or may share a "cultural space"; (3) the complications entailed by shared space, specifically, the modes of sharing space and a set of rules that makes possible living together with a degree of order and cooperation; (4) the consciousness as well as the acknowledgment of the advantages or desirability of humans living within a commonly accepted framework that I call "games of rules"; (5) the understanding that each human being, once a polity is founded, is equal in rights, obligation, and standing as a member or citizen—standing being exclusively a reference to political life and connectedness, not an assertion of biological, psychological, or social equality. As members they are identical; as individuals they remain unique.

But the composition of polities is not a natural phenomenon. Political power is derived from connections that bind people together outside the immediate circle of family or the more or less natural association of friends. Political activities exemplify human creativity in response to plural occupancy of space on earth. The inhabitants, members, partners, or participants recognize that they have common business, concerns, affairs (*res publica*), and problems requiring jointly authored solutions and resolutions not because someone says this is the theoretical or ideological case, but because the actual situation makes it clear to everyone. When the ties wither, the entity weakens or disappears, although its apparatus may live on. This is a phenomenon that seems to be at work throughout the Western world and is most manifest in the United States in decaying urban areas and perhaps in some states. Similar events mark the recent history of Europe and have been at work for centuries in the Middle East.

Nor is politics fixed. What we consider to be *res publica* shifts over time. No discussion of common interest has yet been or ever will be the same for all time. Moreover, even a founding is tenuous in that the presumption of permanence is constantly tested by the death and birth of members. The newcomers are not replicas of their parents but unique, special, demanding in different ways and likely to uncover new needs or ways of looking at well-known needs. Those elements in the humanly authored world that are thought to be subject to general or public direction are altered over time, just as the geographic assumptions about the proper size of a polity or state alter. Aristotle believed a polity should be entirely visible from some central high point; today, in addition to a handful of small political entities, vast states—the United States, Canada, India, Australia, China—are typical, and what is called politics is increasingly disinterested in established spatial divisions and sub-divisions and necessarily caught up in global issues.

To be in power is to be authorized to act. Unless the empowering group continues to acquiesce in or support the government, regime, or leadership, the underlying foundation or base supporting the government's operations begins to vanish. A good example of the complexity of empowerment is the widespread misunderstanding and considerable tension concerning the place and attitudes of African Americans in the U.S. political system. To the extent that the political system treats black citizens as if they have a lesser and different set of rights or are in some "essential" and presumably natural way inferior, one of the responses that inevitably will be heard, given the rising expectations that U.S. governments have been endorsing for the past fifty years, can be expected to sound like this: "If I am not actually a full-blooded and equal member of your polity, then the laws you write, the actions you undertake, the activities you say are consistent with the behavior of a 'good citizen,' do not necessarily apply to me. I am, as you never fail to remind me, 'different,' a breed apart. Why, then, should I obey what you call the law or be bound by your declarations as to what the words 'right' and 'wrong' mean?" In sum, language conjuring up images of equal justice, rights for all, equity and constitutionalism, will be alien to those who, often with good reason, do not believe that they are included in the imagery and who realize that when the words "we" and "they" are spoken, they refer to participation in or exclusion from political power in all three of its aspects. Those treated as if they were second-class citizens cannot be expected to behave on every occasion as if they were equals simply because others insist that this kind of behavior is appropriate. Nor have they empowered the current governments or fully acquiesced in the conduct of affairs, most of which are conducted as if they were exclusively "white men's business." To ask them to say "we," when arrangements divide them from others in the society and degrade them, is foolish and hypocritical.

The impression should not be created that a political arena, because it originates in joining together, is a place where gentleness prevails or independence is always encouraged. A strong exercise of independence is often dreaded by others, particularly those "in power." Since independence may not be derived from a group or pool, but reflects personal development, the independent are looked upon with suspicion by those who hold office. Independence contributes to the never-to-be-eased tension between the individual and the society, between self-interest and the general interest. To put down or reject independence in many instances is to make violence a likely alternative to win attention or to create a political counterforce. For example, when women and children pour into the streets of the Arab sectors of Israel (or Arab Palestine) and throw stones, they are being violent but also making a statement about their coming together as a group—they are at once violent and "powerful." Their actions therefore speak loudly and they become a potent force, not because of strength of arms—they could be quickly eliminated if the Israelis dared—but because of the power actualized by their joining together.

To conclude: political life originates in "power," which begins with recognition of the connections among human beings, develops foundations and a degree of permanence, and engages in what I have called politicking in order to deal with shared problems, needs, weaknesses, and virtues. Americans are regularly informed about politicking by the media, and they have, according to surveys, concluded that they don't care for politicians and politics. Of the initiating and foundational aspects of politics, and their significance, they are not well informed, except in a stuffy, formal way—as often as not innocent of any distinction between foundations and ongoing politics, despite much talk about the Supreme Court and the Constitution. Nonetheless, when their nation's existence or way of life has been or is said to be threatened, assuming the threat is widely perceived—and that is easily managed these days—they respond with enthusiastic support and patriotism. And when annually called upon to acknowledge their membership by producing an accounting of income earned and taxes paid—in most states several accountings—they do so in astonishing numbers without waiting to be commandeered by officers of the Internal Revenue Service. Hopefully, support rather than fear of punishment guides their actions and possibly they have a better grasp of the foundations, the basic order, the framework, than some leaders currently in charge of the day-to-day operations of the system. To see how that might be possible in terms of today's understanding and outlook, we need to examine our politics not exclusively as outcomes of old and long-applauded documents or notions of authority, perhaps better understood hundreds of years ago, but in the light of metaphors that may have some connection with our times and perceived circumstances. Of these, more later. Meanwhile, the obsession with politicking and its many corruptions contributes to the alarming disintegration of the sense of connectedness among Americans. In order to understand these changing attitudes, we have to examine further the significance of the foundational aspect of power and then turn to what has thus far been avoided, the impact of "ideas" upon power and politics.

NOTES

1. One can argue that the experience of initiation is more widespread than I have yet allowed, by using examples such as the decision to purchase an old and broken-down house and reconstitute it completely, turning it eventually into a modern edifice that at the same time preserves the appearance and architectural integrity of an earlier building. Or one might ascribe the same feelings and attitudes in another social or intimate situation, namely, the appearance of a new child.

2. A framework can be derived from the work of the moral philosopher and father of modern economics, Adam Smith (1723–1790). He argued that humans, in addition to being driven by self-interest, possess a "moral sensibility" that enables them both to empathize and deal responsibly with one another. This sensibility takes the form of a detached spectatorship that enables them objectively to sit in moral judgment and approve or disapprove both of their own and others' conduct. Rooted in "moral sensibility," this objective judgment is akin to political awareness and therefore a source of political connectedness, suggesting that humans universally possess a responsiveness to shared space, situations, and standards. They are, accordingly, political animals.

I have not chosen to follow Smith's argument, however, because he posits these internal propensities, tendencies, or sensibilities as natural givens, a view that ultimately pushes the student of political life into a motivational hall of mirrors in search of so-called fundamental motives, impulses, instincts, and so on. Nonetheless, his is an ingeniously suggestive affirmation of the significance of human plurality; of the linkages between "morality" and judgment and, therefore, political life; and of the implications of shared space. See, in particular, Adam Smith, *The Theory of Moral Sentiments* (1759), Part 3, Chapter 1, in Robert L. Heilbronner (editor), *The Essential Adam Smith* (New York: W. W. Norton & Company, 1987), pp. 101–3. Also see "Adam Smith," in David Miller *et al.* (editors), *The Blackwell Encyclopedia of Political Thought* (New York: Basil Blackwell, 1987), pp. 476–78.

3. Hannah Arendt, *On Violence* (New York: Harcourt, Brace and World, 1970), pp. 44, 46. It should be noted, as in Chapter 1, that Arendt's views are central to this commentary on violence and power.

4. Attempts to clarify sometimes exaggerate distinctions and thereby create new confusions. Violence and power are discussed here as if distinct to clarify the differences between them. Arendt wants us to consider whether it is possible to distinguish an unjustified from a justifiable act of violence—even though such justification, irrespective of cause, would never be accepted by those absolutely opposed to violence. And she indicates as well that it is equally important to look

at things from someone else's point of view, to compare justifications, as it were, to achieve a degree of analytical sophistication (see *On Violence*, pp. 30–31, 51).

But this supposed difference doesn't seem to accord with the talk we hear around us in the media or everyday conversation. On the contrary, it has become usual to draw no distinction between violence and power or to conflate them. Not only everyday talk, but also "intellectual" talk tends to use the two words as synonyms. At the beginning of Part 2 of *On Violence*, Arendt notes that there seems to be a consensus among many writers that violence and power are more or less identical (p. 35). Power is seen as an "instrument of rule" (p. 36) that forces changes in the structure, shape, or character of individuals' behavior and that requires them entirely to abandon their own inclinations and substitute those of a ruling exterior entity. She cites one writer after another over the past 150 years who conflates power with domination or command.

5. Nineteenth- and twentieth-century racism attempted to override this condition, stressing racial rather than spatial links among people. These efforts to tie linkage to something other than place or space show up presently in emphasis on ethnic, religious, cultural, and social ties. These, too, may ultimately be destructive to political life as it was once understood; although in some instances, it is clear that individuals whose status in the polity is unclear or clearly less than equal may have no choice but to create, so to speak, their own cultural or racial territory.

6

A Closer Look at Foundations

FOUNDATIONS AND RULES OF THE GAME

Imagine a South Sea island inhabited by a people whose lives are extensively shaped by a gentle and generous Nature. They fish, pick fruit, procreate, and celebrate the beneficence of the gods. They know nothing of war, and their mating and family rituals are sophisticated enough to protect them from incest and consequent genetic damage. Some would say that their rules are "natural," derived entirely from what nature provides and dictates as necessary to their survival.[1] The thesis here, on the contrary, is that even in this simple hypothetical situation, agreements exist that are the stuff of artifice rather than nature's commands. These islanders may have little conflict, but they have discovered and are utilizing power. They deal with one another by means of a foundation of rules—a procedure for exchange of fish and fruit as well as marital and mating procedures enforced by the parents and elders of the community. Their rules reflect and are sustained by agreements, however informal and unwritten, that can be modified by later generations, but our imaginings about such simple existences usually include the belief that their rules are fairly stable. Assuming the presence of a few complications, we can guess that they also exchange artwork and crafts for "currency" representing "value"—something precious, fabricated or dug out of the sand. That, too, depends on the establishment and"enforcement" of rules.

Contemporary "free market" advocates insist that the marketplace establishes significant rules on the basis of "laws" of supply and demand. They may well be correct. The perspective here, however, is that whether or not affected or determined by so-called laws of supply and demand, these cannot operate until they are supported, even tacitly, by agreement to play the game by the rules, to abide by the market's determination of a coconut's value when compared to any other item of worth. Rules in operation depend on this agreement. In other words, political life, molded by power, exists on this idyllic island. *Wherever agreed-upon or accepted rules command, direct, or guide operations, power and political life are present, even if no formal government is visible; that is true whether the rules operate to control family relations, religion, exchanges of goods, or the selection of elders to serve as leaders.* This pattern, which appears to be spontaneous, in fact requires serious and continuous thought and action; in Western thought it is best expressed early and in a sophisticated way by the ancient Greeks.[2]

What, then, of the claim that there is always a spontaneously operating society before there is civil authority? Insofar as any rules operate—exchanges of goods or vows, the presence and usage of money, the appearance of private property and ownership, the existence of servants, pricing arrangements, contracts—they depend on operative rules. There must be agreement that I can claim property as mine, which means that I acknowledge the property claims of others as well. That agreement is "foundational" and is an aspect of power and political life, even though it is easy to conceive of a time, at least in logic, when neither governments nor magistrates existed. Nonetheless, the foundational aspect of power is precisely what is at work when rules are established. Power, not some mysterious natural force, ensures that the game will be played by the rules. Otherwise, the institution of private property becomes merely common sense, which would be fine if one could assume the presence of such a "sense" in every human being. But no science has yet determined its existence, and, to increase our doubts, there are usually some people around who either cannot or will not play by the rules. To describe all of them as malformed is to reopen the question of what we mean by nature and natural rights. We have to conclude that *recognition of ownership demands prior agreement about and acceptance of foundations and instruments that generate political operations, however informal they may be, which in turn generate "rules of the game."*

THE GREEK VIEW OF FOUNDATIONS, IDEALIZED

The ancient Greeks are regarded as the first Western people to compose polities, and we look back to them as early advocates of widespread participation in political life. They also gave us the first political philosophers who, each in his way, took exception to too much participation or to the spectacle of the free-for-all in which the city or community was to be run selfishly on behalf of "mobs." The word *"polis,"* often translated city-state because it refers to specific places, Athens, Thebes,

Corinth, and Sparta, for example, is better understood as a reference both to a shared place or territory occupied by a community that includes the rural area contiguous to it, and to shared or joined-together lives, an arena that is not merely a "place" but a sense of mutual connectedness. To be a member of a *polis* meant to blend one's life and experience into those of one's fraternal co-members and to make those connections more or less definitive for a good or well-lived life. In modern collegiate talk, to be a member of the *polis* is to be a member of a fraternity that exists side by side with equally independent fraternities—the other "Greek" communities—in the midst of non-Greeks or barbarians. Or it is what is meant when people speak of being part of a community or of being community-spirited.

The Greeks regarded the *polis* as foundational. The city or polity was a partnership that attended to problems facing everyone living in it. Political life is concerned exclusively neither with those who rule or govern nor with those who are ruled but is the affair and responsibility of every citizen. In other words, the Greeks discovered what today is called the public realm, the public interest, the commonweal, although some historians and analysts suspect that they overdid it and attempted to interfere with or even deprive citizens of any non-familial or kinship ties that existed outside of the city's boundaries.[3] Yet when they voted to make war, the poor, who tended not to vote, got paid for service if they *agreed* to perform it, while the rich, who participated more extensively in the voting and were *required* to serve, by calling for war gave up their time and possibly lives for a compensation that could hardly have been worth the effort or the danger.

The first Greek rulers were nobles who ran the cities. There were also tyrants who rose to rulership by using tactics worthy of the bosses who many centuries later ruled the large cities of the United States. They "took care of" things. But given the conception of political community that emerged, tyranny was unacceptable. The word "tyrant" is rooted in the Greek for "master," someone who rules without challenge. This is the notion of rulership against which the idea of *polis*—a jointly created place in which citizens share responsibility—was a reaction. Despots or overlords, particularly aristocratic or oligarchic masters, were no longer to hold sway. Their rulership was less attuned to the public interest than came to be thought desirable. Even an enemy of democracy like Plato portrays rulership as attached to the Idea of the Good, which, if it is applicable to human affairs, has to shed light on what is best or just for everyone in the polity; and Aristotle attacks every system in which "class" or segmental interest prevails over concern for the general well-being.

I think it accurate to maintain that the use of the public realm for a single individual's or group's advantage was logically inconsistent with what the Greeks came to believe about life in the *polis*—it was a style of life that distinguished them from barbarians, a superior mode of existence in which voting and equality before the law were fundamental, potentially elevated citizens to equal standing, and brought an end among them to anything that smacked of master-slave relations. Therefore the *polis* was at the heart of "good" or fully developed relations among men as well as fundamental to their outlook.[4] It was the coming together of people of equal standing (adult males, the citizens) who by joining together agreed to face and settle problems of general concern, "everybody's business." The *polis* as place and as gathering of people were one and the same. *Polis* tied every citizen's fate together, reinforcing and providing a vehicle for the connectedness that was equally important to every Athenian or Theban. No one states this with more eloquence than Socrates, according to Plato's *Crito*, who insists that since Athenian laws had nurtured him, they had earned his compliance with them. The sentence of a jury, 501 of his fellow citizens, that he die for subverting the youth of Athens, had to be carried out else he would have joined those who mock the law. Could even his very special life be above the generality and majesty of the law? We have his remarkable answer: civilized humans live together in public realms collectively governed by laws they accept and support individually; respect for the laws is a pillar upon which the well-being of the entire community rests.

Indeed, in marked contrast to modern totalitarianism, the Greek *polis*, though it built markets, conducted trials in open or public arenas, sponsored outdoor theater, and made itself felt in everyday life, separated the public and the private. Matters that in the twentieth century have become the occasion for endless public concern were for the Greeks more likely to be shielded from public criticism. Although Greek sexual practices earned considerable criticism, there was little public interference with those sexual practices. For that matter, even murder was treated as a civil rather than criminal offense. The wall between private and public, between "mine" and "ours," was solid.

From our perspective, this creates something of an anomaly. They drew closely together, believed firmly in a joint or common fate, and understood the meaning of equal standing before the law, but they appear to have protected and respected privacy more fiercely than we do. Their sense of both the private and the public may have been stronger than ours. They were at once engaged in public affairs and conscious that the walls of the household were shields against outside interference. This reminds us that they also made greater strides toward some semblance of freedom than any other ancient people, yet they increasingly depended on slavery as a means for maintaining their economy.

Their household may have been private, but it is not particularly appealing to modern tastes. In the household, hierarchy and domination were the rule. Adult males ruled. Others—women, children, slaves—were ruled. As one writer states baldly, "The primary value of a woman was as reproductive machine."[5] And they readily converted cultural and ideological convictions into biological "truths," maintaining, for example, that males "create" children with sperm and that the womb is merely a nurse or attendant, an interpretation of the female's role consistent with the household structure they concocted.[6] Not surprisingly, therefore, the household could not be an arena in which people competed or displayed their "excellence." It was exclusively a place within which "nature" predetermined roles and in which necessary and natural tasks were to be undertaken—eating, sleeping, procreating, rearing children. Command and subordination were the given forms of relating. They were nature's prescription, not the inventions of human beings.

In contrast, the public arena was evidence of human artifice, invention, and convention. There men stood side by side as equals—as citizens had equal standing before the law—although economic stratification persisted throughout their history. They competed and displayed their uniqueness on that same equalitarian basis: athletic prowess, rhetorical skills, military genius; in sum, their "excellence." Equality and distinction entailed each other, for only among equals was there an opportunity to be seen, heard, and judged as special. One's superiority must be proven in the company of one's equals but was a given among inferiors—slaves, women, children, barbarians. That viewpoint also accounts for the celebration and elevation of public dialogue, which provided an opportunity to convince and persuade one's equals. Even trials took place in large arenas. When Socrates was tried for subverting the young, the usual large jury was empaneled—the number could reach two thousand, an extremely large percentage of the male population of Athens. (The population of Athens was in the neighborhood of 400,000–450,000, more than 200,000 of whom were slaves and 70,000 resident aliens. There were about 140,000 free Athenians, of whom 40,000–45,000 were adult males and therefore citizens.)

Talk filled the air, not one-sided talk as between television set and viewer, but conversation and dialogue. Few probably talked as much as Socrates, if Plato's or Aristophanes' presentations of him are remotely accurate. Plato's works, written as the Golden Age ended, underscore the importance of dialogue—discussion of justice, knowledge, proper rulership, the meaning of death, the character of beauty, and the nature of existence itself. Greek drama likewise reveals that talk and exchanges of views about the human condition and the fate of individuals were a commonplace of their public life. The form of Plato's work, the dialogue, is consistent with the centrality of speech, persuasiveness, reasoning, and logic in Greek public life. Their notions of teaching, of philosophy, of political life, come together in the dialogue, dialectic, exchanges of views, and joint efforts to find the "truth" amidst so many convictions and, above all, in the involvement of so many individuals. The drama was similar.

Certainly, there is an arrogance, hubris, about these Greeks. They react to barbarians (those unlucky enough not to be Greeks) with contempt. They practice slavery and justify it. Aristotle, Plato's pupil and successor, argues that while Greeks may not be enslaved, no such restrictions apply to barbarians, some of whom are fit only to be slaves, as he sees it. Women are "above" slaves, but nonetheless inferior. But nothing compared with life in the Greek *polis*: outsiders could not share in the fraternity and fellowship implicit either in its actuality or "idea"; to be a non-member was to be a lesser human.

The key to these attitudes lies in the already-mentioned differentiation made between the household and the public arena. Private life or business had to do with the world of necessity wherein humans are neither good nor bad. Excellence is displayed or proven in competition with peers or equals in the *polis*. That is the arena for virtue and "goodness," where men's characteristic relation is not as superior and subordinate or governor and governed, but as equal participants—we would say as citizens or members of the community. In public, the truly excellent, the great orators, the best athletes, the military heroes, stand out among their peers. The *polis* is a place and idea in which the notions of equality and excellence are subtly and ingeniously intertwined, where choices and options, not necessity, are confronted. There, men are free; otherwise, they are alone and less than complete. There, the interests of the individual, his or her private concerns, took on meaning within the larger context of the city-state. To have an interest required that one be among others. Without community, individual achievement was impossible; an individual achieved his destiny and fulfilled his potential where others could recognize his skills and abilities. Without the *polis*, no human activity could meet the tests for excellence or justice. To the Greeks, the drawing together of humans in a *polis*—political life or community—is the foundation for human development.

LOCKE AND THE EARLY AMERICANS: A DIFFERENT IDEA OF FOUNDATIONS

The Greek *polis*, despite the architectural echoes in Monticello or the nation's capital, was remote from the early Americans. The writings of John Locke were not. Locke remarks in his *Second Treatise of Civil Government* that "in the beginning all the world was America."[7] He was concerned with the appearance of new space in the world—as were his successors, the Physiocrats and Jean-Jacques Rousseau, and his predecessor Thomas Hobbes. The discovery and opening up of America recalled the biblical Garden of Eden and was therefore reminiscent of the beginnings or imagined beginnings of human society. The "beginning" Locke refers to is that time long ago when men first roamed the earth.

Hobbes had imagined it by employing a logically constructed anthropology, a "natural condition of mankind," and had concluded that it would have been a time when men, without society, law, or government, were unrestrained: They invaded each other's space, coveted each other's belongings, and lived a life "solitary, nasty, poor, brutish and short."[8] Rousseau, who lived after Locke, thought otherwise. During the earliest times that logically could be conceived, there were far more of the world's goods available than the existing population needed. Food was plentiful as in the Garden of Eden. Lasting ties and social organization or connections were unnecessary and non-existent. Humans were totally free to be themselves and to do what they wished without being bound by rules, laws, private property—those chains hammered together by civilization and society to shackle them. Rousseau's imagery portrays men originally, that is, in "nature," totally at liberty, entirely disconnected from one another, completely free, and without ties or responsibilities.

Locke's views were neither as pastoral as Rousseau's nor as grim as Hobbes'. He saw "the state of nature" as a time when land was in great abundance. He developed, accordingly, a theory about property that related it to the natural capacity to labor, in which title to property was earned by those who applied their labor to the land. In such a time, they had little need for much more than what he calls "the laws of nature," which they understood and enforced individually and therefore had neither government nor statutory laws. But the ability of individuals to enforce the rules of the game weakened as the amount and quality of unclaimed land diminished—in effect, men got in each other's way and were forced to be more aggressive. The inconveniences of that warlike condition—an echo of Hobbes' dog-eat-dog "natural condition of mankind"—mandated establishment of governments to adjudicate and settle conflicting claims. These were not, as the Greeks had believed, central to the human condition. Their task was to maintain and protect each individual's preexistent liberties, what Locke described as their natural rights to life, liberty, and estate. Men had built their primary institutions, family, economy, and church before they needed or decided to have a government.

The early Americans' view was generally consistent with Locke's. Whether they came to the New World to earn money in companies (ultimately, plantations) as in Virginia or to set up their own religious institutions as in Massachusetts, they believed the open space made it possible for them to be at liberty to pursue whatever they might desire. In later documents they would describe these rights as "life, liberty and the pursuit of happiness" (Declaration of Independence) and "life, liberty and property" (the Constitution). They believed government secondary, an afterthought to reinforce an already-established society—either by direct support of some economic activities (a conviction typical of the

Federalists at the time of independence, though not at first that of the Jeffersonians who came to control the new Union) or by making certain that no one's excessive zeal robbed others of their right to pursue happiness.

In contrast to the Greek view that humans lived in two arenas, of which the public was the more consequential, the seventeenth-, eighteenth-, and nineteenth-century view reflected the increasing complexity of life. There was now a "social" or "societal" realm that mixes private and public activities and stands between them. This realm includes family, religious, and economic institutions; in time, the economy becomes most consequential. What gives society coherence is an "invisible hand," a self-regulating mechanism governed by laws of supply and demand that function "naturally" in the marketplace—in the "New Zion" even ministers were hired and fired by the congregation; they were employees, however prestigious their positions. Employee-employer relations and the laws that govern them supposedly wove together a social fabric that required no legislation. Humans exchanged one item of value for another under the governance of spontaneously ("naturally") developed rules. The marketplace shaped the rules and taught people that value is extrinsic; "worthwhileness" is equivalent to a price fetched in the marketplace, just as Hobbes had said in *Leviathan*.

The Greeks thought the household was an exclusively biological or natural entity hierarchically arranged; the Americans imposed a similar quasi-biological metaphor, derived from Locke's claim that private property is the by-product of sweat or labor, on society. A naturalistic scenario was seen as being played out on all sides. The Puritans admonish everyone to keep busy and avoid the idleness that is the sign of the devil's triumph over the apparently Godly virtue of "busyness." The devil is seen everywhere in omens, cloudbursts, and signs, culminating, of course, in the literal "sighting" of witches during the hysteria in Massachusetts. Years later, Benjamin Franklin exhorts men to work hard, be thrifty, invest wisely, be inventive, and demonstrate business acumen, all of which he treats as natural virtues. Jefferson personally lives out the text of this nature-obsessed gospel and accompanying ethic of work and "busyness." He engages in a tidal wave of activities as politician, statesman, inventor, writer, architect—enough to kill an ordinary man. He speaks to the glories of nature in *Notes on Virginia*, praises the naturalness of Indian society, remarks on what he sees as the natural "inferiority" of the black man, and ascribes to the yeoman, the independent, laboring, "natural" farmer, the status of a "chosen people"—if, he adds, God ever had a chosen people. This early American attitude, still much praised in verbiage but barely imitated, treats the processes of working or laboring as if they mimic or parallel the body's laboring, eating, and resting cycle. Work and labor are portrayed as the human organism's testimonial to life itself. Moreover, this "organism" best operates—and this is persistently claimed once the Puritan theocracy fades—when nothing "interferes," as if it naturally guarded each human's health. Interference is unnatural or anti-natural behavior.

Very little of the Greek view of politics is visible in this. Political life exists primarily to protect the "natural" liberty to pursue goods, satisfactions, property, happiness. Political life assists the pilgrimage to material happiness embodied in the working and laboring cycle and entails no intrinsic values—they are found in the family, in religion, in the society— but has extrinsic functions, namely, to protect the nation from foreign dangers and shield individuals so they remain free to pursue their own ends. There is little discussion of the general good, except in the Constitution's unclear reference to general welfare, and famous phrases like "to insure domestic tranquillity" (Declaration of Independence) mean precisely to permit the citizenry to go about their affairs without governments getting in the way. Power's foundational moment and the ensuing construction of political life was, and still is, seen in America as a compressed period, approximately from the fifteen years preceding the writing of the Declaration of Independence (1776), through the adoption of the Constitution of 1787, to the settling in of the new Union government by 1830. That foundational moment has significance as long as everyday successes continue—prosperity, accumulation, happiness, the good life however conceived. The foundational aspect of power is treated as an exercise in craftsmanship and mechanics: Build a good "ship of state" and the problem of government is resolved. There need be no living or ongoing rebuilding of foundations.

What I earlier called the foundational aspect of power becomes, therefore, a ritualistic memory of strangely dressed, bewigged men signing immortal documents and defying the assorted follies of King George and his generals. A major holiday recalls but does not reinvest the foundational aspect of power with any substantiality. The real stuff of life, material success, came to be seen as a derivative of the natural marketplace operating, free of government intervention though not of government subsidy, in agriculture, production, and commercial exchanges. Later modifications of this view permitted government to limit or counteract gross imbalances in the society and in the opportunities available to some groups or individuals and to provide a "safety net," President Reagan's term, to help Americans outside the mainstream of business and money-making activities, among whom are apparently one in five people. A further modification substitutes group pressures and the maneuvers of large institutionalized entities—corporations, the financial establishment, educators—for the activities of individuals. In the absence of positive notions about political life and public purposes, what is good becomes an offshoot of passing concerns in the society. The government monitors, leaving all free to pursue their ends but presumably not overstepping loosely defined and constantly shifting boundaries that sway under pressure, which in turn encourages constant testing of the limits permitted to self-seeking at the expense of the population at large. The government is supposedly impartial and allied with no particular interest but welcomes pressure from all private and special interests. The public interest is therefore equated with the outcome of a tug of war among private interests. In the United States, accordingly, economic activity becomes the foundation for the operations of society; political life is perceived as a pesky, unreliable superstructure erected on top of the more serious goings-on in the economy.

In contemporary American life the private world has at least two disparate sectors, often carelessly mixed together. First, the intimate world of the family, household, and friendships, and second, the world outside of that relatively confined circle, the social realm of associations, churches, clubs, universities, groups, unions, and businesses. My right to pursue and accumulate "happiness" is entangled with social rights presumably reflected in the existence of associations regarded as essential to a pleasant, happy, prosperous, or proper existence—the right to operate as an economic entity in the marketplace, to work or hold a job, to buy a house, to own a car, and to play, plus those "rights" involving churches, clubs, pressure groups, educational institutions, and friendships. Rights were reinterpreted during the nineteenth century so as to emphasize a "liberty of contract," nowhere mentioned in the Constitution but clearly at the heart of early American thinking. They were pulled, full-blown, out of nature's hat, but of course they did not necessarily extend to minorities or people of color.

This conglomeration, coupled with persistent disagreements about the proper role of government and political life, confounds all previous views of foundations. Looking at contemporary life from the Greek point of view, it is obvious that the wall between public and private no longer exists, nor is the public arena regarded as fundamental, however crucial it may be in fact as distinguished from rhetoric and ideology. From the point of view of natural rights theory, the elementary rights to life, liberty, property, and/or happiness are now entangled in a web of societally protected rights of employment, well-being, and quality of life. From a nineteenth-century free market or Marxian point of view, the so-called basic and fundamental material conditions of life, what capitalist spokesmen call the free marketplace and the now-vanishing communists called a system of exploitation, which according to both were supposed to evolve and develop their own rules, regularities, or laws, have given way. Technology, organization, and bureaucracy—none of them spontaneous or "natural"—are in fact antipathetic to spontaneity. The institutional paraphernalia associated with them, which from Rousseau's time to the present have been bitterly complained about and which the communists said would wither away and the capitalists thought could be minimalized, are now deeply embedded in every aspect of life. The food, health, transport, and communications industries are obvious examples of how entangled contemporary existence is with organizational and societal contact points without which life can no longer be managed. The older assumptions, which rooted themselves in assorted visions of self-sufficiency, are now entirely fictions or romances. We are part of a web of transactions and necessary linkages, whether we feel disconnected and unfulfilled or actively engaged and happy, or whether we are in fact, whatever our feelings, in neither condition.

In truth, we have enlarged our governments and used them to encourage, support, subsidize, and regulate economic and other activities, to maintain what we call the infrastructure. We have built a protective floor, now unsteady, to shield some individuals from medical and health disasters, thoroughly enmeshing health care with public policy. And we have done the same with "security" and "well-being" at every stage of life, although obviously not every interest in the society has been satisfied and a large percentage of the population, 15 or 20, is uncovered. The same developments have taken place in our educational system and our business activities—in which heavily engaged government is a primary partner. Indeed, the range of public involvement in these activities might convince the casual observer that we mean the opposite of what we say. While rejecting politics, we have made just about everything public to the point where even the most private and intimate of matters have been propelled into the public arena, and the tendency to do so increases as our capacity to transmit information, to "see" and "hear" through every wall and obstacle, improves and increases. In effect, every aspect of the society once considered private has sought or is required to seek public engagement of some sort.

Since how we speak is not necessarily how we act, we are not certain at all about what is foundational for us. What we can be more certain of is the attitudes that developed at an earlier time in the history of the United States.

THE IMPACT OF LOCKE'S AND EARLY AMERICANS' VIEW OF FOUNDATIONS

The combination of Lockean and early American perspectives created views and attitudes that may be summarized as follows. These contributed greatly to and continue to affect America's ideological stance.

1. *The idea of "new space in the world," which is the basis for conceiving of a state of nature in the first place, was definitive for European thought and for Americans once the settlements succeeded and developed their own ways of*

conducting affairs and looking at the world. It shaped the thinking of Hobbes, Locke, and Rousseau and through them the future of English philosophy, the work of the Physiocrats in France, a new anthropology, a new "science" of economics, and eventually the notion that values correlate with demand or consumerability. The American setting inspired comparisons between new and established institutions, between the "primitive" and "the developed." But Americans went a step further than European thinkers. Their enthusiasm for these views was neither abstract nor philosophical. It was practical: They believed Locke's "state of nature" accurately described their experience because the first colonists came here to use "new space in the world." Not only did they treat the New World as unoccupied, they acted as if it could be shaped and constructed in any way they wished. For some, those who settled in Massachusetts, there was an opportunity to build a society based on religious beliefs, particularly the various versions of Protestantism they brought with them. They could practice "Puritanism" unencumbered by Old World political and religious conflicts and frozen economic privileges. Others came because they were in trouble or felt drawn to the opportunity to change their lives. These included some of the Puritan leaders, who took advantage of the chance to play elite roles in the building of what some called a New Zion. This was more clearly the driving force in the settlement of Virginia, where some came to work off their debts and others were sent as agents of a company established to make money on the basis of the New World's as yet untapped and uncharted opportunities. These economic lures may have varied from individual to individual and group to group, but they have a certain unity about them: all who came to America under the auspices of organizations like the Virginia Company were in effect promised an economic beginning, though not necessarily a new political life, since, theoretically at least, control remained with the proprietors of the company. So both early groups, the religious zealots and those who wanted or needed a new beginning for themselves, came because the New World represented opportunity. In other words, what Locke had written as a speculation— because the idea of new space, of America, excited and intrigued all the thinkers who witnessed its colonizing from afar—was for them substantially real, a constantly validated news story. In both instances, the economic potential was increasingly recognized and itself became a primary stimulant, factor, and foundational fact.

  2. *In addition to initiating a new way of life, the early settlers and their immediate successors, simply by venturing across the ocean, were given a tremendous sense of "doing something" or attempting to get things done.* The idea of "pushing on," which became a mainstay in the American view of the world, came to mean that it was always possible to change, transform and reorder the world. Willpower and opportunity, a willingness to go

to work, the conviction that anything is possible, and the presence of as-yet-unclaimed land were required. And as the entire world was to discover, there was plenty of "unoccupied" land just waiting for settlers. This optimism paralleled, grew out of, and fitted into the notion of new space in the world, making promise and potential quite concrete.

3. *If beginning over is always possible, if destiny yields to human intervention, then life is a never-ending series of opportunities, of doors waiting to be opened, of frontiers.* As the colonies developed, people moved further inland and set up still-newer colonies, thereby reinforcing this view. This moving frontier existed literally until the twentieth century. If there were disputes, and they were endless among Puritans with respect to religious ideas, the presence of still-unoccupied territory made it possible for dissenters to move on. If the best land was already occupied on the seaboard, there was plenty more inland, a cornucopia. That possibility convinced early Americans that opportunity was boundless.

Furthermore, abundant space meant that the sheer movement of people, which can give rise to rootlessness and placelessness, also encouraged the notion that here there was a "good" place for everyone. The theme of spaciousness thereby reinforced the promise of progress for everyone. In the older settlements, the best places were soon filled; but what of it? There were additional "empty" territories. Only slavery raised questions about this in early days, just as minority impoverishment and isolation from the mainstream do today.

Not only was there beautiful and open space, and the attendant promise of plenty, but the very grace of God was obviously the cause of this bounty and promise. This could be a land in which brotherhood itself might prevail "from sea to shining sea" and the promise that no one need want for food could be fulfilled. The new land was "America the Beautiful": "O beautiful for spacious skies/for amber waves of grain/for purple mountain majesties/above the fruited plain/America! America! God shed his grace on thee/And crowned thy good/with brotherhood/from sea to shining sea."

4. *Fulfilling these optimistic expectations encouraged the idea that success was always possible in human endeavors.* "Anything is possible" became a favorite theme for those who wrote and spoke optimistically of America as the land of opportunity where, they insisted, every day proved that new and better accomplishments were always possible. As the country expanded westward, as its dynamism, energy, remarkable climate, and natural resources continued to unfold, as new immigrants came, this message was repeated over and over and widely believed—as well it might have been, given the contrasts between the United States and Europe— except among those who for one reason or another never quite "made it" in the system. In the beginning it was the Indians; shortly thereafter it was the slaves; after they were freed but prevented from exploiting their

freedom, it was the blacks; and aside from blacks, it was the newest immigrants to arrive—each group in turn for a time being left out. But the view persisted that all would succeed, with the possible exception of American blacks, whose visibility and continuing history of struggle kept the issue of their place and role alive generation after generation.

5. *If newness, beginnings, getting things done, developing new land, moving across the continent, and simultaneously moving up or making it became central themes in the early and also later American view, there developed an accompanying notion that if one had to choose between change and tradition, one almost inevitably chose change.* Except for that one brief founding period, approximately 1770–1830, which remained frozen retrospectively as a triumphal and increasingly hallowed moment, traditions were seen as restrictive. Ironically, individuals from each new group, once successful and more or less accepted, came to believe in their turn that the current situation ought to be maintained. Periodic struggles arose, ostensibly over the preservation of tradition, in the face of pressures for change. And, of course, in the twentieth century, with many locked into and some locked out of high places, more explosive struggles loomed as possibilities, though successively interrupted by the Spanish-American War, World Wars I and II, the Korean conflict, the war in Vietnam, and the Persian Gulf War.

6. *Finally, the Lockean-American view suggested that in "the state of nature," the pre-civil condition, self-maintaining mechanisms were already operative and encouraged people to be productive.* This implied, and many Americans came to believe, as many still do, that these social and societal institutions were "natural," that they are rooted in the biological and physical order of things and are to be tampered with only at great risk. The conviction was widespread, and persists, that action by the government is at best a last resort and is always, when one speaks about the internal and domestic life of the nation, dangerous and counter-productive. In plain English this means a persistent view that "that government which governs least governs best." That was Jefferson's view, just as it appeared to be Ronald Reagan's, however different their respective times or the one's supposed radicalism and the other's conservatism. And it remained the view of Americans even in the presence of government activity and subsidy throughout the country's history—from the bargain basement purchase and later giveaway of the huge Louisiana territory, through the era in which westward expansion and railroad building was ensured by the government and in which the Constitution was put to work on behalf of industrial and financial development, to the present, in which government subsidy, support, and outright bailout have become the hallmark of a system whose leaders constantly speak of individual effort and private enterprise.

In contrast to these convictions, many "political" rules were in place—to accept private property, to exchange money, to sell crops, to build churches, to exploit a colony, to have servants, to "buy" slaves, to make and trade rum. These rules are evidence of the existence of "power" and therefore suggest a political foundation of which only the revolutionary generation, with its obvious concern to establish a new nation, seemed cognizant. Other Americans, including a chorus of experts among whom can be found members of corporations, governments, and the academy, seem little aware of this facet of the nation's history.

Thomas Jefferson's point of view dominated U.S. politics within fifteen years of the Constitution's adoption, even though again and again it was the activities and perceptions of his opponents—especially the early Federalists, the prematurely killed Alexander Hamilton or the long-reigning chief justice, John Marshall—that shaped much of American life. However, whether we have followed Jeffersonian ideas or not, and even he violated them as president, Americans tend to insist, even as they regularly ignore them in favor of their selfish interests, that Jefferson's words respecting limited government represent something akin to a biological truth. But there is much else in Jefferson's view of society that they have adopted as slogans:

(a). That men can live without government for the most part as long as there is land enough to go around. A variation on that theme (Madison) is that government exists only because many humans require control and, if need be, punishment. In other words, government is something that happens to us because men are not angels; but even that does not do it. Trouble begins when space either disappears or society becomes over-crowded with those who are different.

(b). That the society could stay harmonious provided a more or less consistent and relatively homogeneous style of life prevailed everywhere. The style or way of life was to be agricultural rather than commercial and revolve around the values of the yeoman farmer. Furthermore, the coun-try had to be culturally unified, even if there was diversity and in spite of the importance of individualism. Too many urban workers (Jefferson called them "sores on the body politic") were not healthy for the com-munity because they had customs, a way of life different from the yeomen he regarded as a chosen people. Black slaves also were a danger, for they were biologically different. If they physically intermingled with whites, they became a threat to the homogeneity of the population. (This was perhaps as much a commentary on what had happened, even in his own bed, than a prediction about the future.) His solution was to get rid of slavery by shipping blacks back to Africa. In sum, the concern for homogeneity is very strong in his writing and shows up in the work of other early Americans. Benjamin Franklin, for example, railed about the habits of German settlers, citing their persistent retention of the German language and resistance to the use of English as a menace to the well-being of the society.

The overarching theme of this Jeffersonian perspective is that society, with its diverse but largely economic activities, is natural and political life is artificial. Now this is true enough in the view of this writer, but it overlooks differences between the natural and the artificial except to the detriment of the latter. Early American thinking is understandably biased in favor of "naturalism," given the luck of the ex-Europeans who had stumbled on a natural gold mine, a partially occupied space in which they could expand without regard for present occupants, and therefore a chance to "make it" never before seen on earth. They had come to the right place at the right time.

Not satisfied with that, they invested this good fortune with all the sanctity of the religious and theological texts some of them, at least for the first years, spent so much time assessing and disputing about. So they came to believe that their good fortune and God's blessing were but two sides of a single coin and that what they did in the pursuit of success or "happiness" was naturally ordained by nature and nature's God. And in an endlessly abundant natural setting, there for the taking, just as Locke had noticed, it followed that they hardly needed to be governed, not too much by their own governors, still less by the once and distant mother country. What was done in society became equivalent to the body's biological rhythms and therefore took precedence over what was done in political life. Americans deviate from that conviction only with respect to dealings with outsiders where the prevailing view is that the government is always entitled to approval, a generosity not extended to domestic policies unless our group, town, industry, or state happens to be in trouble. The views of early Americans are modified, however, in two critical ways. First, the nation's leaders became more intense about international politics and the populace, after some resistance to overinvolvement in external affairs, finally accepted the idea of a *Pax Americana*. Second, despite anti-governmental rhetoric, enough Americans are apparently willing to give the government a strong hand at home when the benefits to them are visible in the form of tax breaks, land grants, or special favors.

The artificing and imagination that go into the building of human relations in that general, public entity known as political life or government has never been esteemed to the degree that business activity and farming have been, except at the moment of founding. Those who extol laboring, Jefferson among them, have confined their admiration to the fields, unless they run for office in a district with a preponderance of laborers. Rarely has the worker received ringing endorsements, though we have set aside a holiday to celebrate the virtues of laboring. In no instance, except as a reverie or dream about the past, has politics received much praise, certainly not since the Civil War. That that is now costing us dearly is a matter perhaps of dispute, but clearly these revered Lockean-American ideas have too little in them to resolve the kinds of problems that escalate while we maintain that old "truths" will see us through, forgetting that what accounts for America's success is not so much wisdom but the unmatched resources of this blessed, spacious land and the human energy set loose on it in a remarkable movement of peoples. Furthermore, whereas the Greeks saw politics as the generation of power, one aspect of which was foundational and required continuous support, the American view has never seen the renewal of foundations or support as significant except as the nation faces outward. The internal dynamics that create support systems have been seen as located elsewhere, in business and the marketplace, in farming and the cultivation of the soil, in town life and the separatism of the fifty states. As a result, the idea of government is a withered plant, parched for water and serious attention, though, somewhat incongruously, our governments are enormous in size.

NOTES

1. David Ritchie's *Natural Rights* (London: George Allen and Allen Unwin, 1894; 5th impression, 1952) argues that the appeal to nature has two usual sources. The negative source questions authorities and institutions once regarded as sacred or useful. The positive source is a version of "common sense" or "universal reason" that substitutes for inherited or conventional wisdom the "judgment of every individual" derived from one or the other. Although individual judgment and input are important if ever advances are to be made, these so-called natural rights raise the question of equality in such a debatable form—everyone's judgment is *ipso facto* equal to everyone else's—that controversy is inevitable. It also tends to substitute a new tie, commercial or cash transactions, for the old one, a permanent mutual obligation commanded by higher authority. When this new natural rights theory ages and is handed on as dogma, it too turns out to be dogmatic, except that the new authority or standard by which everything is measured is the well-being of the economic and social order, from which all true obligations and rights are now said to derive. See pp. 3–20.

2. For an excellent view of ancient Greek practice and outlook, see M. I. Finley, *Economy and Society in Ancient Greece*, edited by B. D. Shaw and R. P. Saller (New York: Viking Press, 1982). With respect to this comment see pp. 77–94.

3. See Gabriel Harman, *Ritualised Friendship and the Greek City* (Cambridge: Cambridge University Press, 1987), which argues this thesis. See particularly pp. 2–11 for a discussion of the inferences.

4. This is what Aristotle means when he asserts that the *polis* originates in the need for self-sufficiency—is the unit large enough to provide for "everyone" in contrast to the smaller necessary units, household and village?—but actually survives because above and beyond "mere" necessity, it provides for the good or "full" life. *Politics*, 1252b, sec. 8. Translated by Ernest Barker (New York: Oxford University Press, 1962), pp. 4–5.

5. Robert Garland, *The Greek Way of Life* (Ithaca, N.Y.: Cornell University Press, 1990), pp. 1–31.

6. Ibid.

7. John Locke, *Second Treatise of Civil Government* (1690; Indianapolis: Hackett Publishing Company, 1980), sec. 49, "Of Property," p. 29.

8. Thomas Hobbes, *English Works* (Molesworth edition), vol. 3, *Leviathan*, Chapter 13.

PART TWO
EMPOWERMENT AND ITS MAINTENANCE

7

Myth, Theory, Ideology: How We Attempt to Make Sense of Political Life

SCIENTIFIC AND HUMAN LAWS

Scientific laws predict behavior. They derive from application of appropriate methodologies and processes and events that are or resemble natural phenomena. They are human constructs that recapitulate cause-and-effect sequences, "forces" that, irrespective of human wishes or desires, occur predictably in nature and cannot be eliminated (but may be overcome by creating offsetting forces) *or* describe a human behavioral tendency. The law of gravity, which expresses the observable, measurable behavior of bodies in accordance with mass, distance, and attraction, is an example of a cause-and-effect sequence derived from observation of other than man-made or controlled phenomena. The "iron law of oligarchy," which states that *leaders tend to free themselves from the constraints and wishes of the membership that selects or consents to their leadership* (Roberto Michels, 1876–1936), is typical of constructs that attempt to describe human behavior.[1] Obviously, laws that describe physical phenomena and human behavior differ in their predictive precision. They are similar, however, in that they require validated, reliable descriptions of cause-and-effect relationships. Observations must be replicable to be validated; to be reliable, they must withstand disproof with respect to the causal relationship they predict. In other words, if I report a result based on observations that no one else can duplicate, in or out of the laboratory, the "law" I have discovered cannot be validated. But if validated, reliability is established only if predictions stand up.

However, human laws or rules are unlike scientific laws in important ways. They are not descriptive constructs but directives, encouragements, or warning signals. They threaten; punish transgressions; force and/or reward compliance; establish sanctions to discourage or prevent undesirable or unacceptable behavior. Human law may command people: "thou shalt not kill." That is, don't do what you are known to be capable of doing. Or it may require people to do what they otherwise might not do, for instance, observe a speed limit when driving an automobile.

Human laws are not reliable or valid descriptions of the way things are. On the contrary, they interrupt or control conduct, either to prevent what is possible but undesirable or to stimulate what is desirable but might otherwise not be done. They grow out of fears, hopes, and expectations and anticipate, regulate, shape, reorder, and color behavior and activity. We post a speed limit of fifty-five miles per hour because we know drivers prefer higher speeds which contribute to traffic fatalities. We forbid (most) killing because humans have always arbitrarily killed one another. In sum, laws are promulgated and enforced precisely because humans otherwise might or might not behave in certain ways. They give us a different order of probability than scientific laws: *what they forbid will occur*. And they generate an entirely different atmosphere than "nature's laws." Humans cannot alter the moon's gravitational pull on the earth, but they can alter life on earth. They transform as well as inherit the earth and do so on the basis of beliefs and convictions that help shape their judgments.

BELIEFS, CONVICTIONS, MYTHS

The word "myth," according to one writer, refers to "valuational responses [good! bad! better! worse! best! worst!] men give to the circumstances and trials of their lot, whatever conceptions guide their behavior, spur their ambitions or render existence tolerable."[2] These responses may be technically sophisticated philosophies, confused impressions, religious convictions, mature or immature responses to experiences. Mythic beliefs, irrespective of their truth or falsity, guide people when they make choices or act. This is not to say they are either true or false—they are true enough for those who believe them. What is crucial, however, is that humans cling to and act upon "valuational responses" not tested for scientific reliability or validity, nor necessarily consistent with common sense or the principle of non-contradiction (when two propositions are diametrically opposed, one is wrong). To a believer the claim that a myth is false is irrelevant, irreverent, or both.

Convictions, such as the belief that one race is superior to another biologically or genetically and therefore intellectually, appear to be as congenial and necessary to human beings as is the generalized sense among them that they are "naturally different" or "better than" others. That tendency makes possible the belief that a flag should not be "desecrated," a word that surrounds it with the aura of a religious icon. The flag reassures me, establishing my proximity to some and distance from others on the planet. "Old Glory," my flag, is a comforting blanket that warms me and the others who share my feelings toward it—and simultaneously connects me with them. Beliefs, such as sentimental and "valuational responses" about the sanctity of the flag, cannot be waived away or jeered at. They are significant.

Mythic beliefs do not lend themselves to the evaluations that science favors, in particular disproof, nor do they fare well if subjected to tests that rely on "reasonableness" or empirical validation. They are articles of truth and faith for the believer—and here I am concerned primarily with how they affect political relations, with their sheer presence, and not with analysis of that presence on the basis of any particular theory. During the Salem witch hunts, while many claimed that witches were pinching them, the atmosphere was such that an insistence that so-called agents of the devil cannot have substantiality, and therefore cannot "pinch," proved to be futile. A skeptic's failure to be pinched or to see witches swinging from church rafters did not alter what the victims felt or believed and what their supporters solemnly confirmed. On the contrary, the accusations multiplied, and failure to see made the doubters suspect. Were *they* in league with the devil? Believers, meanwhile, hailed the accusers for their defiance of the devil, thus placing themselves squarely in the ranks of true believers who recognized the ever-present danger of Lucifer's triumph and giving them an opportunity to accuse skeptics of undermining the community's unity.

Some see McCarthyism, the mid-twentieth-century belief that communists were well placed in major institutions—the military, the government, the schools—as similar. Using the threat of Soviet-controlled Bolshevism, accusers attempted a public cleansing of the body politic through loyalty oaths, confidential investigations, and congressional hearings that drove people out of their jobs. In time, critics of the hunt were attacked; they were said to be allied with the accused. By that route, critics, like the earlier Salem dissenters, were silenced. In time, such episodes can only be ended by those whose credentials are impeccable enough to place them beyond the reach of the accusers. Members of the military, President Dwight Eisenhower, and conservative senators in the end finally silenced Senator Joseph McCarthy.

Untestable convictions may be of dubious merit, but they are not always beneath contempt or irrational. They also celebrate freedom; whisper to people that migration will take them to the holy or promised land or a better job; suggest that to die for one's country is heroic; portray judges as impartial; maintain that education will enrich their lives and make them better human beings. Faith in them helps people cope. If they lose the array of shared beliefs that convince them to be cooperative and supportive, society might come apart at the seams. Neither internal order nor external relations can survive in the absence of a populace convinced of certain myths, which are part of what sociologists and political scientists call political socialization, a process that spontaneously goes on as the child becomes an adult and absorbs the values and beliefs that tie him or her to the political system. No process of this kind is ever total— were it otherwise we would simply replicate past convictions and attitudes. Some people do come to believe in different, opposing myths.[3]

At the simplest level, such beliefs are typified by convictions such as the now-little-esteemed "spare the rod and spoil the child," a homily that can be neither proven nor disproven. Such simple convictions may have little impact on politics. Turn instead to one that often buoys up Americans, to wit, the once widely held belief that the (U.S.) electoral system always produces "the best person" (formerly, "the best man") as the presidential nominee of the two major political parties. Disproving this is difficult. Partisan Republicans and Democrats can be persuaded or dissuaded only with respect to their own party's process. And even if they concede that their opponents do the same, the term "best man" permits no validation. Does it refer to character? Is conduct in private important? Is there something called "public character"? Do we mean best actor, athlete, political scientist, or philosopher? These are not questions to which valid answers can be given. So it is with all myths that affect political life. They are the conventional wisdom that operates on a day-to-day basis without serious appeal to evidence. Adolf Hitler repeatedly claimed that Germany lost World War I not to its enemies, but because of a "stab in the back," the treachery of certain German citizens who wished, he claimed, to see their own country defeated. Acceptance of Hitler's assertion by a large number of people typifies the non-susceptibility of such beliefs to proof or disproof as well as the presence of convictions that prepare the ground for the acceptance of accusations that, to outsiders, have no basis in fact. Hitler was thereby able to shift blame for the war's loss to scapegoats, absolve "good" Germans from responsibility, and obscure the foolishness of a policy that insisted on making war on two fronts. Millions of Germans enthusiastically agreed.

To speak of myths is to move as far away as possible from theory as conceived by scientists. Myths are "facts" in that people hold them, swear by them, act on them. Their importance cannot be overstated. Much of what we say, what we do, how we react in the context of political life, indeed, in all of our activities, is governed by these beliefs whether they are simple or complicated. To ignore them is to be constantly surprised by what happens within the political setting. These days the mass media feeds, enlarges upon, distorts, changes, modifies, and revises those convictions, often at lightning speed, in what can never be a totally objective way. To believe for a moment that the dictator of Iraq, however much his words are reported, will be presented on American television as supportively as the president of the United States is to deceive oneself. Our media builds up world events and affects our understanding accordingly, and they do not always present us with testable evidence. In this electronic age, they have become a ubiquitous source of beliefs and myths.

Since much that we do is dependent on untestable propositions, myths are inevitable. Theory, on the other hand, reflects the desire and willingness to test beliefs, convictions, hopes, and expectations. In hard science—physics, chemistry, biology—this leads to regularities that we believe can be counted upon forever. In the softer sciences—sociology, psychology, political science—a similar search for regularities is constantly under way. Advocacy of theory and science means a willingness to be disproven. For the scholar or student, for anyone who wishes to know in accordance with the rules of science, that willingness is mandatory; but, of course, myths are also a form of "knowledge."

Despite science fiction fantasies about a future governed entirely by hard-headed reasoning and theoretical conclusions, humans are likely to need and use myths. There is little difference, in the final analysis, between Plato's myth, disguised as theory, that there are fixed external Ideas that can be substituted for malleable, fallible human judgment and futurists' pretensions about a fact- and theory-driven universe. Human activities are partially shaped by the untestable, by articles of faith, by convictions that people believe in, share, and act upon as well as by the sheer contingency of the human condition. To overlook or make fun of this, to insist that political affairs are or ought to be largely a matter of theoretical propositions revealed to the uninitiated by the learned, is to arrogate to an elite of so-called clear thinkers the right to govern. Although many claim the title, no such group has yet appeared.

THEORY AND FACT

Coming to grips with the word "fact" is difficult. Confronted with the oft-stated cliche "the facts speak for themselves," we find ourselves giving the unsatisfactory if accurate reply, "facts require interpretation."

What, then, is a fact? To answer, we ask ourselves, "what does it mean to describe something?" and this precipitates other questions. Where do we start? With what information? If someone is asked to "describe the weather," how to begin? The answer seems simple: pick locations, report temperatures and conditions, rain, snow, degree of humidity, barometric readings, and so on. But what are these "facts"? They are what they are, in this instance readings consistent with systems of measurement that have been standardized or objectified plus less precise but widely understood qualities. Statements about the weather may be factual but as meaningful as one of the oft-heard BBC forecasts for Britain, "inter-mittent sunny spells." Moreover, if it is raining but I say, "the sun is shining," two problems show up at once—either I am an inept observer or I have chosen to misstate the facts.

If I ask, "how did the Korean war begin?" specifically, "what event initiated the actual outbreak of full-scale hostilities?" the answer is that "North Korea invaded South Korea." Facts, that is, are direct and presumably indisputable, although often imprecisely expressed truths, and that is why people say they speak for themselves. In the case of the Korean War, however, some dispute the factuality of the statement I just made. The "fact" of an invasion by North Korea, they say, will turn out to be anything but simple and direct. North Korea might have been pro-voked into an attack, in which case the discussion of "the facts" must move to an entirely different level. There has to be an evaluation and interpretation of available data. My original answer is factual only with respect to the moment of invasion. The same is true of other so-called factual statements respecting the instant the German army crossed into Poland, Japanese airplanes attacked Pearl Harbor, Hawaii, or the hour rain began to fall in Peoria, Illinois. Each responds to a specific question with an answer that states what indisputably *is* or *was* the case and can-not be altered unless lies are told, there is no one to tell what happened, everyone's memories are wiped away, or all records are destroyed.

To decide whether or not the North Koreans were provoked requires evidence and inferences. The difference between stating the facts and making a valid statement about them is easy enough to see in an exam-ple drawn from logic textbooks, as in the syllogism "All men are animals. Socrates is a man. Therefore Socrates is an animal." But "what precipitated the invasion of South Korea or of Poland or the bombing of Pearl Harbor?" is an evaluative question, the response to which depends on the availability and construction of valid answers. It is not as simple as the textbook syllogism.

This neither lessens the importance of facts nor frees us from the obliga-tion to recall them. Indeed, if we fail to save the facts we lose our bear-ings in the world, since they indicate "what is the case" and are storehouses of memory and therefore expectations. But facts as such neither have nor carry with them any necessary meaning. In and of themselves, they explain nothing. They have no built-in meaning. Without some organized way of understanding, they are a mass of inexplicable data. Even the most hideous and expressive of facts—the existence of a murderous concentration camp or killing field—is mute, though power-fully suggestive. Phenomena that startling, unless explicable, leave the observer silent, shocked, and speechless, overwhelmed by the sheer unbelievability of what the eyes see.

In sum, facts require interpretation and treatment, and these depend upon judgments as to which are and are not important as well as the assignment of "meaning" to them. This assigns them variable weight. To reach a judgment, the members of a jury will each weigh the facts differently, screening or sorting them to isolate what is relevant and telling. They then collectively work out interpretive disagreements, a process that resembles what goes on when any collective decision is made: there is dialogue and exchange and a mutual effort to persuade.

What if factual information is scanty? For example, a disease spreads extensively throughout society, but the method of transmittal is unclear. An investigator hypothesizes, setting up propositions that can be tested. To do that effectively often depends on experience that leads to "hunches." The good diagnostician who says "I suspect that X is the culprit" is the one who has command of the literature and sufficient experience to rule out the least likely hypotheses.

Diagnosing and hypothesizing are sorting-out processes akin to what we mean by the term "theory." Theories attempt to organize, explain, or give meaning to what otherwise would be masses of unrelated or random facts or experiences. A theoretical statement or proposition presents the facts in such a way as to clarify relationships among them. The symbiosis between fact and theory is crucial. Theory derives and is construed from facts; a proposition has no theoretical standing if it contradicts the facts it employs; a theory can only contradict the facts it does *not* employ. While in everyday affairs facts are immediately confirmed by shared observations and comparisons, the stuff of historical, social, and political life requires memory (the means to preserve "the facts"), research, clarification, and assessment. When one seeks explanatory constructs, theory is the general term that covers successful efforts. Theory is "good" when congruent with the facts—its claim to explain is validated and reliable—not because it is pleasant, likeable, or preferred. Good theory coherently represents the facts: it synthesizes or pulls them together and its summation is consistent with them.

If a non-fact (error, distortion of information, lie) is utilized to explain something, then the theoretical structure dependent on that factual foundation collapses. Someone may claim, "'intelligence' correlates perfectly with 'race'" (i.e., "race" X is more intelligent than "race" Y), and if a series of observers perform similar tests and statistical analyses that produce deviations from the generalization, we have no choice but to conclude that the theory has no basis in fact and therefore no standing as a theory. If the assertion is insisted upon, it is not a theory but an untestable—and many of us would argue, false—belief.

The commonly heard complaint, "you're being too theoretical, just give me the facts," assumes that theory is a form of unsubstantiable speculation, therefore remote from the facts, and that facts not only exist but also somehow explain themselves. Both assumptions are incorrect. The individual who theorizes is not being impractical. On the contrary, he or she remains as close to the facts as is possible. Theory, therefore, is not dreamy stargazing, shapeless speculation, or fuzzy thinking, but a practical exercise whose aim is to make sense of the world being examined, be it the workaday world, the microscopic worlds of cells or genes, the telescopic universe of heavenly bodies, or the humanly constructed world of politics. None of this excludes the obvious variance in theories that seek answers to different questions and therefore seek out different facts. Theories, after all, involve valuations and choices and they do not exclude the possibility that certain speculations, consistent with matters humans feel compelled to explain, may never lend themselves to scientific fact gathering and are handled by other means—faith or myth, for example.

Normative or prescriptive theory, which deals with what "ought to be," prescribes rather than describes; it seeks to remedy a condition or reach toward a goal. It looks to a better or improved future; whereas theory as defined above attempts to read the past coherently in order to say, "if the future is an extension of the past and present, then this is what will happen." Nonetheless, prescriptions also require attention to what is and has been the case. If I say that people ought to behave in a moral way and ought always to seek "the good," I am also suggesting that it is possible to know, factually, what "the good" is and act accordingly. Statements about what ought to be are no less dependent upon a factual base for verification and support than are theories about the world as it is.

Theory may develop by a method that stresses observation—in what we call good diagnosis—but it may also develop by insight and deductions growing out of principles isolated at a time when the facts in no way seem to suggest them. A case in point might be Albert Einstein's initial assertion that space is curved, for which no regular observational evidence was then available and which depended on mathematically derived principles that some but not all mathematicians and physicists understood. Empirical evidence, in the form of photographs, followed some years later.

The use of statistical materials, so important in current behavioral science, complicates the problem of dealing with and interpreting the facts. Statistical data is mass data; that is, it incorporates information by classes or categories, of which the terms "race" and "people sixty-five years of age and older" are examples. These categories make statistical analysis possible, but they also swallow up the individuals who in aggregate make up the category. We can speak statistically about race X or Y, about "blacks" or "whites," about people who are sixty-five years of age or older, but no one has ever seen the black "race" or white "race" or the group "people sixty-five and over." We see individuals who are black or white, who are younger or older than sixty-five. That distinction is often lost in our haste to generalize, and there is the consequent danger of assuming that the category "white" is real; whereas the individual who is white, a discrete and unique person rather than the representative of a category, is merely a statistical deviation from some mean, average, or norm that aggregates all individuals who are white. Other behavioral observations, as noted earlier, create a similar difficulty: sexual preferences, for example, may be used as a description of an individual's entire being or character. This perhaps reflects the growing impact of statistical data on our thinking, that is, a habit or tendency to evaluate by category rather than individuated act. It is understatement to point out that that has been the fate of the vast majority of Americans of African origin.

IDEOLOGY

Confronted with the vast array of human happenings, ideology and the ideologue or ideologist suggest that everything can be sorted coherently, that things fit together, that there is a structure and/or pattern in human affairs that accounts for, explains, and even predicts sequences of events.[4] The "idea" in ideology therefore tends to be somewhat general and sweeping, presuming to explain broadly all human social, political, and economic processes and occurrences.

Marxism, for example, explains the operations of society using ideas originally brought together by the philosopher and social scientist Karl Marx (1818–1883). Marx's central notion is that human misery and degradation are neither the result of some universal, ordained plan nor the accidental by-product of a series of diverse, individually correctable problems, but an outgrowth of the structure of society. Society is a vast, coherent system whose many complexities are reducible to persistent structural patterns or "structural imperfections."[5] These regularities in all their complexity were detailed by Marx in a corpus of publications that include newspaper articles, pamphlets, historical analyses, and lengthy scholarly books. Marxian ideas, including what are called "laws of class struggle," presume to explain the way human society develops and functions, in particular the layering of society into classes that compete with one another and a consequent exploitative situation whereby the ruling class depends upon a laboring class it simultaneously controls and reduces to a condition of misery.

Ideology is reminiscent of what we have called theory. As explanation, Marxism synthesizes significant facts that come to serve as the explanatory key to the current and future development of society. A general idea or conceptualization drawn from study of social, economic, and political relations describes the past and present and, insofar as nothing alters current economic and social relations in the society, predicts the future. But ideology differs from theory because discovered regularities are utilized to predict the future and to change the very conditions that gave rise to the regularities. Ideology may begin as a theoretical construct but adds in a political and social program: eliminate, alter, or accelerate the core phenomenon that in the first instance yielded the explanation. If the central idea or condition that drives human history is now known, then insofar as suffering and injustice have been systemic and structural, a correction must be made. Theories clarify and recapitulate systemic phenomena that are inherent in the system. They can foster adjustments but do not change circumstances. Ideologies are different: They lead directly to programs for change, to political action. If one discovers, as Marx claimed to, that the productive system had generated an oppressive class structure and further discovers that over time the struggle narrows, leaving only two warring classes, then the ideology first predicts an outcome—a single surviving class followed by a classless society, therefore the end of class warfare—and then decides to take action, as Marxists did, to speed up the historical process. Some might claim that ideology is therefore akin to biochemical and medical research in which infectious processes are discovered and antidotes developed. But the analogy is false. Antidotes may in time eliminate a disease, but the natural processes that account for the disease remain viable even if a specific agent of a particular disease is forever banished from the earth.

Ideology attempts to do away with and/or enhance ongoing processes. In other words, although ideology may be rooted in a desire to explain and clarify, it moves on to political action. Prescriptions in ideology presumably derive from descriptions; the ideologue supposedly stands in relation to the theoretician as the practicing physician does to the medical researcher. But critics see the ideologue differently. They believe that proposed changes in the order of things are unacceptable because they interfere with what have been seen as natural or reasonable processes whose alteration might damage society beyond repair. Critics also note that ideologies, since they move theorists out into the streets, provoke premature experimentation with the social order and assume, rather than prove, that society is responsible for human ills and therefore needs to be transformed.[6]

My view is that ideologies may also be committed to the preservation or even the restoration of social, economic, and political practices. American ideological positions often celebrate or romanticize a past in which individualism flourished and men and women succeeded largely on their own. At the heart of this view, and common to strenuous ideological commitment, is a belief in change—in this instance coupled with a glance backward to a presumed pristine and better time. If ideology attempts to explain and then offers programs in the light of the explanation, there is no reason why these cannot celebrate and venerate the past or present, why a so-called law of history that has been pushed aside or stymied by untimely interventions ought not once again be allowed to operate. The past can be looked upon as a time of virtue and beneficence and the present as a time when society has reached a zenith, as if what is good in life had been achieved. If so, if a society is at the end of development, an ideology might indeed urge us to stand pat. Or the present may be seen as constantly progressive, therefore leading to the never-ending betterment of life. Ideologies are packaged in various ways—as humans choose.

The ideology of the *invisible hand*, which has played a very prominent part in Western economic development, calls for preservation, restoration, or installation of an unregulated or free marketplace. It originally arose in conjunction with the marketplace economy of early capitalism, a critique of feudal and mercantilist practices, particularly the fixed places, statuses, and relationships that threatened to interfere with newly exploding market forces. It asserts that society is governed by self-regulating laws, such as the law of supply and demand, that function best when unimpeded. The accompanying political program insists that self-regulation is consistent with "nature" and produces an "invisible hand" that operates automatically in the marketplace. The complex theoretical grounding of this ideology owes much to the work of John Locke (1632–1704).[7]

In his *Second Treatise of Civil Government* Locke maintains that each human possesses the energy or labor power that makes human existence and survival possible. Labor power is concurrent with life itself and is valuable not simply as the basis of survival; it also is each individual's exclusive property. The earth itself, however, the space in which humans have been placed, is initially shared by everyone. God thereby authored the two dynamic principles that govern the human condition: collectively, humans once owned the entire earth; individually, humans possess (own) labor power. A third idea, ownership of property, is the implicit but necessary foundation of the other two. And a fourth, the idea of exchange, is implicit: with ownership comes control of disposition. Locke believes, then, that individuals are "propertied" at birth: They possess their lives, which he equates with energy or the capacity to labor, and they own property. At first, they jointly hold title to all land but now maintain joint title to all unclaimed or undeeded land, of which the huge "empty" spaces of the New World represented the latest and most exciting example. Given the abundance of land "in the beginning," and the appearance of this untouched space, he asserts further that any man who applies his labor to a portion thereof is entitled not only to resulting crops and produce but also to permanent title to the land itself: *application of labor to a portion of common land creates title to that sector*. One possession (labor power) is exchanged or expended for another (exclusive title to formerly common land). Thus Locke justifies private ownership.[8]

To this he appends the idea that the rights to life, liberty, and estate are also natural, God-given, and irreducible. Humans may choose to give up their lives or exchange their properties (labor power, land that they have earned through its use, or resulting wealth—money having come into existence in this early natural state), since they have the right to dispose of whatever property is theirs, but the rights themselves—life, liberty, estate—can never be bartered or bargained away, not even in civil society. The proximity of these ideas to the "life, liberty and property" celebrated in the United States Constitution is or ought to be evident.

Locke elaborates his story:

He who appropriates land to himself by his labour, does not lessen, but increase the common stock of mankind: for the provisions serving to the support of human life, produced by one acre of inclosed and cultivated land, are . . . ten times more than those which are yielded by an acre of land of an equal richness lying waste in common. And therefore he that incloses land [ten acres] . . . may truly be said to give ninety acres to mankind.[9]

In other words, by removing property from mankind's common storehouse and making it private, an individual takes nothing away, but adds something to mankind, has made a gift, land that is productive rather than fallow, to his fellows.

This is the original core "idea" in the invisible-hand ideology: *when I use land, that is, labor energetically, I am rewarded by the produce and title to the land, but at the same time, others are rewarded; by making the land fertile, I have made a contribution to everyone else. Whatever benefits me, benefits everyone.* To state that differently: whatever I do to improve my own economic situation, my own welfare and well-being, automatically unites my efforts and everyone else's into a system that benefits all people who live in the society. The more selfishly I pursue my private ends, the more altruistic I become. Friedrich Hayek offers a contemporary version: "the acquisition by any member of the community of additional capacities to do things which may be valuable must always be regarded as a gain for that community."[10]

Might not acquisition of additional land harm someone in the community? Locke responds by setting limits of a sort to my acquisitiveness, while Hayek answers that although some may be disadvantaged, the majority of the community gains. But through what mechanism? That can be discovered by noting the way in which Locke's successors, notably the Physiocrats, French agricultural theorists of the eighteenth century, developed capitalist economic theory. They shifted attention away from the individual and his labor, focusing instead on the importance of productive or cultivated land as the source of value, and they argued that free labor applied to privately held land was the primordial source of wealth. For the invisible hand to function properly, however, government intervention was prohibited absolutely. The Physiocrats and their successor economists, among them the founding father of classical political economy, Adam Smith, maintained that the market was a self-regulating entity that when left to it own devices produced the best distribution of goods and services and therefore the general betterment of the society at large.[11] For Smith and the Physiocrats, the so-called invisible hand, the presumably natural laws that governed the marketplace, is the result of self-developed equilibriums between demand and supply and price and production. To them this is a process as inevitable and natural as gravity itself that works automatically in the absence of interferences from governmental regulation or monopolies. Karl Marx, also influenced by Locke, accepted Locke's ideas about the value of labor and reworked them into an alternative theory that all value was derived, not from land or capital, but from labor. Marxist ideology, with its historical basis in class warfare, thus derives from the same source as capitalist, invisible-hand ideology.

To sum up, the invisible-hand ideology asserts a God-sanctioned right to private property, then adds the claim that exercise of property rights—including use of land and of the individual's labor in a free market—produces general benefits above and beyond self-regulation. The accompanying political program is simple: eliminate government activity that in any way interferes with unfettered operation of these forces in an open, unregulated market.

Explanatory theory develops in a research space protected from everyday calls for action and is as close to pure scientific effort as is possible in the social sciences and humanities. Calls for action, in contrast, are public and must involve dialogue with people unfamiliar with elaborate historical and scholarly theses. The result is simplification. This is as true of what we called the capitalist or invisible-hand ideology as of Marxism. No formulation of free market ideas and their political platforms can be as simple (and distorting) as the ideological demand that business operations be permitted to proceed unencumbered by any sort of intervention or regulation. Adam Smith, an originator of the invisible-hand ideology, rejected competitive free-for-alls and total elimination of governmental intervention. But the later view typifies what happens when an idea is cut away from theoretical moorings and made part of a public dialogue. Marx's theories suffered similar simplifications, among them the assertion that only a vanguard or elite, namely, members of the Communist Party, understand the historical dialectic and therefore have the right to operate as the high priests of developing socialism. Not surprisingly, while ideologues continued to debate "truths" derived from the past, capitalist and communist nations abandoned them. In invisible-hand societies, the state's hand touched everything; in Marxist societies, the cry for private ownership is heard everywhere. Inherited ideologies can be dinosaurs; try as they will, they may not fit today's facts.

An ideology, we have said, does not merely explain the way society, culture, civilization, and politics work but attempts to justify and/or change human affairs. It connects ideas to action and either claims that "things are as they ought to be and therefore are going well" or "society is defective and ought to be changed" (as often as not, radically). Ideology transmogrifies theory and becomes an *agent provocateur* in, rather than mere observer of, human affairs. The convinced ideologue studies not simply nor even primarily to increase human knowledge but to change the world. The task of even the most impractical of subjects, philosophy, is not to study the world but to contribute to its betterment, so Marx, who opened the door to modern ideological formulations, believed.

Furthermore, since ideology adds political programs to analysis and actively engages the world, it produces intense commitment and conviction well beyond the level reached even by the most dedicated proponents of new scientific theories. Theories—even new theoretical constructions being urged upon skeptical scientists—suggest detachment: explanations presumably follow the facts wherever they may lead. Ideology is more intense and can, like a virus, weaken its carriers' defenses and neutralize them. Ideologists, like theorists, begin by seeking a verifiable appraisal of the facts, but the compulsion to act grows stronger. Ultimately, action becomes all important. Moreover, since advocacy is as important as explication, the ideologue who is exposed to disagreement is unlikely to retreat. Nowhere is this better illustrated than in the exchanges that have beset international politics during the latter half of the twentieth century as an outgrowth of constant face-offs between the Soviet Union and the United States, particularly since each insisted that what is also at stake between them is not only their particular point of view and ideas but also the survival of a decent world. It follows that dialogue stagnates. Phrases like "capitalist exploitation," "communist totalitarianism," "crime in the streets," and "free enterprise" are emptied of content. Commitments and convictions threaten to displace genuine exchanges of view. Totally convinced ideologues become puppets whose words are placed in their mouths by their own unwillingness to take another look at evidence.

CLASSIFYING IDEOLOGIES

Human beings live a good part of their lives shielded from the world of political talk. Much of what they cherish has little to do with governments. Yet someone who is skilled, an Adolf Hitler in the Germany of the 1930s, for example, can whip up thousands of people and for a time move them to expend as much energy on the state of their nation as on the condition of their finances or love lives. Perhaps symbols and beliefs that are tribal, national, and religious are as important to people as the concrete and visible persons and objects that surround them in daily life. It is more likely, however, that when times are ordinary and unexceptional, human beings will be occupied more with the people and things that are part of their personal, private lives than with the abstracted symbols of flag, nation, movement. Under these conditions, ideologies can be extremely valuable in maintaining individual involvement with general and public concerns. They convert a maze of appearances and an abundance of speculations into a more or less orderly view of the world.

In hard or turbulent times, the balances change because the outer world, the elements larger and more general than family and friends, impinge more directly and heavily on personal lives. Domestic troubles now closely mirror community and national issues.[12] The urgency and impact of issues creates a pressing need for quick understanding and simplifications, and here ideologies become a potentially explosive phenomenon.

Ideologies, therefore, are an important part of political life. Many seem incomprehensible, extreme, even dangerous to non-advocates. But the attempt to link theory with political action, which is the source of ideologies, is a contribution to human dialogue. Ideologies provide an opportunity to proximate theory in political dialogue. This does not mean, however, that they are guaranteed to remain untainted by excess or fanaticism. In keeping with the view that ideologies are necessary but sometimes excessive and destructive, I distinguish two types. My purpose is not to create fixed categories but to point out tendencies.

Exploratory Ideology

Exploratory Ideology is pliable with respect to changing conditions and evidence. Like all ideological phenomena, it is supported by explanatory generalizations about the world but permits, even encourages, alterations in those explanations. An example is the widespread belief, expressed by Thomas Jefferson, that "that government is best which governs least," the origin of which we have previously discussed.[13] Government was to be reined in by barriers expressed variously as the right to life, liberty, and estate, or life, liberty, and the pursuit of happiness. The rights exist prior to government and remain intact after its establishment. While many Americans advocated a much larger role for government, this view well expressed a theory of government consistent with conditions prevailing in the new nation and therefore both described a present America and prescribed a political program for future progress.

Americans have repeatedly moderated this view. Government resources might be used to encourage private development or tackle problems too large for non-governmental entities. In the Populist era (late nineteenth century), governments applied controls to railroads and other interstate businesses, hoping to bring these interests and farmers' concerns into equilibrium. Progressive urban reforms (early twentieth century) further enlarged government activity. During the New Deal era (1933–1972) government stimulated the economy and protected workers from the operations of marketplace laws Americans once believed best left to operate without government intervention. The modern American state and bureaucratic apparatus had been born. But Americans maintained that their original ideological formulation was still valid. The basic Jeffersonian formula was now said to be broad enough to permit the government to protect individuals from circumstantial disabilities or the excesses of oversized private interests.

The ideological formulation modified as conditions changed. While some complained that the true original theory of government had been twisted out of shape, these modifications demonstrate how an exploratory ideology adjusts to and takes into account new facts.

Another feature of the early Jeffersonian ideology was the proposition that the backbone of a good society consisted of hard-working, independent farmers and yeomen. The accompanying program of the Jeffersonians called for the maintenance of a yeomen-dominated society. Not long afterward, even Jefferson gave up on that possibility. While he may have continued throughout his life to believe that the "best" American society would be free of congested cities, he recognized that events encouraged a mercantile, commercial, urban America. And that indeed came to pass. But the heart of early Jeffersonianism persists: What was once said to be true of the small farmer was simply transferred to others, workers and businessmen. The ideological residue enlarged the virtue of the farmer into the idea that those who work, in whatever capacity, are primary contributors to the well-being of the country. This group of hard workers also fits the early Puritan work ethos, despite the inconsistency of a machine and service technology with these ideas. In exploratory ideology elements do not harden to the point where deviations are rejected in the name of the ideology. It might be argued that this flexibility is the hallmark of a non-ideology, but the belief system expounded by many Americans fits the definition of ideology. It has a credo built upon an explanation of the human condition and an accompanying program, however remote from contemporary conditions. Exploratory ideology stretches out and incorporates new factors and facts, but it depends on a central idea and offers a program.

Orthodoxy

Orthodoxy is characterized by doctrinaire allegiance to an explanatory or theoretical foundation regarded as a fixed set of truths applicable throughout history. The orthodox will, if need be, push, mold, or color interpretations of events and structures to correspond with the ideology's expectations. Nazi orthodoxy identified "inferior" (non-Aryan, Semitic, and "dark" or "colored") races as the source of degeneracy on the planet and proposed either to eliminate or enslave them. The mere existence of "inferior" races threatened the purity of the "superior" Aryan blood and exposed the world to wily degenerates who exerted influence everywhere and whose elimination was a holy task calling for nerves of steel and a special kind of courage. Lack of evidence to support these preposterous assertions meant little, and wholesale murder could now be justified as ideologically necessary. The idea of racial purity became intertwined with a monumental disregard for the sanctity of human life or the right of humans, other than those selected by the Nazi leadership, to occupy space on the planet.

Joseph Stalin's Soviet Union was similarly disinclined to deal with a reality other than that which ideologues conjured. Stalin's belief that everyone close to him in the apparatus or organization known as the Communist Party threatened his life and the system led to murderous purges in the party and wholesale expulsions to the gulag. That this activity was simply the result of Stalin's paranoia is worth considering. However, orthodoxy is not a personal view of the world but an ideology that purports to explain everything. Stalin's confusion between his own leadership and the course of Russian, Soviet, and even human development became, for the longest time, a hallmark of the Russian Communist Party and its satellites around the world—and is not entirely unheard of wherever there is hierarchy. Suspicion of the motives of others, particularly of close supporters, became part of what was said to be Marxist ideology. The members of the party, ostensibly leaders of the historical movement toward a classless society, became the luckless victims of the fear that highly placed groups and individuals carry the virus of dissent within them and must be eliminated before history can proceed toward its predestined outcome. At the same time, Marxism, in the Russian version, adapted and outdid the tactics of czarist Russia. The persistent use of secret police, spies, efforts to penetrate enemy organizations, and similar tactics, commonplace in the last decades of the czarist regimes, influenced all sides in the struggle for control of Russia.

The paranoid element in Soviet communist ideology is consistent with orthodoxy. Wherever there are true believers, there is bound to be a search for false believers, hypocrites, enemies, and those who claim that current facts no longer justify the original theory. But even constantly evolving paranoia may finally be forced to reconsider reality. One of the most remarkable events in the late twentieth century has been the gradual weakening of communist orthodoxy, culminating in radical transformations in eastern Europe and the current tensions with the Soviet Union itself. It is too early to tell whether these can fairly be ascribed to ideological rigidity or simply reflect the system's inability to maintain productivity. A settling down and time to analyze are required.

At its most extreme, orthodoxy demands total commitment from advocates and substitutes mindless endorsements for thoughtfulness and reexamination. The totally committed become an inner circle or elite, priests who guard and enforce the orthodoxy's truth. Within the elite certain individuals emerge as high priests. True believers form a circle around them, shielding them from contact with the world and from would-be attackers. Exploratory ideology, on the other hand, demands commitment from large numbers of people and wins their general support not so much for detailed programs but for the major explanations and viewpoints of the ideology. The phrase "capturing the imagination of the people" may describe the degree of commitment and conviction required of advocates. This is a flexible, changing phenomenon. Orthodoxy is more formal, fixed, and demanding and tends to give rise to organization, which means membership, dues or duties, leadership groups, and propaganda sheets reporting the activities of the leaders. Wavering supporters threaten unity; therefore orthodoxies' elites seize every opportunity to purify and purge membership.

Exploratory ideologies cohere minimally. The theoretical element—willingness to test and weigh interpretations in the light of evidence—survives. Most U.S. political liberals and conservatives could be considered advocates of exploratory ideologies. They are serious advocates but not yet committed to an all-embracing explanation of the entire human universe. The orthodox, in contrast, believe that truth has been uncovered for all time. They are found not only in the Soviet Union and China but also in the United States, where some maintain a doctrinaire opposition to the Soviet Union more pertinent to Stalin's time than to the present, while others discover "eternal truths" in ancient philosophers, convert them to doctrines, and apply them, willy-nilly, to every context. But the real hallmark of orthodoxy may well be intellectual and political elitism, the circle of true believers. In the final analysis, orthodoxy disfigures ideology by petrifying its theoretical foundation, which then becomes mere doggerel, doggerel strong enough to support the use of terror to work its will on non-believers.

Ideologies do not necessarily have developmental or evolutionary histories that drive them inexorably from theory and science to fixed, unyielding orthodoxy. They are advocacies of a kind that apparently first appeared during the French Revolution and have been with us ever since as an operational fact of modern politics, representing programmatic hopes, desires, and expectations. Twentieth-century orthodoxies, meanwhile, warn us of the ever-present darker side of ideological thinking.

Thus far, even in choice of words (theory, fact, ideology), I have opted to remain within vocabularies reflective of the old physical sciences and old social science, which tends to link ideology and theory, the one being partisan, therefore bad, the other supposedly neutral, therefore good. However, neither neutral theory, which has little impact on government, nor ideology, which has greatly influenced government policies on both sides of the suddenly lifted Iron Curtain, has checked the apparent loss of confidence—visible in Europe as well as the United States—in the capacity of current polities to solve problems. This suggests that altered images and words are needed, for it is the contention here that shared beliefs and ideologies, in some form, will always exist to support political systems and that they are equivalently vital to the ongoing foundation building and politicking aspects of power.

NOTES

1. "Organization implies the tendency to oligarchy." Roberto Michels, *Political Parties: A Sociological Study of the Oligarchical Tendencies of Modern Democracy* (1915; New York: Dover Publications, 1959), p. 32.
2. The quotation—but not the exclamatory interjections—and the paraphrased sentence that follows are from R. M. MacIver, *The Web of Government* (New York: Macmillan Company, 1947), pp. 4–5.
3. See entry for "Myth," *International Encyclopedia of the Social Sciences*; see also Gilbert Morris Culbertson, *Political Myth and Epic* (Lansing, Mich.: Michigan State University Press, 1975).
4. Following Kenneth Minogue's commentary in *Alien Powers: The Pure Theory of Ideology* (New York: St. Martin's Press, 1985).
5. The phrase is Minogue's. Ibid., pp. 31–32.
6. Ibid., p. 44. Minogue apparently regards ideological transformation as always devoted to progressive change. My view is different: ideologies may look to the restoration of a "better" past.
7. We have already looked at one aspect of Locke's thought (see section entitled "Locke and the Early Americans" in Chapter 6).
8. Locke, *Second Treatise of Civil Government* (1690; Indianapolis: Hackett Publishing Company, 1980), Chapter 5, "Of Property," sec. 15–51, pp. 19–30.
9. Ibid., sec. 37.
10. F. A. Hayek, *The Constitution of Liberty* (Chicago: Henry Regnery Company, Gateway edition, 1972), p. 88.
11. On the Physiocrats and Smith see the appropriate entries in David Miller, ed., *The Blackwell Encyclopedia of Political Thought* (Oxford: Basil Blackwell, 1987), pp. 372–73 and 476–78, respectively.
12. On "troubles" and "issues" see C. Wright Mills, *The Sociological Imagination* (New York: Oxford University Press, 1959), pp. 8–15, 128–31.
13. See Chapter 6.

8

The Political Process: How Politicking Works and What Makes It Work

Every person in the United States is subject to at least two political jurisdictions (three if local and other governments are included) and therefore has dual citizenship, state and national, and two "sovereigns." No single government in the nation is responsible for every rule, statute, or law, or for applications thereof. Nor is there a single court system. This arrangement, called "federalism," originally intended to salvage the states while establishing a single nation or Union, is perhaps the most intricate system of governance ever devised by men.

The structure of U.S. governments guarantees additional complications. Decision-making authority is allocated to the several branches—legislative, executive, judicial. Nebraska excepted, state legislatures consist of two houses, with members elected for terms of different duration. Jurisdictional boundaries are often in dispute among governments—local, state, national—as well as within them. Turf fights are common. The Supreme Court of the United States has often been at odds with one or another branch, and it can be scuffed up when a battle ensues. Congress and the president are often at odds, particularly since the president has constitutional rights with respect to legislation and is subject to Congress' constitutional authority to pass budgetary and other legislation. Friction is built into the system's machinery.

But friction is a small part of the complexity. The presence of huge numbers of extra-constitutional players further complicates U.S. politics. There are political parties—often differing in character and outlook from state to state—and there are thousands of pressure groups operating both within and outside of the government. Furthermore, quasi-governmental status has been conferred on non-governmental groups. Bar associations are involved in selection of judges. Medical associations control the licensing of physicians. Linkages exist between health insurance companies, which differ from state to state, and the Medicare system, a national plan providing health care benefits for people over sixty-five. Hospitals, too, however independent they appear to be, depend on the government for funds and are affected by and affect public policy. Similar complications occur in the states as well as the nation's territories to the point where the phrase "the government of the United States" has no fixed reference point.

Furthermore, the Union was founded by thirteen states strung along the eastern seaboard with a total population of four million; the remaining thirty-seven were admitted to the Union and in this regard are its "creatures" rather than the other way around—including, West Virginia, torn "illegally" out of Virginia during the Civil War; Nevada, admitted with a very small population during that same conflict; Texas and California, once independent republics; and a number carved out of cessions or purchases following the war with Mexico.[1] Beyond, and presumably above all these, are "the people" who supposedly ordained the Constitution, eventually won the right to participate directly in the election of senators, indirectly choose the president (following political parties' nominations, of course), and in some states directly participate in governance through the initiative and referendum.

In the face of their political situation, the founders did what they had to, namely, acknowledge sovereign pairs of governments—the Union and each of the states. But what was a remarkable compromise then is a mechanical and political nightmare now.

No one can say precisely what the attitudes of the people, 250 million of them, are toward any of these governments. Opinion polls, regularly cited by television announcers, reveal little except the constant and quick rise and fall of support and opposition as measured by responses to questions that are gauged to measure particularities or are structured on the the basis of a three-choice response—"approve," "disapprove," "don't know"—that reveals little. But recall the scene in Mark Twain's *Adventures of Huckleberry Finn* in which Huck, a reluctant and frightened prisoner of his father, reports the old man's attitude toward "the government."

Whenever his liquor begun to work he most always went for the government. This time he says: "Call this a govment! Why look at it and see what it's like. Here's the law a-standing ready to take a man's son away from him. . . . Just as that man has got that son raised at last, and ready to go to work and begin to do suthin' for *him* and give him a rest, the law up and goes for him. And they call *that* govment! That ain't all, nuther. The law backs old Judge Thatcher up and helps him to keep me out o' my property. . . . They call that govment? A man can't get his rights in a govment like this. . . . Oh, yes, this is a wonderful govment, wonderful. Why, looky here. There was a free nigger there from Ohio—a mulatter, most as white as a white man. He has the whitest shirt on you ever see, and the shiniest hat; and there ain't a man in that town that's got as fine clothes as what he had; and he had a gold watch and chain, and a silver-headed cane. . . . And what do you think? They said he was a p'fessor in a college, and could talk all kinds of languages, and knowed everything. And that ain't the wust. They said he could *vote* when he was at home. Well, that let me out. Thinks I, what is the country a'coming to? It was 'lection day, and I was just about to go and vote myself if I warn't too drunk to get there; but when they told me that there was a state in this country where they'd let that nigger vote, I drawed out. I says I'll never vote ag'in. . . . I says to the people, why ain't this nigger put up at auction and sold?—that's what I want to know. And what do you reckon they said? Why, they said he couldn't be sold till he'd been in the state six months. . . . Here's a govment that calls itself a govment, and lets on to be a govment, and thinks it is a govment, and yet's got to sit still for six whole months."

We're left to wonder if Pap knew which government he was after, Hannibal's, Missouri's, or the Union's, though Missouri clearly is the weak government that has to wait six months to sell this "uppity p'fessor." Pap was no student of politics, but Twain is saying that he was well attuned to the antebellum view of "rights." For in the United States there are many bodies that thinks they is governments, says they is governments, and is called governments, but a good deal of what they do is dictated or shaped by groups and elites and parties and bureaucrats as well as other "govments" and, of course, the people themselves. *And anything governed by something or someone else can't be, in the purest sense, a government.*

I am reluctant to give a name to this collage of offices, agencies, unofficial participants, citizens—many of whom don't vote—officials, civil servants, and labor, business, and other pressure groups. It is not a democracy, except where direct voting determines policy. Nor is it fully "representative" or "republican," since it is too often unclear who the decision makers actually represent. It is a corporative polity, meaning that citizens' lives are now directed by thousands of "corporate" units, including the businesses that employ millions and are treated deferentially by officials at every level and in every agency and the less visible individuals and entities that always shape and sometimes make political, determinative, and authoritative decisions that are often equal in impact to public laws. Among those I include the newspapers, television stations and networks, and their co-workers on the radio. This elaborate complex is our "government," the operational powers that, as tradition and earlier chapters would have it, depend upon a bedrock of support and approval—this in a nation that has always spoken of itself as the world's leading advocate of minimalist government.

So the turf on which the political process is played out is thick with governments and quasi-governments, official and unofficial actors representing the public, part of the public, or none of the public. You "can't fool all of the people all of the time," but you certainly can confuse them most of the time.

THE POLITICAL SYSTEM

Designated agencies make and execute governments' policies. In the United States, these include Congress (a legislature responsible for passing statutory laws); the president (an executive charged with carrying out the law, suggesting policies to the Congress, making and executing foreign policy, commanding the armed forces); a judiciary (courts to make findings on a day-to-day basis about alleged violation of the civil and criminal codes, and, at the highest level, a Supreme Court to rule on the constitutionality of the other branches' policies and lower courts' construction of the law); and an administration or bureaucracy (a fourth branch of government often associated with the executive, barely mentioned in the Constitution, but now, seemingly, an all-but-independent branch, making and executing policy, including, among countless thousands of agencies, divisions, bureaus, and departments the Internal Revenue Service (IRS), the Federal Bureau of Investigation (FBI), the Department of Housing and Urban Development (HUD), the Immigration and Naturalization Service (INS), the Veterans Administration (VA), the Federal Reserve System (the Fed), and the Environmental Protection Agency (EPA)). Under the federal Constitution, in addition, there is a similar array of branches, agencies, and so forth, in each of the fifty states as well as miniature versions in territories under federal jurisdiction, and still others operating as regional units among several states. These are the official, more or less visible instruments of government.

In the United States there is, furthermore, a larger collection of involved entities: organized pressure groups, unorganized groupings, political parties, and political action committees representing corporations, business associations, and labor unions, probably more than one hundred thousand in all.[2] In no instance, however, can today's snapshot of these activities exactly duplicate yesterday's or tomorrow's. The political process constantly changes, although in societies resistant to change on the surface everything appears to be frozen in place.

Since the system is so complex, we must borrow from the social sciences to examine the process by means of which "the government," surrounded by satellites, parasites, clients, and would-be supervisors, reaches decisions. By examining the process, rather than concentrating on the classical definitions—Congress legislates, presidents execute, the judiciary "applies" the law—we imply that the activities authored by and "surrounding" government usually follow a regular, visible pattern, that public policy making replicates other processes by which something is made or constructed, that identification of the elements or ingredients that go into it in effect explains it. Although this exaggerates the regularity of the process, one hopes it also clarifies it.

The blast furnace, the invaluable "engine" in the production of steel, works well as a metaphor for the operations of the political process, particularly from the vantage point of explanations that assume that political decision making in the United States results from group pressures coming from all layers and levels of society, although with a few modifications it also works well for "elite theory."[3]

The outer walls and boundaries or framework of the "furnace" consist of the institutional paraphernalia of society, which in turn reflect the needs, demands, and expectations of the population—influenced by their convictions, beliefs, hopes, fears, desires, myths, and ideological dispositions as well as those generated by government and other artificed institutions that supposedly represent them. That is to say, there are pressures within the inner walls of the firebox and reflections outside it. The inner walls of the furnace consist of the responsible agencies of the government, the political apparatus—the Congress, president, courts, administrative agencies, bureaucrats, and civil servants. Inputs or pressures come from within as well as from outside the firebox.

For example: citizens expect the country to be protected from foreign threats. But that expectation is manipulated by agencies within the national governmental apparatus as well as defense contractors outside it. The Navy maintains that a navy, complete with the latest and most costly aircraft carriers and nuclear submarines at the ready, is necessary; the Air Force makes its claims; the Army is "indispensable" for police actions, limited wars, and rescue missions. Then there are special groups and forces with long histories and strong support, the Marines for one, and to a lesser extent the Coast Guard and National Guard. Further pressures come from communities where contractors maintain office and production facilities, from defense workers, and from military contractors, recipients of a goodly percentage of the current $300 billion a year allocated to the military, each offering expert advice that leads to the purchase of their materiel.

Pressure works its way through the system, affecting both the formal governmental bodies and the organizations that exist exclusively to put the squeeze on the government. As a blast furnace produces an output by combining ingredients, pressure, and heat, so the political process produces outputs in the form of policies, laws, administrative findings, court decisions, rules and regulations, allocations of contracts, awarding of research and developmental grants for new weapons, facilities, student aid programs, housing, health services, rules that mandate cleanups and government expenditures for the same, bailouts of savings and loan associations or of corporations in financial difficulty, educational policies, wars on poverty, on drugs, on crime, foreign policies, granting trade parity for some countries and setting up barriers against others, permitting or forbidding oil exploration in the remaining areas of wilderness, and so on. These policies may infringe upon individual liberties or enlarge them. They protect citizens from harassment by police and security forces, encourage the latter by finding that there is a national drug crisis or, in earlier years, a national drinking problem or national and local subversive problem. They may declare that home is the individual's castle or may find, as did the Supreme Court several years ago, that invasion of the bedroom in search of what some in the society insist are unnatural acts, even between consenting adults, is constitutional.

Whatever a policy's source or impact, it is an *"output,"* the result of the political process that in turn affects the society at large, satisfying some, irritating others, and inevitably having unforeseen consequences—in any case producing "feedback." In summary, the political process refers to the procedures and structures used in a political system to meet needs, demands, expectations, goals, and desires; in contemporary Western governments and perhaps now in central and eastern Europe, it is a set of decision-making operations that delivers public policies to deal with, correct, and/or anticipate problems and that involve non-governmental participants whose stake in outcomes may be given priority. In less open societies, the difference in the political process relates to access, which is far more limited, since policy conflicts are hidden from public inspection. In this society, there is access for selfish interests at every turn.

WHO IS IN CHARGE?

Many believe that at the time of the founding of the American system, men of good will, committed to public service, peopled the government, weighed issues carefully and fairly, and then acted on behalf of the public good—and that may well have been true of a Washington, Adams, Jefferson, or Madison as well as lesser-known public officials and servants of the founding period; it may also be true of many government workers today. The many scandals of the post–Civil War era produced an entirely different view based on "realities" that seemed to have turned ugly. At one point, for example, Commodore Cornelius Vanderbilt and the Erie Railroad appeared to "own" the New York State legislature. In the late nineteenth century progressive scholars—reacting to the situation—called for a new realism, which meant abandoning emphasis on the operations of official agencies and greater focus on forces in the society that might generate effective pressure to shape political conflict and outcomes. This realism ultimately produced two theories that remain the most widely used explanations of policy making in Western democracies. They not only assess how the political process works but also characterize U.S. and other modern systems of governance. Both portray society as a coherent system with identifiable routines and practices; and they see the polity, like the economy, as an agent of societal forces.

Interest-Group Theory

James Madison, in the *Federalist* No. 10 (1786), outlines the view of human tendencies that drives interest-group theory. He argues that men form factions, groups linked together by similar interests, in order to press their concerns upon the public and in governmental bodies. Madison thought such factions "evil" yet necessary. Their presence, which divides the body politic, proves, as long as they exist, that society permits men of divergent interests to press for policies favorable to their perceived needs, even at the expense of others and of the general good. The problem for Madison was not to suppress these "evil" factions—counterproductive from the point of view of the harmony and cooperation necessary to the operations of a successful polity—but to create a situation in which no single faction would sweep away all other interests in the society and thereby convert the polity into little more than an agent for a self-concerned part of the society. Madison based his views on the observation that men have different capacities; therefore they succeed differentially in life and develop distinct economic perspectives and interests. The Constitution, he claimed, solved the problem by balancing each faction against the others and through the federal mechanism, which kept interests contained within state boundaries. Given their current noisy presence, factions have surely been preserved, as Madison contended they should, under the Constitution.

There are echoes of Madison in the commentaries of Southern advocates of slavery, particularly John C. Calhoun's proposal that the Union adopt a system of rulership by concurrent majority and veto that, in Madison's terms, is an effort to prevent a factional majority, in this instance the Northern non-slaveholding states, from crushing the interests of the minority Southern slaveholding states. But Madison's view was not fully revived until the early twentieth century. A new industrial class had appeared. Immigrants had entered in record numbers between 1840 and 1901 to fill the ranks of labor, just as labor began to wrestle desperately with the new industrialists and financiers who viewed America as a wide-open invitation to become wealthy. Farmers had come to blows with railroad operators over transport to and rental of grain storage facilities in the Midwest. Cities grew rapidly and developed a physical ecology that literally separated people of different class, ethnicity, religion, and values into neighborhood pockets. Poor men struggled with other poor men for a relatively small share of the pie, but on occasion they found a common enemy in the rich. The rich, having survived ferocious competition, learned that they were better off when united in restraint of trade or monopoly than when they competed. The federal and state governments found themselves in the middle—defending the railroads against the farmers; sometimes protecting workers against capital, but more often allied with financiers, and yielding at times to popular pressure. Madison's theory of factions came back to life. Three books—Arthur F. Bentley's *Process of Government*, Charles Beard's *Economic Interpretation of the Constitution of the United States of America*, and J. Allen Smith's *Spirit of American Government*—invigorated the study of factionalism, of separation, of group ranged against group.[4] Beard's book was the most successful, since it persuaded American historians to give up their obsession with legalisms and grapple with underlying economic and social realities. But Beard was heavily influenced by Bentley's lesser-known work.

Arthur Bentley (1870–1957) is now credited with the effort to incorporate the study of interest groups into political science, but he did far more than that. He attempted to find a general procedure to assess the ways in which humans were bound or connected to some of their fellows and distanced from others. For purposes of analysis, he argued, society and politics consist not of individuals or feelings, states of mind or outlooks, but of transactions that tied together and separated humans and created both harmony and conflict. These were the relevant data for political study.

Bentley argued, in his own books and later, in association with the philosopher John Dewey, that, historically speaking, three modes of analysis could be identified. Each of these, like all attempts to explain social and political developments, is keyed to a central idea. The first or pre-scientific approach saw action as derived from internal mechanisms in individuals. Bentley ridiculed these inner forces or impulses, calling them "spooks." Why did men act? Because an inner man, thing, or "spook" impelled them. Bentley calls this analysis *self-actional* because it relies on interior guidance systems, implying that human beings simply carry out their historical or genetic possibilities, a view that leaves little room for change and development. As an acorn is destined to be a tree, so a man is destined to become a citizen. There is a further implication in self-actional thinking, namely, that human conduct can be explained by inner states, which Bentley also rejected.

Self-actional thinking, at least in the physical sciences, was abandoned by Galileo and Isaac Newton. They moved on to *interaction*. Galileo's conclusion that a body remains at rest unless or until some force strikes it or Newton's conclusion that there is a law of motion that determines that a body not interfered with will continue in a straight line exemplify this interactional theoretical construct. The physical world as they portray it becomes a series of colliding forces shoving bodies and particles this way and that.[5] Bentley, first in *The Process of Government* and later in works influenced by Einstein and Dewey, moved beyond these earlier views to *transactional* analysis. "Transaction is the procedure which observes men talking and writing with their word-behaviors and other representational activities connected with their thing-perceiving . . . and which permits a full treatment . . . of the whole process."[6] To put it in terms that Dewey and Bentley use, "no one exists as a buyer and seller save *in and because of* a transaction in which each is engaged." Each is indubitably connected and chained to a manifold or environment; our conduct is not the result of individual impulses (self-action) nor of forces that shove us this way or that (interaction), but of the fact that we are part and parcel of elaborate activities (transactions) constantly under way among human beings. Above all else, human activity is a complex, changing web, never capable of being reduced to any fixed, previously discovered or accounted-for group, group attitude, essence, state of being, or mind-set.

Bentley treats groups as constituting a fluid, unstable, changing system that results from continuous transactions among human beings. Some are responded to again and again by a complex of fluctuating groups and some deeply involved at one time, dormant at another; some temporary, some permanent but only intermittently engaged in the political process, and none fixed or mere statistical categories. We have, he says, "one great moving process to study."[7] What men want and the men who want and the acts of those men as well as the institutions and the world in which these wants occur are not parts of a machine, but "different phases of a process."[8] No single classification of a society or polity into groups suffices to explain the process. Allies on one issue turn out to be opponents on another; in yet another instance, one group is concerned and involved, the other indifferent and uninvolved. The group array evolves and changes.[9] As he saw it, "For most of us all of the time, for all of us most of the time, it is quite sufficient to regard human beings as 'persons' who possess qualities or motives which are phases of their character and who act in accordance with these qualities or this character."[10]

To see a person who performs a kind act and conclude as a passerby that we have witnessed someone whose "inner being" or "state of mind" is "decent" or "kindly" is good enough for everyday relations. But to rely on such observations to explain what is going on in society at large and what statutes and policies win approval explains events by individual interior qualities, be it a question of intellect, kindliness, or any other so-called personal trait. That, he believed, was as useless for analysis of societies as Aristotle's observations that some people are slaves by nature.[11] If we take the legislature for what it purports to be, namely a deliberative body, little sense can be made of it. Rather, law making has to be traced from "its efficient demand to its actual application"; it is, in other words, the product of a real social-economic-political situation, and that situation has to be understood, rather than the pretenses of the legislature to deliberation or of individual legislators or presidents to public-spirited conduct.[12]

The raw material we study is never found in one man by himself, it cannot even be stated by adding man to man. It must be taken as it comes in many men together. It is a "relation" between men, but not in the sense that the individual men are given to us first, and the relation erected between them. The "relation," i.e., the action is the given phenomenon, the raw material. . . . We know men only as participants in such activity.[13]

That is, analytically speaking, we know them only insofar as they are involved extensively as participants in transactions. We do not know men and women as buyers, nor as sellers, but as part of complex buying-selling transactions. It is improper to speak of their activities with one another as interlaced. Rather, "the interlacing itself is the activity. We have one great moving process to study."[14]

According to Bentley, the analyst looks at the society as a whole. The mind's eye has to be retrained for the job—the entire mass of Americans (or any other society, community, or grouping) is envisioned as a spinning sphere that can be looked at from above, much as astronauts on space vehicles can see the planet as a whole. The mass of people consists not of things or entities, though obviously that is what people look like when they are dealt with on an everyday basis as individuals, but of activities (transactions) that are the events that make up social and political life, occurrences that turn out to be substantial and durational. They are actual happenings that take place over a time sequence. As we look at these activities, we begin to uncover, to detect, to assess what is going on—what makes society and therefore politics tick.

If society is pictured as a spinning mass of activities, within that mass, people are bonded or linked together by those activities, connections that bring some together while separating them from those not similarly engaged. The initial categories appear simple enough and obvious. We can identify Catholics and non-Catholics; separate blue-collar workers from non–blue-collar workers; Indians and non-Indians; Irish Americans from non–Irish Americans. And we can continue in the same fashion separating automobile workers, bankers, bank clerks, educators, students, college administrators, college teachers, Italians, Jews, blacks, whites, Orientals, and WASPs. The list is finite but seems endless.

And we can go further by linking and dividing people with respect to attitudes, for example, those who regard abortion as sinful from those who regard it as a legal and moral option. To do so is to understand why Bentley saw the groups as fluid: these last groupings were non-existent fifty years ago.

Activities and attitudes bond individuals into what Bentley calls an interest. They are linked to one another not by the observer but by the activities that give rise to the category (though one runs into difficulty equating religious, ethnic, and racial bonds with "activity"). They do not share an interest if they are not linked by an activity—though again we have to note the special difficulty of ethnic, cultural, and racial categories insofar as they may not produce similar activities but only similar perceptions either within or outside the "group." The image Bentley creates, accordingly, is of two aspects of social relations: human beings pulled together by their activities and therefore into categories, groups, and interests; those groups in turn separated from all other groups.

There is potential for confusion and misunderstanding here. Some bonds seem as natural as the connection between the gall bladder and liver. Others appear to be accidental—automobile workers, providers of service, those who share opinions. Furthermore, these categories, as Bentley discusses them, are analytically valuable only insofar as particular issues develop that produce an array of groups that become active in the political process. A mere statistical category may suddenly become important politically. At one time "people over sixty-five years of age" meant nothing politically; now the category refers to a group with considerable political clout. The claim that such a grouping might become politically significant would have been greeted in earlier times with laughter. But Bentley realizes that the constant development of society generates shifting issues and therefore groupings and will create an entirely new group that may or may not last, depending on the tractability of the issue. Prohibition groups and temperance leagues have long since ceased to be important in the United States, but at one point they stampeded the nation into an amendment to the Constitution. Any category we can identify— whether it be through the palpable linking activities Bentley discusses or the result of statistical analysis and classifications of the population— may become consequential in the political process. It follows that the number of *potential* bonds is enormous. But politically speaking, some categories will never be other than statistical and have no present significance in the political process, though they may be very important to market researchers. In contrast, some potential groupings, first identified as mere statistical categories, have been activated politically. The example used earlier—so-called senior citizens—will suffice. Passage of the Social Security Act in 1935 made the age sixty-five important. Over time, as the youngsters who were around when the law passed reached their sixtieth birthdays, as more and more Americans were covered by the provisions of social security legislation, this grouping became visible in the political process.

How, then, do Bentley and his successors (many of whom deviate markedly from his "hydraulic" approach) purport to explain the activities that lead to political decision making in all forms? They regard policy making as the result of a series of conflicts that surface in the form of political issues that in turn activate an underlying or potential interest-group pattern. According to those who believe that interest-group theory is a decisive tool for understanding U.S. politics, interest groups structure the society, whose politics otherwise would be chaotic and incoherent. This structure, that is, the array of groups that become active in the presence of issues that touch their interests, makes politics representative while preserving diversity. Presumably, politically active groups mirror the varied needs, and sometimes the desires, of the general population.

If the existence of many permanent groups and the potential for many others is regarded as an operative characteristic of a pluralistic society and polity, it follows, according to Bentley's analysis, that no fixed array of groups determines policy outcomes. For each dispute, there is a corresponding pattern or *gestalt* that develops and that engages various groupings.

This image of the political process is direct, simple, clear. Society's linkages, the threads that tie it together as an operating unit, determine the character of political life, the political order that prevails and decisions that are made as imbalances, difficulties, new problems, arise periodically. Furthermore, interest-group theory, as it has been employed by American and other political scientists, maintains that the key to American democracy is its special brand of pluralism, that is, encouragement of groups, even dissenting groups that become the vehicles for pressure and over time for change. Although the basis for formation of groups is self-interest—the connecting thread after all is each person's status, ethnicity, or concern—the overall result is representation of everyone's interest, since the field is, presumably, always open for the appearance of every potential or possible example of self-concern. Concern for self, as in the ideology of the invisible hand, to which this pluralistic theory bears some resemblance and to which it may owe its origins, gives rise to like-minded group after group and therefore in due course, to an equilibrium of groups. Underneath the surface—*in the working machinery of society*—interests develop; at the surface—*in politics*—as occasion demands, groups representative of those interests, on both sides of every issue and also in the form of third parties whose interests might be affected if one or the other side prevails, join in combat and ultimately resolve their conflicts. Thus the system's invisible hand, a self-operating adjustor that, pushed this way, pressed that way, finally comes to a decision that is as good as it can be, given the varying and often mutually hostile interests that have to be served in an open society.[15]

Critique of Interest-Group Theory

Theories of this kind are closely related to our view of the economy. Madison rooted factions in the differences among human beings and thus they were seen as more or less the result of natural talent, which eventuated in different economic postures and positions. Interests were therefore economic in origin, but success was linked with "natural faculties." Bentley's speculations, while enormously fertile and rooted in a sophisticated grasp of the complex ways in which each human's existence and activities meld into patterned transactions, also are heavily oriented toward economic concerns and hint that societal activity is a kind of organism. Later efforts in political science, once interest-group theory made converts, endorsed that conception. The group struggle in politics is largely, though not always exclusively, depicted as a struggle for economic advantage or protection and that seems to square with the realities as they might be perceived from a seat in Congress or an office in the White House.

The link between the evolution of capitalism in the United States and interest-group theory in the study of politics is well understood by some writers.[16] Capitalist theory portrays rational individual decision making as selection of the least expensive among competing items of equivalent intrinsic value—whether the unit is goods that one requires or a laborer offering services. In modern speculations, the individual is replaced by groupings and the government becomes the adjudicator who both holds the system together and keeps it in equilibrium, rationalizes it by encouraging the formation of protection of groups as they bring pressure to bear, then referees among them when they come to blows or become the potential detonators of serious internal explosions. The melding together of capitalist and democratic theory is particularly striking here, as is the tendency over time to conflate the two. While capitalist theory originally left little room for government, as per the invisible-hand ideology, interest-group theory parallels up-to-date capitalism, which recognizes segments and groupings among the population—including corporations, financial networks, unions, and government purchasing units, not the smallest of which is the military—rather than trying to explain everything by the unlikely claim that each and every individual decision moves society and the political apparatus. As a result interest-group theory becomes an attempt to say that each citizen "votes" in groups and gets results insofar as his or her groups win access to the government, which is both the handmaiden of and the referee among the varied interests that make up the society. Also, the government is now just another grouping, first among equals, perhaps, but by no means singular in its orientation or apparent concerns. In the final analysis, the only real differences among society's units insofar as interest-group theory is concerned is that the government has more general and greater favors to dispense than anyone else—it is bigger than churches, universities, and businesses, awards more contracts by far than any other corporate unit, has control mechanisms that can be applied to any individual or group in the society, and makes war or prepares for it—over the past decades to the tune of trillions of dollars. In other words, the government is fair game for every hunter but also provides protection for the other units, groups, and individuals that make it a target.

This tale is more bizarre than might once have seemed likely. For one thing, the government grew inordinately. Second, it parceled out goods to develop or stimulate economic activity and surrendered authority to individuals and groups. Call this a policy of divestiture whose purpose can be summarized in a slogan: "if it is a possible source of wealth, give it up; if it costs money to maintain, keep it." Land was given away—to individuals as well as to would-be railroad builders, oil and lumber interests, and so on; the right to control their professions was given to lawyers and doctors; the right to supervise excesses and execute public policies designed to check them was given to new departments like Commerce, Agriculture, and Labor, which were quickly captured by their "clients"; control of elections was partially ceded to extra-constitutional entities, political parties; the right to influence elections to donors and, recently, to corporate, union, and trade-association political action committees; the right to pollute was claimed, in the name of productivity and profit, by industry and ignored by government; the right to control and maintain national highways was divided up with the states, who in turn have permitted contractors to rip off the public treasury; the right to regulate money has been handed off to a committee representing fiscal interests (the Fed); the right to regulate savings and loan institutions was permitted to deteriorate into a savings and loan bailout scam; the right to operate a postal service, one of the few constitutionally specified mandates of the government, was parceled out to private agencies and transportation specialists by subsidies (for carrying mail, for example) and by giving the public postal service all the unprofitable tasks. Much of what is or should have been included in the public realm has been handed over to groups and the balance is regularly sabotaged. In the United States not only are private foxes asked to guard the public chickens, but they are paid handsomely for their efforts.

If the assorted groups that flourish and maintain offices in Washington, D.C., and the state capitals resembled those portrayed in interest-group theory, academic explanation of the political process as a democratic group struggle might make sense. These are not groups as Bentley portrayed them but privateers and lobbyists for privateers whose purposes are clear enough and straightforward, namely, self-advancement at any cost provided others pay the bill. The claim that each man's gain automatically improves everyone's life, however true, collapses under the weight of unchecked greed and selfishness, individual or group, and is remote from one of the practices critical to public institutions—discussion of ends, goals, and purposes suited to, important to, and valuable for everyone in the polity. For such dialogues, we substitute discussions concerning "who gets what, when, and how." The result, as Theodore Lowi points out, is that the contemporary version of Bentley's theory regards as necessary and good the notion that the policy agenda of the nation and the public interest of the entire community can be defined exclusively in terms of the well-being of interest groups, to whom control of public policy is in effect ceded.[17] What follows is that every potential or possible interest becomes a status around which many believe "power centers ought to organize."[18] And this tendency has been reinforced in the last two decades by the encouragement the government has carelessly (or is it deliberately?) given to political action committees (PACs).

This means that legitimacy is in effect privatized—given over to private agencies. For the citizen who looks to government for representation of the general interest, disappointment is inevitable; he or she has to turn to whoever has been given control of his or her sector of the public realm, be it a private interest or a supposedly public bureaucracy. Government instruments abdicate in favor of whatever forces currently drive the society and, as in a state like Massachusetts, the government atrophies, which really means that support for taxing policy and sustaining of state governments has all but vanished in contrast to unchecked (private) consumer spending and escalating individual indebtedness. A steady disintegration takes place in the capacity to govern in the public interest. Meanwhile, the public becomes less and less attuned to what has been understood as everybody's business. Whatever currently arouses the media and society, as often as not an obsession with drugs, crime, and overseas "crises," substitutes for general public matters. Concern with public issues, which shape the quality of life in the society, lapses, and with it goes any real feeling for the state and state government, although the boasting continues unabated. In a state like New Hampshire, where people "live free or die," that comes to mean "we will not pay an income tax" or "we will protect our individual liberty to carry rifles or automatic weapons," but we will avoid, if possible, general problems once thought to be essential to the commonweal.

This is perhaps the inevitable result, audible in the words of politicians but buttressed by interest-group theory, of the insistence that the character of society governs and even creates the standards for the conduct of public life. The notions of public good, common good, or public well-being give way, as they have tended to do since the founding of the Republic, to efforts to equate public well-being with individual happiness, or the satisfaction of special interests, or whatever society is currently said to believe—the notion that a neutral government moderates among special interests or the newer view that there is a positive link between the welfare of groups and good governance. Government is no longer the agent of a public will. It either responds to or establishes the diverse pressures represented by organized and unorganized groups. If interest-group theory explains much of what goes on in this society—and who can doubt that it does?—it is also the case that the theory has been given such credence as to have been converted from an analysis of "what is" into a prescription for what "ought to be." In short, it has begun to resemble an ideological program. As long as this is the case, there remains the danger that this faith in groups makes impossible direct confrontation over the well-being of all, the commonweal, other than by aggregating selfish interests. And that means, first, no general perspective, such as is someday going to be required of this country and others with respect to pollution of the earth, and, second, that those unrepresented in this happy playground of groups, the one-fifth or one-tenth of the nation with no access to the instruments of governance, are left out in the cold. These days to be "those left out in the cold" is no mere phrase and its meaning can be observed in streets and ghettoes across this rich nation.

Without an understanding of or attempt to discover the general good, we grow increasingly indifferent to injustices that affect unrepresented or relatively invisible groups of human beings. Interest-group theory correctly records that we are pulled together into groups that contest with one another, only to infer incorrectly that selfishness is always good for the society. That an aggregate of selfish pressures adds up to the general good or public well-being is at best a distortion and at worst a self-delusion. Nonetheless, interest-group theory reveals much about the processes and pressures that produce governmental policies, not only those of congresses and legislatures but also those of executives, courts, and administrators. It demonstrates that left unchecked, what we today call "politicking" is little more than an exercise in selfishness and self-seeking that attempts to violate or do violence to political power in its foundational aspect.

Elite-Mass Theory

Two Italian sociologists, Vilfredo Pareto (1848–1923) and Gaetano Mosca (1858–1941), contributed to elite-mass theory; C. Wright Mills (1916–1962) developed the American version.[19] But a theoretical construct does not develop in a vacuum. Present-day elite theory reflects governmental growth and the rise of modern bureaucracy, although elites—the rich or the best people (*aristoi*)—were well known to the Greeks, and bureaucracies have existed throughout history, though not on the scale with which we have become familiar.

As society becomes more complicated, bureaucracy introduces rules and rule-by-management techniques, the rules representing elaborations and extensions of public laws or high-level corporate decisions. In government, as laws attempt to deal with problems that affect larger and larger numbers of people and institutions, since legislatures cannot deal with the detail of individual cases, they pass more skeletal legislation laying down general rules. Rule-making and decision-making authority are delegated to agencies whose sole task is to manage specific areas: enforcement of safety regulations; operation of transport systems; supervision of health and safety regulations affecting agricultural commodities, manufactured and processed foods and drugs, occupational hazards in mines and industry, and fisheries; or any of the thousands of other general problems that accompany growth of a more sophisticated economy and a consequent enlarged polity. The rule of law, administratively speaking, means refinement of statuses by administrative decree and bureaucratic supervision. In simpler times, legislatures and executives could act more directly, though hardly in person; but now government has layers of agencies. Courts also are involved, no longer simply rendering decisions under statutory law, precedent, and convention, but including the substance though more often the procedures and due process associated with orders issued by the bureaucracy. Bureaucracies are entrusted with quasi-judicial and quasi-legislative authority, that is, given *de facto* legislative and judicial legitimacy that *de jure* resides elsewhere. As a result, rulership comes to mean control over millions of lives by an ever-growing corpus of appointed and increasingly anonymous officials, less recognizable to members of the public than judges, legislators, kings, party chieftains, and presidents.

At the same time, bureaucracy, since it is organized hierarchically, adds layers of command between the government and its constituency. The bureaucracy, increasingly the *persona* of government seen by citizens, not only is an extra layer in and of itself but is organized internally into a series of command levels, reminiscent of the military and the Roman Catholic Church, which first employed these structural principles on a grand scale. What government brings to bear on the lives of citizens is not so much the "King's peace" or "King's justice" but a hierarchy. Over time, of course, this hierarchy not only stands in for the legislature and executive and courts but also becomes the primary interpreter of their intentions and executor of a control system these constitutional bodies have been forced to hand over because of the size and complexity of contemporary governmental tasks. A similar pattern prevails in business. Faceless governments and corporations confront and regulate the population. The common television image of the government in action may be the cop on the beat or the crime-busting prosecutor in court, but a meeting with an IRS investigator, and more than occasional arbitrariness amidst the thicket of rules, regulations, and interpretations, or a visit by a social worker is a more likely experience than a cheerful hello from the local policeman—even in those places that still assign policemen to localities. Another setting for citizen-government interaction is the offices of the

Social Security Administration, where bureaucrats, well shielded from appeals (one of the few safety valves is direct appeal to one's congressman for help of some sort), represent the agency. There, they inform citizens, whose incomes were tapped along with their employers' for building what is ironically called a trust fund, of the good news and the bad—what to do, when to do it, how they are going to be docked or have their checks withheld. Bureaucrats are the officially designated authorities whose control extends in at least two directions. They have a considerable amount to say with respect to citizens' rights and obligations; and they usually outlast the birds of passage who hold appointive titles such as director of the Home Loan Board or chairman of the Federal Deposit Insurance Corporation. Many titled public figures are no match for the permanent civil service.

Bureaucratic growth accompanied the increasing participation of masses of citizens in government as well as the extension of taxes and military service to all levels of the population. As the electorate expanded, the control of government was drifting into the hands of an entrenched officialdom.[20] Struggles could have been foreseen between these bureaucratic elites, as they came to be known, and the populace they attempt to regulate. As the government grew still larger, the struggle to see who was in charge intensified both within it and outside it. And given the organizational tendency for control to drift into the hands of a small group (the "iron law of oligarchy"), contemporary awareness of elites grew. Elite theory, as it emerged in Europe, had a message similar to interest-group theory's in the United States. Both stressed the importance of segments or groups in the political process, giving less and less credence to the formal structures and types of government or so-called systems of rulership—democracy, monarchy, aristocracy, and the like—and more weight to decision makers who controlled the government either from inside the bureaucracy or through outside pressure agencies.

The American version of elite-mass theory was developed independently by a number of writers, but it is C. Wright Mills who most concerns us here. Mills agrees with his European academic predecessors that high positions within institutional structures or "orders" translate into domination and control of political decision making. The institutions he regarded as important are the industrial-financial complex; the educational system, particularly high-powered, prestigious research-oriented universities; the military; strategically placed governmental bureaucracies; the top elective layers of the political system; and the older, now less dominant orders such as the family and the church. In elite theory, exercise of control, distributed pyramidally, is equated with operational power. A handful of people dominate each institutional order; they are, accordingly, in position to control the polity as well; that is, they shape the policies of those who hold offices and appear to be "in power." Many are unseen by the public because though highly placed in the economy and society, they are not public figures nor "covered" by the media—and they prefer it that way. Even to those largely unaware of the way things are, the potential for excesses in these linkages surfaces in scandals such as those involving savings and loan institutions, their executives, senators, and bureaucrats. A mixture of people with recognizable public personae or faces, such as senators, and hidden influentials further complicates an already-complex arrangement.

Elites may be cohesive or non-cohesive. If the former, the people at the top of each order work together; if the latter, those at the top compete with one another.[21] History records past moments when elites in various orders did contest with one another, for example, during the struggle between church and state for priority before the modern nation-state triumphed. There have also been struggles between elites representing different sectors of the economy, although Mills contends that that changed in the United States. Elites here overlap and are interconnected—namely, the visible political elite as well as business and financial leaders, research and technological leaders in the university world, members of top legal systems, and command-level military brass are tied together and fully aware of one another as well as their positions in the society and control of the polity. The academician Henry Kissinger, the financier David Rockefeller, and the politician Jimmy Carter talked and worked together to iron out the details of their mutual concerns and to speculate about their possible adoption as policies. In the United States, participation by the masses in the political process probably acts as an added stimulus to elite cohesion.

Here is a brief recapitulation of Mills' argument:

1. Position in the structure(s) or orders is the basis for control, domination, and power (the three words are synonyms for him). To quote him: "Power is not of a man. Wealth does not center in the person of the wealthy. Celebrity is not inherent in any personality. To be celebrated, to be wealthy, to have power requires access to major institutions. For the institutional positions men occupy determine their chances to have and to hold these valuable experiences."[22]

2. Achievement of position is determined by skills, by previous membership in already-dominant classes, or by personalities, attitudes, or skills that win deference. Scientific, technological, and management skills now increase access to high positions, but old money still counts.

3. Domination of society's institutions is achieved by a small group of individuals. Those who do the guiding are called the elite; those who are guided are the mass. Mills expresses this in opening his book: "The powers of ordinary men are circumscribed by the everyday worlds in which they live, yet even in these rounds of job, family and neighborhood, they often seem driven by forces they can neither understand nor govern."[23] There

are other men "whose positions enable them to transcend the ordinary environments of ordinary men and women."[24] They make the decisions that shape political and societal life.

In sum, a combination of skill, circumstance, and manipulation places some in the "higher circles" within each institutional order. Since these orders are interconnected, those in high position in one order are part of the elite network governing society. They go to the same schools, they enter the same law firms or board rooms, attend the same special seminars, consult the same high priests of world affairs, share the same values, and come together whenever something vital is at stake. And as a supplement to Mills' argument one writer, Philip H. Burch, Jr., has effectively demonstrated that "family interests still play a fairly prominent role in the conduct of big business affairs in the United States."[25] That phenomenon, he says, is pervasive, which means that in addition to the orders Mills describes, there is also a moneyed order, rooted in fiscal and family connections, which has more clout in the world of business and finance and therefore in government than the stress on managers or computer experts has led us to believe. According to Mills, the higher circles make the key or central decisions, leaving other issues to be resolved by congressional squabbling, bureaucratic infighting, pressure-group conflicts. Meanwhile, a much larger group, convinced that they rule because they have the right to vote, in fact constitute the manipulated and dominated mass of people in the society.

There is nothing startling in elite theory. Most people recognize that someone sits above them in the world's hierarchies. There is a difference between old Siwash College and Yale or Harvard in terms of elite presence. To declare that someone is in charge is hardly to bring fresh news—there is only one pope, a handful of cardinals, a small number of bishops, a fairly large number of priests, but a massive flock of parishioners. Elite-mass theory, however, goes well beyond the obvious truism that society is stratified. When it speaks to politics, it says not only that there is one chief executive officer in every organization but also that there is an interconnected web of those who hold the highest positions in important institutions or orders within any society. Those cohorts in the higher circles, according to this theory, effectively control the American polity.

Elite-mass theory maintains that in the United States there is a circle of individuals who sit atop the important "orders" and together make the primary decisions that shape and control American life and government. These orders include what President Eisenhower called the military-industrial complex—that is, the "higher circles" that control military research and purchasing, which means the scientific-technological order; the primary research university order; leading military figures; academic experts whose specialty is international and defense policy and research;

and top foreign and defense policy-making institutions, some of them governmental and housed in the Pentagon, others privately owned, and often government financed, such as the Rand Corporation and the Hudson Institute. Similar structures dominate the balance of our politics. All key decisions—Mills speaks primarily of those concerned with World War II and the cold war period, but his observations can be extended in time—have been and are made by this elite: the decision to build and use atomic bombs; to develop hydrogen bombs; to maintain a large military presence in the world; to research missile technology; to enter the space race; to rely on federal control of the money supply to maintain economic stability; to encourage redevelopment of former enemies Japan and Germany; to work out programs for revitalization of Europe after World War II; to succeed to the roles of Britain and France in maintaining Western hegemony over large sectors of the globe; to face off against the Russians in a cold war; to emphasize air and automobile transport and deemphasize mass transit; to support industrial and financial growth and cut back on the commitment to conservation; to develop and encourage mass education at the higher levels; and to work toward an American imperium or Pax Americana. The visible part of this apparatus is governmental only because government has the necessary authority to carry policies out; therefore, members of the highest circles in government also participate in the making of decisions. But doesn't Congress have to pass legislation? Mills' answer is that most congressmen sit at what he calls the middle layer of power and that Congress is given control of such legislation as the elite cares to allow it to play with; otherwise elites manipulate Congress and the presidency, and Congress ratifies whatever it is presented with, be it a savings and loan bailout or military decisions reported to it minutes before the bombers and troops take off. Later exponents of elite-mass theory suggest that the same pattern applies to all levels of governance in the United States.

Critique of Elite-Mass Theory

Elite theory holds that politics is little more than dominance by elites. For example, all presidential candidates are acceptable to the elite or perhaps, to express that differently, are of equal insignificance to the elite. Whether Jimmy Carter or Ronald Reagan wins the election of 1980, Michael Dukakis or George Bush in 1988, is inconsequential, since basic U.S. policy and expenditures will turn out to be similar in either case. But if that answer does not satisfy those who see personality differences, party distinctions, or different abilities among candidates, the argument of elite theory is that elections are charades, the modern equivalent of Roman bread and circuses. They are popularity contests that, whatever the outcome, will not change the essential character of American society or political decision making. The candidates of both parties are acceptable; the system in any event will be dominated by the highly placed. Electoral outcomes are unimportant. While citizens may fight for a new road into or around their city, elites will determine where the road is placed and who reaps the profits from its construction. So, too, the struggle to win the presidency; it is irrelevant, as are all contests that appeal to the masses.

Despite the illusions and delusions of democracy, elite theory holds that a small, partially hidden group is in control. Whatever appears to be the case, only study of the influential, the highly positioned, the higher or ruling circles, can explain the operation of the political process in any society. Are elites fixed in place, entrenched permanently, exclusive occupants of the highest positions? The answer of elite theorists is that in modern society, given rapid changes in technology and education, given also the loosened class structure, elites circulate. No elite is permanently entrenched, though access to great fortunes and entrenched family wealth obviously have an impact. But the issue is not who lives well—the answer to that is always the same, "those with the means to do so"—but who is in charge and who shapes the society, and when that is seriously studied it is clear enough that elites refresh themselves not only because they choose to do so but because events force them to keep certain doors open. Evolving circumstances, skills, attitudes and problems provide opportunities for new members to be drawn into the old, or constitute a new, elite. Indeed, an intelligent elite will always recruit, train, and co-opt talent. Although the sources of prestige and position change, an elite makes fundamental decisions in every society; it is in charge of what we have called politicking. The question "what is to be done?" is easy to resolve; the elite always acts on behalf of what is perceived as its best interest and is in a position to have its way. The institutions others regard as significant in the political process—a city council, a congress, a state legislature, a president, a prime minister—are elaborate facades that convince the masses they are represented when significant decisions are made. Not so, says the elite theorist.

Is the elite, then, always united and single-minded? Not necessarily. Mills and others point out that the nation's elite includes important businessmen, bankers, real estate dealers, professionals, and, in some instances, old money. They are not always lined up in a phalanx on every question and may come to blows, since the sources of their position will be differentially affected by decisions. That usually does not, however, produce a public brawl. Rather, a behind-the-scenes dialogue takes place, sometimes taking years to conclude, rather than permitting the public at large to settle matters in terms of its perceived interests. This, of course, grows increasingly difficult given the ubiquitous presence of television.

There is, however, a question to put to elite theorists, and that has to do with whether the elite in fact has enough skill and insight to control an elaborate system such as ours that now interfaces with global economies and the higher circles of other societies, among them those of the European union that is emerging, the East Asian elite, which has in the shortest possible time emerged as one of the world's most potent forces, and the soon-to-emerge new elite of eastern Europe. Is the present elite so all-seeing that it also can deal with those other worlds—summarized in the terms "third world" or "developing nations" or represented by the oil interests of the Middle East—whose actions and decisions affect the entire globe? The answer, one has to guess, is that the American elite, often hard-pressed to maintain control over what it supposedly dominates, certainly does not appear able to control the rest of the world other than by means of a nuclear or other military threat that is ultimately self-destructive. There is no evidence that the current elite had even an inkling of the changes that were soon to take place in eastern Europe and little that it can resolve the intransigence of Middle Eastern combatants. Nor is it able or willing to deal with the "third" and "fourth" worlds within our borders, where the homeless and otherwise disenfranchised live.

It is evident that neither elite-mass nor interest-group theory by itself fully explains the political process or tells us who, if anybody, is in charge, in part because of the inevitable presence of human possibility and the happy persistence of the human propensity to do the unexpected. Although on a day-to-day basis events follow a regular pattern and elites or pressure groups have their way, the unexpected is always potentially with us. This may appear to be accidental but should be accepted, with relief, as a sign of stubborn, irreducible humanness, which is creative and produces in every new human being an original. Originals may do original things. That will remain true, unless we breed or propagandize novelty out of humanity. Furthermore, though the elite may exercise tight control, in specific instances their reactions range from indifference to intense involvement. Both those who analyze and those who dream of change are often surprised. Elite theory can in no way explain recent events in eastern Europe, where an entrenched circle of communists found the very fabric of society being pulled apart and their rulership suddenly and unceremoniously threatened, then terminated. What looks like an unorganized grouping overnight becomes the majority's political party, like Solidarity in Poland, and wins control because a "totalitarian" leadership either does not choose or cannot manage to call in the army to use violence to overcome the people in the streets. Even were a military dictatorship to be established in the former Soviet Union, the old elite will have been pulled from its perch. Nor can interest-group theory, however much admired by democratic pluralists, explain the persistence in the United States of decisions that reflect and favor an elite. In the final analysis, elite theory reduces power to a single aspect, politicking, then reduces politicking to a combination of conspiracy and circuses, that is, empty public shows, during which hidden hands manage the controls. It also leaves no room for the public good or tells us that it has been redefined as equivalent to the well-being of a handful.

Is there a way to make use of these two theoretical statements? They are fairly reliable indicators of how things work. On occasion pressure formations determine political and social outcomes, particularly those issues where the diversity of the American population makes differences of opinion likely. The abortion issue, perhaps, illustrates the truth of American democratic pluralism, since it is an issue about which one can expect relative indifference or comparative sympathy among members of the elite who are informed about birth control, likely to control the size of their families, and able to afford abortions, whatever the law. They are a mirror image of the anti-abortion groups more likely to be influenced by vocal religious leadership pushing them one way or another. Among the very poor, where birth control tends to be less practiced and possibly less understood, the incidence of pregnancy and the assortment of pressures to terminate or not to terminate are much more profound. That issue lends itself to interest-group combat and leads to an open struggle during which politicians move this way and that to harvest votes. On the other hand, when questions about the overall character of the society are at stake, not "merely" as moral questions, but as bread-and-butter issues, elites act. Suppose, for example, we imagine the country at the onset of the contemporary transportation revolution. The nation has at its disposal the wherewithal and the space to build more and more rail lines for mass transit or more and more highways for still greater numbers of automobiles. Obviously, there are interests on both sides and good reasons for either decision. But there are also consequences that flow from a decision to come down in favor of one form of transport at the expense of the other, and at that point, those at institutional command posts— whether in banks, bureaucracies, industries, universities, or munici- palities—are likeliest to make the primary decisions. Elite-mass theory is better equipped to explain outcomes realistically when issues clearly definitive for the future of the society arise; interest-group theory and democratic pressure may be most telling when elites abdicate and in effect say, "we are indifferent to the outcome. Let 'them' fight it out." This suggests that both interest groups and elites are important, but an elite network has final say-so in the staging of society's development. In a society so large and fragmented with so many points at which decisions are made and so many access points to those who at any instant legiti- mately hold decision-making authority, simple pressure at times either by organized or unorganized groups will carry the day. But it ought to be obvious that decisions cannot be taken by fragmented authorities. Rather, the American elite's position in major financial institutions and corporations, legal firms, the bureaucracy, the White House, the military, and universities becomes critical. These elite positions shape and direct decisions. They constitute a contemporary ruling circle, a non-territorial polity within the polity, a community of "knowers" and would-be philosopher-kings. They squabble; they are not always capable of seeing the consequences of what they decide—who is?—but they do make the major decisions without which this huge society with its endless motions and energies would be even more like a rudderless ship traveling in ever-faster circles. This "establishment" now represents what Mills was trying to expose (and condemn) when he wrote *The Power Elite*.

This establishment is not always visible. Nor are its views fixed—once, the American elite opposed all welfare and support efforts, and then it learned that such programs had economic as well as possible moral implications that were to the good. But even when it is visible or its outlook is fixed, the elite is affected by the communications revolution, which has altered its overall control. The media can foster or develop outbreaks of opinion that can carry the day, and this is a volatile force in American life.

Both interest-group and elite-mass theory, however, are limited. It may be true that decision making reflects the ongoing structure of society, but the question of what the society's structure really is, if it has a single coherent structure, remains open. If we have a corporative polity, as I first suggested, then the arenas of control have multiplied and dispersed. Neither theory can truly account for this phenomenon, since both seem to rest on a one-dimensional description of American life, on an imagery that speaks certainly of small-town America, middle-class life, industrial preeminence, family values, and regional idiosyncrasies. None of these are fully present any longer, from which fact we have to assume that explanations of the political process that assumed their existence may still have some merit but are, nonetheless, less than entirely satisfactory. We need ways of looking at our political connectedness, institutions, and policy making.

NOTES

1. The following states became part of the Union following the Mexican-American War of 1848 (year of formal entry in parentheses): Arizona (1912); California (1850); Colorado (1876; eastern part from Louisiana Purchase); Nevada (1864); New Mexico (1912). Texas had previously declared its independence and been admitted to the Union in 1845.

2. In other countries there are also official and non-official agents shaped by their customs, experiences, and inclinations. In some polities, the political process appears to be closed off from the public in whose interest power is presumably being exercised; in others the process appears to be open.

3. I'm following David Easton's attempt to portray "the political system," although he doesn't use the same metaphor, the blast furnace—of whose source

I am uncertain. See David Easton, *A Systems Analysis of Political Life* (New York: John Wiley & Sons, 1965), p. 32, for a simplified sketch of the political system. The balance of his book is an elaboration of that sketch.

4. Charles Beard, *An Economic Interpretation of the Constitution of the United States of America* (1913; New York: Macmillan Company, 1962); Arthur F. Bentley, *The Process of Government* (1908; New York: Harvard University Press, 1967); J. Allen Smith, *The Spirit of American Government: A Study of the Constitution: Its Origin, Influence and Relation to Democracy* (New York, Macmillan Company, 1907).

5. John Dewey and Arthur F. Bentley, *Knowing and the Known* (1949; Boston: Beacon Press, 1960), pp. 105-7.

6. Ibid., p. 123.

7. Bentley, *The Process of Government*, p. 178.

8. Ibid., pp. 196-97.

9. Ibid., pp. 203-5.

10. Ibid., p. 4.

11. Ibid., pp. 16-19.

12. Ibid., p. 163.

13. Ibid., p. 176.

14. Ibid., p. 178.

15. See Appendix A for discussion of a procedure for classifying interest groups.

16. Theodore Lowi, *The End of Liberalism* (New York: W. W. Norton and Company, 1969). See, for example, Chapter 2, pp. 29-54.

17. Ibid., p. 58.

18. Ibid., p. 83.

19. See C. Wright Mills, *The Power Elite* (New York: Oxford University Press, Galaxy Books, 1959), and Garaint Perry, *Political Elites* (New York: Praeger, 1969). See also Philip H. Burch, Jr., *Elites in American History*, 2 vols. (New York: Holmes and Meier, 1980).

20. Perry, *Political Elites*, pp. 17-18.

21. Mills, *The Power Elite*, p. 19.

22. Ibid., p. 11.

23. Ibid., p. 3.

24. Ibid., pp. 3-4.

25. Philip H. Burch, Jr., *The Managerial Revolution Reassessed: Family Control in America's Large Corporations* (Lexington, Mass.: D. C. Heath, 1972), p. 9.

9

An Overview of Our Situation

We need to look at the present situation to judge whether it is as unsatisfactory as many people seem to believe. To do that we use a window—the word is used both in the old sense, a glass pane through which we look at a particular vista, and the new, peering at a sector amidst an enormous "spread sheet" of information. I am specifically concerned with the "speeding up" of life, the consequent weakening of stable attachments, by no means a novelty in this country, and the apparent near collapse of the "games of rules" that once constituted our version of order and generated enough support to keep the political system functioning successfully.

I take for granted widespread awareness of the transportation and communication revolution, which has shrunk time and space and brought us into immediate, even instant contact with the rest of the world. But what seems less well understood is that as we draw closer together, we do not necessarily retain our ties with or knowledge about those who are near or proximate to us. The idea of neighborliness has changed accordingly: the proximity once implied by the word "neighborhood" has been altered as our world widened to include people who remain strangers to us. Our habits and "life styles" have changed, particularly in cities and metropolitan areas, which in fact account for a large percentage of the total population of the United States.[1]

CHANGING CITIES

The old cities of the United States, following immigration, developed class and ethnic dynasties. Their streets were busy, crowded with people day and night. Neighborhood meant people living together who both knew and monitored what was theirs. Neighborliness meant watching over the streets and the people who lived and did business on them. The accompanying politics was class- and ethnic-oriented, and the political history of U.S. cities can be written as a sequence in which individuals of different class or ethnic identification, representing or symbolizing the groups from which they were drawn, won control of City Hall. Cities once dominated by an Americanized, that is, native or assimilated, class came to be ruled, as a consequence of the historical immigration pattern, by organized descendants of German immigrants, or Italians, Poles, Irish, or Jews, all of whom at different moments learned to use the cities as a means of advancement paralleling the economic mobility available to their predecessors.

This has changed. Areas of cities have been trashed and made all but uninhabitable. The remaining ethnic or racial enclaves are ghettoes— perceived as racial, since both "blacks" and "Hispanics" are viewed as racial categories—walled-in areas marked by poverty, internal divisions, and open hostility that flows in two directions, from and toward the outside. Folks outside the wall encourage and at times enforce the "containing" function of the ghetto, controlling and patrolling the outer boundaries. Inside, gangs, forming miniature quasi-polities, play the game according to their own rules and freely employ violence, while other residents try to maintain order. To outsiders and city residents the streets are now forbidding; non-residents exercise caution and residents struggle for a degree of calm. A city like Washington, D.C., except for the Georgetown area, appears to close up at night, everyone retreating into his or her own protected place. Visitors are not welcome. Parts of New York City are similar, although there remains, as in most of the traditional immigrant cities, a street life of one sort or another—entertainment areas, shopping places, banks, and so on. Neighborliness, in either instance, is a pleasant word whose exact meaning is less and less clear. Old-machine politicians, whose involvement with the daily well-being of constituents is now often sneered at as little more than low-level bribery, but who in fact did "take care of" their people, are gone. In their place are bureaucratic welfare systems despised by the recipients of aid and held in contempt by many working and middle-class people. Whereas political machines offered support and hope to struggling families, the post–World War II welfare systems trafficked in hopelessness, granted that welfare and social workers are motivated by positive feelings and for a time believed that they could make a difference. The old barrier to mobility was a lack of good jobs coupled with few opportunities to get at those that were available, which could be overcome with the help of educators and politicians at various levels, including union leaders. Today's barrier seems to be an inability to cross the great divide between impoverishment and the lower working class, with the black and Hispanic poor often blocked, excluded, and driven into greater indifference to the values that are said to have pulled their predecessors out of earlier ghettoes. Some new members of the middle class, however, are ex-ghettoites.

We need only add that the old alliance between City Hall and the streets, persisting as each group established hegemony over local politics, is now pretty much a remnant of the past. Today's mayors and bosses have few real friends in the streets, and the people who live in the city are not certain that they have allies in City Hall, except when single or restricted issues carry someone into office and a temporary alliance is formed— soon to be destroyed by the broad problems that resist solutions and force the city's leaders to turn this way and that looking for solutions that will maintain support. In the past, support was purchased with a series of individual and city-wide improvements; today, it is keyed to narrow issues affecting groups with separate leaderships. A similar situation can develop in the State House. A new governor, extremely popular, as in New Jersey, once he acts and advocates a comprehensive and costly problem-solving approach, soon finds former supporters snapping at him in anger. As long as elites remain satisfied, electability means to play the interest game to the point where only the most meager and inexpensive efforts to solve problems will be tolerated by middle-class voters, who are understandably obsessed with preventing tax-based solutions to any difficulty unless the solution benefits them directly rather than generally and are either indifferent to or ignorant of built-in protections of elite interests. The discontent, lack of neighborliness, and disinterest in anyone other than "me and mine" are municipal, state, and therefore national problems and will continue to increase as deferred maintenance and a decaying infrastructure envelop larger and larger areas. Furthermore, it is sad to note that even in the Far West—Reno, Nevada, will serve as example—the old "downtown" areas, in this case once the site of the larger gambling casinos, have suffered from a deterioration reminiscent of large, Eastern cities. Here the problem is not related to ethnicity, but stems from unchecked growth and greed. The old town spreads out, newer clubs and hotels are built at the outskirts, and all of this is accompanied by an endless flight to what elsewhere might be called suburbs, with people moving outward from the center in order to get "better" housing while others, newcomers, are unable to find reasonable apartments or homes at the center and settle, when possible, in tracts at one or another edge of the city. The result is the arrival, over approximately three decades, of all the problems of the flight to the suburbs, including indifference to neighborhood, a sense of disconnectedness, anger over escalating taxes, and a general sense of political and social chaos. Add in the Western-American enchantment with direct voter participation in electoral decisions and the absence of an adequate water supply and the result, on one day, is a referendum decision to build new facilities for the city and to deny funds for buildings and staffing.

THE AUTOMOBILE

The automobile has been an important force in the alteration of city life as well as our political and social culture. As cities grew and became industrial and commercial centers, they developed mass transit systems; and as metropolitan regions—clusters of cities—grew, these systems expanded beyond city limits. Although never completed, a rail complex was once contemplated to serve a huge metropolitan region including central New Jersey, four of New York City's boroughs, its northern suburbs, Long Island, and western Connecticut, terminating, probably, on the northeast in New Haven, Connecticut, and in the south at Trenton, New Jersey.[2] This regional system would have been equipped to move millions of people daily throughout this large and crowded area, thus unifying it. The automobile ended that. As it moved into mass production, the stage was set for decisions to be taken, many of them extremely popular, to restructure the transportation system in favor of highway building.

The allure of the automobile is easy enough to understand. Property had once consisted of land, buildings, and paper, and these were largely in the hands of rich and upper-middle-class folk. The auto expanded ownership of tangible property. In time, once mass-production techniques were mastered—and as more and more highways were built—the poorest of human beings might own a car or at any rate buy one on credit. The perception of this possibility breathed fresh life into the existing American faith in individual mobility by invigorating the capacity to reach beyond neighborhood without public transport, although public building of roads was necessary, proving that far more than individual initiative was involved. In any event, cities exploded outward, suburbs grew, and, in time, the inner city was damaged. A subtle change in the notion of ownership and the sense of "mine and thine" took place. The auto offered every human being potential ownership and control of his or her space and the possibility of moving that space around at will—provided roads were available. It also offered a new arena for privacy. It is "mine," and I fill it with the people and the music I want. The people next door no longer need be central to my life; the road out of town is. It is now open. All I need are the wheels and a little change for gas. Above all, within that framework I and I alone pick and choose those with whom I am willing to share space. Not only am I propertied, but in a sense, I am in charge, on my own, subject to no higher authority—unless one counts the ceaseless efforts of highway patrols to keep speeding to a minimum.

This new-found privacy and sense of control travels with me. Though others are on the road, the space my car occupies at this instant is mine, and the sense is one that early discussants of private property, like John Locke or his successor Karl Marx, could never have imagined. Property is now a box on wheels that I direct. Furthermore, privacy is severed from what had been its other necessary half—being able to wall oneself in to be shielded from unwanted outsiders, from "the public." In a world of stationary properties, walls and boundaries are sanctified. Protection is a task of government and politics. In a world of moving properties, priorities reverse. I come to believe at an early age that my property goes with me. It is no longer a function of walls, but entirely personal, and the feelings that Americans have developed for automobiles resemble the pride so often reported in the past by land and estate holders. Public space, which, it can be argued, is the necessary foundation for privacy, private property, and rights, faced now with privacy in motion, is once again following an older American pattern, given a subsidiary place in the scheme of things. The public world, so this way of seeing things suggests, is something I support or ignore, since I regard myself as little dependent on it. Neighborhoods, communities, towns, governments, these are the residue of an older time when people sat still, more or less. Now this public realm depends on my willingness to accept its importunings and interventions. At long last those who portrayed human beings as free-moving particles speak the truth: enclose everyone in a moving space and each is free, the "owner" of whatever space he or she occupies at any given instant. I am, after all, the nucleus of a world that moves around me. I am free at last when on the road—and being an American, I am on the road often.

If one adds in other forces that have been at play in the United States since World War II, the possibilities for tension become transparent. The cheap house, the new suburb, the inner city's desertion by whites and occupation by African Americans—all of them related to cars and highway building—plus the flight of the rich out of the city or skyward to its lofty, expensive, and "secure" apartments combine to create a very different environment that, coupled with racism, becomes supercharged. In sum, the car has been a landscaper grooming the country for the possible loss of all but the most entrenched patterns of connectedness. In a world of highways crowded with cars—Los Angeles in general, New Jersey in most places, and even relatively deserted southern New Hampshire will do as examples—everyone is on the loose, in motion, less restrained or bounded, less connected except by the frustrating presence of others on the road. In the face of this phenomenon, traditional views of individualism, of property, of public space, of privacy, cannot sustain themselves. The highway and the mall replace the neighborhood and old polity. Add in astonishing changes in communication that obliterate distances, and yesterdays's truths become unreliable.

The car came to represent property, independence, mobility, and "prosperity" for the middle class and, later, for poorer Americans. It thereby became the vehicle of choice for an overwhelming percentage of the population. It also bred new sources of pressure in the society—the manufacturers, their allies in the steel, rubber, and oil industries (now being hard pressed by the Japanese), road builders, and, still later, automobile clubs. Accordingly, efforts to upgrade mass transit were brushed aside in the push to expand highways and roads. Bridge, tunnel, highway, and superhighway building became the order of the day.

The effects of all of this are still unfolding, but some are visible. The suburbs—originally places for families of means to escape the noise, dirt, changing ethnicities, and suspect energies of cities—owe much of their contemporary character to the automobile. Mass transit in and out is limited. The clusters of neighborhood shops found in the old city neighborhoods, such as one still finds in Manhattan, Brooklyn, San Francisco, or Chicago, were not replicated. Rather, centers or "malls" were developed in which the stores clustered together, opened and closed down at set times, leaving nighttime pockets of deserted parking lots. Neighborhoods never came to exist in suburbia—in the older sense of clusters of people who together develop a street life and relationships with one another, or parts of cities in which people occupied sidewalks in good weather and circulated in a comparatively small area to shop or run shops and occasionally traveled "downtown" by bus or trolley for major shopping at larger stores with more heavily stocked and variable departments. The automobile took over. In some places, the idea of walking to the store, along with daily shopping for fresh groceries, vanished. In others, sidewalks either were not built or not well maintained. People moved by automobile rather than by foot. And for a time fresh groceries were replaced by goods heavily larded with preservatives.

With the automobile also came changes in social relationships. Sexual mores were altered by the existence of a newly discovered place where young people might, free of the prying eyes of parents, learn about the pleasures and trials of intimacy and privacy. Old-fashioned middle-class notions like "calling on young ladies," preserved for us in books and films, gave way to dating patterns that were governed by the car. The authority of parents weakened while the young's independence grew. The so-called sexual revolution, if indeed such a thing has any reality, may have begun in the relatively shielded back seat of an automobile, that is, is as much rooted in the presence of an increasingly ubiquitous artifact, the automobile, as in "liberal" ideas about child rearing, or permissiveness, or the suggestiveness of films.

The automobile, so much interwoven with visions of ownership, property, and individuality, may well be a primary contributor to the apparent lapse of our awareness and appreciation for things public. Are we indeed connected to other human beings? Do all people understand that they are "in polity" and "in commonwealth" with others? "Only," the automobile driver responds, "in the sense that we are forced to share the parkway and streets with them." (Ironically, this indifference to public matters has now turned into a potential nightmare for motorists and therefore all taxpayers. The nation's bridges and highways, which, of course, are built by governments with public funds, are said to be in such disrepair that some $33 trillion is needed to return them to first-class condition. Such expenditure is highly problematic for the foreseeable future.)

There is yet another consequence. As these suburban developments grew, urban political ties loosened and the infrastructure seemed to collapse. Planning to build in the city had meant planning to maintain, although the effort was often insufficient. Nonetheless, the political organization and community were in place to work on problems. As focus and funds shifted to building new roads and extensions of and rings around the cities, increasing indifference developed respecting the future costs of what was being built and to the question of responsibility. As developers built mall after mall, little attention was paid to traffic jams and consequent costs they generated or to their contribution to the need for still more roads. Meanwhile, deferred maintenance within the old cities, from which "better-off" citizens fled, leaving behind the poor and their problems, meant large areas of urban blight. The question of preservation of old buildings was raised, but it was a special interest of the few, since the poor, given the deteriorating inner city they lived in, could hardly be expected to enthuse about that kind of expenditure. These new inhabitants inherited areas that increasingly fell into disrepair and whose absentee landlords no longer felt compelled to maintain them. The sense of neighborhood, which among the poor had kept places intact and habitable, in alliance with City Hall, began to evaporate. There was now almost no one to protect the old inner city. City Hall, meanwhile, resembled the bridge of a sinking ship, with orders barked out to increasingly self-concerned groups of officials and police officers who, in addition to their lack of connection with the new population, saw more reason to shout "save yourself" to one another than to work on the escalating general problems. The new immigrants—blacks and Hispanics in particular—found that the city was not something of which they could be proud. Instead of concerning themselves with the disappearance of neighborliness, community, and upkeep, they had to focus on mere survival. That attitude, soon enough deplored by those who waxed nostalgic about the good old days (but who themselves had long since moved away or upward to the highest reaches of huge apartment buildings protected by security guards), was in fact but a mirror image of the "meism" that would triumph everywhere in the United States during the 1980s. In sum, this left just about everyone, politicians and voters alike, more indifferent than ever before to the public weal, which was now looked upon as a piece of merchandise—as goods, goodies, stopgap measures to keep things afloat, at best at the material level and at worst at no level whatsoever.

BREAKDOWN OF THE DISTINCTION BETWEEN THE PRIVATE AND THE PUBLIC

The idea of being shielded from the outside world, as vital to individuals as it is to that outer world, has been under steady attack thanks to changes in how life is lived and what is valued. Every household is now prey to constant messages from the outside—telephone, radio, television—and the desire to be shielded in many instances has been weakened or replaced by the apparent wish of many individuals and groups to display their (formerly) private business and/or themselves in public.

One aspect of this, apparently as old as humanity, has to do with the need for recognition, acknowledgment, deference, and, these days, celebrity. To some extent this relates to the sociopolitical milieu, which fosters an attempt to achieve visibility or display because the media are now available to make it more widely possible. Another, reflective of changed cultural attitudes that may relate to changing attitudes toward film, is the virtual disappearance of the idea that some things might best be shielded from public display, that things done in the dark (other than felonies) ought to be kept there. Apparently, the contemporary desire or need to project everything onto a screen, to display oneself even in odd circumstances, has replaced the older view that some things were supposed to be private or intimate. To be displayed means to have achieved one's place in the sun, to have become celebrated or notorious (these two words are now used regularly as synonyms, though they refer to opposite reputational outcomes).

The desire to be identified, known, displayed—however widespread it may be—in addition to reflecting a primal concern to be acknowledged may now also relate to the twentieth-century growth of the psychological and sociological disciplines as well as to the spread of their messages into every recess in the society. Freud's notion, for example, that each life story is a revealing sequence that, if examined closely enough, will yield an etiology of disorders, neuroses, and even psychoses not only contributes to a new medical-psychological discipline but also enlarges the significance and weight now given to each individual's story. Everyone becomes, potentially at least, a case worth recording; no fetish is too minor to escape the conviction that it marks its originator as special. Details, originally in the hands of doctors, are kept confidential during treatment. But sooner or later, albeit encoded, the stories have to be shared with colleagues—science demands public discourse. And sooner or later, historians (and now journalists) attempt to discover the identity and details of the "case," if the author has not already sold the story or given it away. In developing this technique of analysis, modern medical science, I suspect, has reinforced a new desire, breaching all former boundaries respecting inner "secrets" and the dialogue between me and myself. Now those who cannot afford or do not have the means to engage psychiatrists also want their stories compiled in the register of revealed human uniquenesses. This adds to the attack on privacy, an attack as likely as not to be endorsed by those whose privacy has been violated and, if "interesting" enough, sold off to the highest bidder. Privacy, once highly prized, apparently is not as well regarded and is clearly less well rewarded than publicity. And yet the simple truth is that "private" and "public" are words that refer to related opposites. If there is no "private," then there can be no "public" arena.

VISIBILITY

There is also the phenomenon of "visibility," an outgrowth of our societal and political situation, rooted in the incongruous presence of "invisible" human beings in a society convinced that everyone has a special identity and ought to be seen, responded to, noticed. At the present time, given the wealth and/or sufficiency that characterizes the standard of living of about 80 percent of our people, the gap between "well-off" and "impoverished" seems to have widened. Current evidence contradicts the early American view that in this society every man could find food, make a living, buy a piece of land, and live a life in which extremes of neither poverty nor wealth would be important. The impoverished, including the homeless, are now "there," in large numbers, a phenomenon practically unknown in the America of Franklin's and Jefferson's time. They live in stark contrast to those who are well-off or comfortable; and they generate both a reaction that something ought to be done and a tendency to look away. By observing the reaction to them, we learn that plainly visible human beings can be ignored, looked through, treated as if they are neither present nor fit to be heard, seen, or touched. We have witnessed such things in other societies—Hindu untouchables, for example, a caste or category relegated, from others' perspective, to a living non-existence. But we no longer need look to other places. Colonies of people can be found at the darkened ends of New York City subway stations, lying under piles of newspapers and rags. They have no regular housing and are part of no apparent social structure or place. A gust of wind comes along or a sweep of law enforcers, and the cardboard and people beneath it disappear from the spot, only to turn up in another temporary place. Meanwhile, we find ourselves learning not to see, so that such people or non-persons seem to be in the world but somehow do not appear. That singularly human combination—the appearance of persons who as persons are not acknowledged by others whose senses are otherwise unimpaired—is the phenomenon of invisibility, which has often been of consequence in this society even before the need to be visible (not as "saints" as in Puritan America, but as persons), the need to be seen and acknowledged grew and became part of what is called the American Dream. It begins, not recently with the homeless and impoverished, but at the beginning, with slavery and people brought here from Africa.

Not surprisingly, the significance of invisibility in America was first grasped by African American writers, among them W. E. B. DuBois (1868–1963) and Ralph Ellison (b. 1914). They understood that the white world tends to identify black individuals by attaching pre-set images to them. The stereotype lives; the individual is absent even when present. "Who is there?" becomes a meaningless question when the answer is presented exclusively in group or racial terms, "a black man or woman." Regarded only as representative of a category fixed *a priori* in the mind's eye and therefore the mind of the beholder, the black woman or man becomes, metaphorically speaking, invisible. But soon enough the metaphor becomes literally true in the world of appearance. In the days of slavery, those who were chattel were no longer seen as persons; they were living property, stripped of personhood. When the law finally forbade property in persons, Negroes were then addressed not as men but as "boys." They had less standing than house pets. These are merely the obvious, exterior effects of non-status. The "invisible" person has his or her own interior reactions.

The "Invisible Man" who knows he is invisible may choose to behave as befits his status; that is, he may flaunt or defy society's rules.[3] How, after all, can rules apply to those who are not there? Or he may withdraw into a silent, bitter acquiescence. But whether or not actively conscious of the "Veil" behind which each lives, he or she will be dominated by invisibility.

Every individual is identical in that he or she is separate from all others. Indeed, absent others, no single human can be present in the world because what we mean by "the world" is precisely that conjunction of things and others around each human being, that is, the objects, humans as well as traditions and habits, that are present in the environment. To be singularly oneself and to comprehend that singularity, to know oneself as a "somebody," means, in the words of Herman Hesse (1877–1962) to be "the unique, quite special, and in every case the important and remarkable point where the world's phenomena converge, in a certain manner, never to be repeated again."[4] However, when the world treats an individual as representative of a category (and it has apparently done so for as long as the categories "sameness" and "difference" have been around), the individual's self-identification becomes a problem. Each human's presence, insofar as he or she represents category rather than person, becomes antipodal, or more precisely, ambiguous; each individual is separated from all others by a wall that we call skin (in this instance thickened by the category "skin color").

All humans, to reiterate Hesse's point, depend in part on others to confirm their identities. But if we listen to all the current talk about groups— the elderly, the homeless, yuppies, women, African Americans, Latinos, gays, the ethnics—his simple observation seems to lose its impact. However, he is correct. What "really" exists are not groups, but individuals linked together by some characteristic regarded as distinctive enough to distinguish them collectively from all other humans. But in response to the emphasis that this culture and society places on these differences—and claims to see in them—what people expect to find inside themselves has come to reflect what the world celebrates or sees as singular or notorious in the supposed characteristics of their group (see earlier section, "The Gospel of Reified Groups," in Chapter 3). Identification tends to become synonymous with outer or statistical characteristics, possessions, or acts; when they ask themselves, "who am I?" an inner search is no longer apparently satisfactory. We are, many seem to believe, largely what we are perceived to be as members of a group or class. The result is self-identification in terms of the surface characteristics that others stress and a possible consequent sense of inner emptiness. Hesse's comment about social reality—that an individual is a point at which the world's phenomena intersect—is not the same as the conviction that we are no more than reflections of so-called group characteristics. "Identity" is connected to context, but our obsession with ethnicity, race, gender, religion, and pre-American cultural heritage as well as symbols of difference, success or wealth, creates an "identity crisis" because it looks to exterior phenomena, allegedly rooted in "natural" differences and connections, for answers. When that happens, human beings qua persons become "invisible."

The "Invisible Man"—generally a reference to African Americans but these days possibly applicable to everyone who lives in a bureaucratically governed setting—is condemned to a curious non-existent being. Denied individual existence, the invisible person reminds us of the young Rousseau's warnings about society, namely, that it forces persons to seem to be what they are not, that it separates "to be" from "to seem to be." Identity or the inner sense of worthwhileness is then governed largely by the outer characterizations of society at large; that is, "black is ugly" becomes not simply a prejudiced statement but for blacks, a serious characterization that they find themselves believing. Where invisibility operates, those who are invisible measure themselves against stereotypes (unless they develop a strong antidote to the negative group characterization), and they are so measured. The sense of individuation is distorted for them. In other words, those unseen as persons are viewed as mere reflections of "group characteristics." Existence becomes, in DuBois' phrase, "two worlds within and without the Veil." In his example, black people lead ambiguous, stress-filled lives because they are robbed of the normal sense of interior or individual strength. Outside the Veil, the invisible person has no personhood or individual identity; behind it, singularity and specialness clamor for attention, but attention to the person is never fully given, not even from other blacks, who ought to but cannot be empathetic because they have fallen victim to the same phenomenon and in time, in too many cases, to self-loathing. Where the Veil is operative, not only do whites perceive black persons as "blacks," but other black persons are pushed into a similar perception. The world becomes a kaleidoscope of stereotypical images and reactions to them.

African American writers have best captured the effect of this non-status—that to be alive is no protection against invisibility or guarantor of visibility. Invisibility, however, is not the unique burden of one group but is a possibility for all human beings: even genetic uniqueness does not immunize individuals against this "non-existence." Those who cannot "see" the invisible also suffer; that is, they become the victims of their own insistence that the world is made up of categories and types rather than persons. Socialization and conditioning also foster difficulties similar to those resulting from "invisibility"; to wit, individuals are pushed to conform to social norms. But in the white middle-class milieu the absence of racial stereotyping makes likely different reactions, among them the attempts to throw off norms and assert differences in values, beliefs, and individuality that achieved considerable notoriety in the 1960s and, for a time at least, created a new group of "dropouts." However, for African Americans, thanks to widespread and deeply held attitudes toward them in the United States, the internal sense and strength of individuality, which brings with it visibility, is much more elusive.

The visible person is not merely distinguishable physically or because of individuating behavior. He or she is not seen as a large or small, dark or light pebble on some collective beach, but as a person, as a unique presence, a somebody distinct from, and distinguishable from, all others. There is an element in visibility, however, that has to do with and largely depends on others. That is, there must be a context, a space that accepts, encourages, and even treasures difference and individuality. Visibility, in other words, is contextual as well as individual. And it is that context, political, racial, and social, with which Americans are familiar and to which they have turned in order to make it possible for their so-called group characteristics to become supportive of, rather than an impediment to, their visibility. In the second half of the twentieth century, in the United States and elsewhere, the effort to accomplish this has repeatedly sought to "politick" it into existence, whether at the level of the Supreme Court or Congress or local school districts—everywhere in the society where some kind of political entity has existed. ("Politick" here refers to what we earlier called the operational aspect of power; but it is in the "initiational" and "foundational" aspects that the problem can really be located, for black Americans are not regarded as initiators, co-founders, or co-members and therefore are not accorded equal standing as a matter of course or common treatment as fellow humans.) In the latter years of the century, however, a reaction set in that emphasized individuality *per se* and attempted to reverse changes aimed at underwriting visibility for minority groups. These programs, with their effort to bring to bear the full force of the law to provide individuals with real opportunities—affirmative action is an example—were repeatedly attacked, somewhat ironically, given a structure that now featured almost unbridled activity by thousands and thousands of organized groups and political action committees each seeking special favors or protection for "their" particular interests. (Readers interested in an effort to clarify the role of groups in the political process see Appendix A.) Meanwhile, many black Americans, the leading victims of invisibility, remained invisible, though some made considerable progress (and among those a group emerged condemning these very programs.) In no other area of life did it seem quite so evident that economic success *per se*, in most Americans' view the key to unraveling all problems, meets its match in racial prejudice.

OUR "WINDOW" AND CURRENT AMERICAN ATTITUDES

What, then, can be said, using the window through which we have looked, of the condition of contemporary politics? I think the answer is that politics today is an art form whose purposes and virtues are no longer understood, that at its best it meets needs sporadically, that indifference to domestic problems often seems as prevalent in the United States as elsewhere in the world, and that at its worst politics concentrates on external problems, bringing distant dangers near in order to rouse up feelings of patriotism, nationalism, religious zealotry, and ethnicity rather than confront issues. Actions that bespeak an awareness of the positive uses of power and politics are all but non-existent. Even our leadership achieves office by attacking the governments they presumably hope to serve. All that seems to be left of our politics are the extensive maneuverings of pressure groups and elites and the manipulations of bureaucracies.

We find ourselves, accordingly, driven toward self-concern and protection rather than by a universalist or global or even community sensitivity, in other words by the narrowest conceptions of "me and mine" or "we and they." What was earlier called "connectedness," the relatively conscious choosing of linkage to others, has weakened to the point where we have to fall back on more primal, emotion-packed, and so-called natural connections. Changes with so much potential for good—material success, electronic communications, high-speed transport—have been accompanied by an inability to maintain political connectedness or replace it with something that concentrates on general well-being rather than my or my group's climb up the economic ladder. We have also been caught up in a kind of voyeurism that substitutes itself for active efforts to resolve problems. We think of involvement as a cross between watching a screen and expressing opinions on every possible subject that momentarily flickers across it, and our actual contact with good or decent general governance has been reduced to grousing about or paying tax bills. We are not in contact with one another or with *our* political instrumentalities. Even our language has lost contact with politics. Television commentators, individuals of obvious intelligence, think nothing of sentences like this one: "Soon, we have to adopt some kind of national health care plan, but we have to keep politics out of it." But it is precisely politics in its rightful meaning that has to decide whether or not to adopt that kind of policy and, if so, what the character of the policy should be.

The presence of various invisibilities has damaged our capacity to understand the implications of politics. In the United States, trivialized social visibility has been substituted for genuine understanding that humans as humans stand together when they choose to, thereby conceding to one another that they are visible as persons and realizing that to do so is the necessary condition for maintaining an ongoing, relatively orderly framework within which we do our "personal" business. Instead, "personhood" is related to celebrity, skill in sports, wealth, success, and "life styles of the rich and famous." Rather than a political guarantee, namely, that every member of the polity stands on equal footing, this new social visibility stresses difference, uniqueness, being "better," being "Number One." The visibility about which American writers have spoken so eloquently, applying it initially to black Americans, stresses equality of footing, of foundation, of opportunity, each accepted as a necessary and deserved element in the development of political power in a democratic society. To be unable to develop that visibility and accompanying sense of community is to open the door to a different order of things, a stress on group identities from which each individual's identity derives. The consequence is a concentration on politics as a divisive group phenomenon, a game wherein each group gets its appropriate or reasonable share—fairness being determined by the exercise of group pressure, influence, threats, money, what have you.

As a consequence, the older political notions are pushed aside. The agreement to agree, which initiates power and maintains support, is but a dim recollection, displaced apparently by celebration of an agreement to disagree, of the right of each to exercise something that resembles veto power. The foundation that includes the rule of law, the participation of citizens, an honest attempt to achieve representation, and insistence on public and open processes, which needs constant reinvigoration, is weakened. And the realization that people "get their share" by coming together, engaging in dialogue, giving a little as they argue and effectuate compromises, is all but forgotten.

The new point of view, with its stress of societal position and eventual linkage of that position with group presences in the body social, makes personhood dependent on group identities and clusters. Our slogan is "we are what we achieve," when it ought to be "we exist, therefore we are human and politically equal, and that standing is more fundamental than social standing or an excess of possessions and luxuries." The broader identity of human beings provided by the public realm is lost. When personhood becomes dependent on social achievement, we run immediately into the obvious problems: not everyone can be a great basketball player, hit baseballs, knock down quarterbacks, be externally or physically "beautiful" or "handsome," make a killing on Wall Street, win the race, or be in position to be acknowledged for any of these. Logic tells us that if someone is to be the most beautiful or able to hit the most home runs, then there are a host of others who cannot by that route become visible. Many, even with society's best effort to educate and a maximum effort to succeed, will not do so. Indeed, the price of this societal-achievement version of visibility is high because it raises expectations to the point where many people inevitably become frustrated, resentful, and violent. "Others," the majority of people of color, females, and, for that matter, white males, failing to "achieve," are pushed toward substitute comforts. Non-minority individuals may feel a deep sense of failure or weakness. To watch million-dollar, two-million-dollar, twenty-million-dollar celebrities tossing footballs, chasing a small white ball, or appearing on television, and to regard those activities as significant while ignoring the political test that says otherwise, or to ascribe "greatness" to those personalities who palmed off nearly worthless junk bonds on a gullible public—another version, until recently, of "great achievements"—invites discontent and backlash. For the poor, invisibility in the form of "failure" can be a permanent pathway to disablement and worse.

We ought to celebrate contributions and advances in society, be they on Wall Street, at the office, in the classroom, or on the playing field. But politically speaking, we have to operate in a way that provides each person with a sense of worthwhileness and pride that comes from sources other than the nation's victories on distant battlefields or being top dog. For a time the automobile may have been a substitute for that sense, albeit a trivial one that just happened to be within the grasp of millions, and perhaps their cars still do this for the young, but traffic jams, pollution, and highway expenditures have taught the rest of us that like other material things, automobiles provide only a shallow sense of "pride." As they have become universal, so they decreasingly serve to prove that anyone has achieved much more than what has now become necessary.

Ironically, on battlefields the sense of connectedness does prevail because soldiers have always known that they have to rely on one another. But this is neither a viable nor a desirable means of instilling feelings of connectedness among members of the general public. Rather, there have to be ways of internalizing a similar sense of worthwhileness that, I believe, comes in part from realization of equal political standing and awareness that life is a series of "games of rules" rather than mere televised war games. The political sense with which this book has been grappling has to do with being a somebody among many somebodies— citizens, fellows, equals, joint tenants, connected and sharing human beings aware of each other and, hopefully, of the millions with whom they share the planet. War and wealth cannot be the only metaphors that do this unless we can only think of problems, domestic or foreign, as potential targets for violent assault or for unstinting applications of money rather than as subjects of thoughtful resolution.

We have to concede that a still-not-clearly shaped world exists, although we use an old vocabulary to address it and make an effort to restore political life so that what is yet to be can be nurtured in its time. One is tempted to say, "concoct some alternative transforming activity," some "authority" that changes the basic conditions of our lives and societies, but to say that is no more than to find a different name for a good part of what we once meant by politics. The discussion here takes us in other directions, in search of fresh imagery and metaphors, which are required to understand the positive uses of power—the sense of coming together (and later remaining together and supporting decisions responsibly reached), the building of a foundation, and politicking reasonably. We need, in short, not to reinvent but to restore politics.

NOTES

1. As of 1 July, 1988, something like 245 million Americans lived in the top 150 Metropolitan Statistical Areas, to use the Census Bureau's designation. These ranged from the largest five—Greater Manhattan (New York City, northern New Jersey, Long Island, western Connecticut (18,120,200); Los Angeles–Anaheim– Riverside, California (13,769,700); Greater Chicago, Gary–Lake County, Illinois, Indiana, Wisconsin (8,180,900); San Francisco, Oakland, San Jose, California (6,041,800); Philadelphia, Pennsylvania, Wilmington, Delaware, Trenton, New Jersey (5,963,000)—to the five "smallest" (over 108,000 in population)—State College, Pennsylvania (115,700); Wausau, Wisconsin (113,400); Santa Fe, New Mexico (112,500); Fayetteville-Springdale, Arkansas (110,600); Danville, Virginia (108,100). The estimates are taken from Bernhard H. Ross, Myron A. Levine, and

Murray Stedham, Jr., *Urban Politics: Power in Metropolitan Areas* (Itasca, Ill.: Peacock Publishers, 1991; 4th edition), Appendix B, pp. 449–55.

2. As per note 1, the current population of this area is now approximately 20 million. Anyone who has traveled in this region is familiar with the havoc that has been wrought by highway building and the neglect of mass transit. The New Jersey Turnpike and Garden State Parkway, which cross one another and are two major "north-south" monster highways in the state, demonstrate an almost total absence of political judgment, but pressure for such highway building is the responsibility of the auto industry and its allies as well as a public unaccustomed to decent public transit and crazy for more automobiles. A trip through New Jersey on these roads, and others, is almost enough to convince one that the population there is bound to have or has had a collective nervous breakdown.

3. "Invisible Man" is, of course, the title of Ralph Ellison's superb novel, first published in 1947: *Invisible Man* (New York: Vintage Books edition, 1972); the "Veil" is a notion developed by W. E. B. DuBois in his definitive *Souls of Black Folks* (1903; New York: Signet, New American Library, 1969).

4. Herman Hesse, *Demian: The Story of a Youth* (1923; New York: Henry Holt and Company, 1948), p. 2.

PART THREE
RESTORING THE AMERICAN POLITY

10

Tired Images, Defunct Ideologies, Forgotten Games of Rules

OUR INAPPROPRIATE IMAGERY

The political and social imagery we have inherited originated in ideas that contrast nature with artifice, the primitive with the civilized, the isolated, particle-like individual with the civil partner. In their time, these were fresh images used to explain and justify emerging ways of organizing human life.

Following the "discovery" and colonization of the New World—our view of these incidents arrogantly implies that its existence depended on Westerners' coming ashore and settling it—a new "natural history" of civilization was imagined. The Western Hemisphere, half the globe, came to be regarded by Europeans as newly appeared, all but free of people, and ripe for colonization and application of their commercial energies and appetites. Thomas Hobbes helped shape this new metaphor, maintaining that the original world was reconstructed by men in stages—pre-civil, formative, and post-contractual. Primitives or pre-civil beings understood little, not even the commands of nature or the virtues of sovereignty, nor the advantages of civility and order over an uncivil free-for-all. The English Civil War also helped author and confirm his views, but its third source is cultural ethnocentrism—the idea that Europeans had been handed a virtually empty space to develop. That their own societies were exploding with commercial inventiveness provided the impetus and justification for seeing other territories as nature- or God-given opportunities.

Particle and impact theory, so central to seventeenth-century scientific thinking, also played a part. Hobbes' political theory and that of his successors emphasized separation and boundaries—separate phases of development (pre-civil and civil society); separate arenas of life (private and public, in addition to which successors would separate the economic from the political and disengage the intimate from the social)—with each area exhibiting a pattern unique unto itself. This stress on separateness portrays life as a container filled with free and uncontrolled entities constantly in motion and at risk of collision.

Hobbes' predilection for geometry helped. Like geometry, the polity or commonwealth was man-made. The two could be treated as analogues and the result is a geometry of politics. Furthermore, though Hobbes doesn't say this, the New World's occupancy by "mere" savages suggests the existence of "natural" men, and therefore the "natural condition of mankind" he wrote about. The New World—both its existence and the idea of a vast empty space waiting to be dealt with—might be treated as a blank page on which Europeans as authors and settlers could write, thus echoing the blank pages on which the first geometers drew their points, lines, circles, and triangles. Hobbes also affirmed the conviction, visible in his contemporaries' new experimental sciences, of which he disapproved, that men made the commonwealth as an experiment precisely as God had made the universe. He thereby helped to instigate the arrogant thesis that the New World was a God-proffered blank slate on which Europeans would do the writing. The evolution of this newly discovered space might parallel the deductions he made respecting the transition from the most primitive and war-torn to the most civil and orderly society wherein governance depended not only on discovery of the laws of nature that command peace but also on the proper "construction" of a Sovereign who maintained order. Later, perhaps in an unwitting echo of Hobbes, Thomas Jefferson described Europe as a failed experiment, one conducted before the Maker had fully learned His craft; but since God was no longer seen as the prime mover of human affairs, Jefferson was actually talking about progress in human science and the uses of reason. It was men who had learned how to build society— America was the "empty" arena in which they could refine their craftsmanship and conduct an experiment in the pursuit of happiness.

John Locke had prepared the way by reshaping the metaphor. Philosophically, he expanded upon Hobbes' idea, treating the mind as a blank tablet on which experience in the form of sensations writes and prepares the way for "knowledge." Similarly, his political theory rests on Hobbes' notion of a "natural condition," a logical "early" time when fertile land is empty, unused, and the property of all—a blank page with potential waiting for the application of human labor. Eventually, the land is occupied and labored-upon, its title passes to individuals, and a struggle breaks out between those who became propertied through their expenditure of labor and those too lazy to do the same. The struggle grows more intense as the quantity and quality of unclaimed land diminishes, since even those willing to labor can no longer find fertile land on which to expend their energies. He places the institutions of property, exchange, money making, and accumulation of wealth logically and chronologically in pre-civil society, which thereby is given a far more significant status than the succeeding stage, polity or commonwealth. In Hobbes' metaphor the founding of the polity is the basis for all other activity, including the operations of society itself; in Locke's the commonwealth is an afterthought. The commonwealth is not the basis for society, but a step taken to preserve, protect, and extend the blessings of property and an already-existent society. The polity merely administers natural law, that is, protects the "natural" rights to life, liberty, and estate that he alleges operate before there is government.

Jean-Jacques Rousseau, writing later, further explored the metaphor, at first excoriating what so pleased Locke, private property, and celebrating what terrified Hobbes, primitive, natural man who lives in blissful liberty doing as he wills. Rousseau opened the door to the romantics, to the idealization of primitive man and his presumably natural inner feelings, which differed dramatically, he believed, from the inferior socially induced pretensions of civil men. While concocting this new primitive source of individuality, Rousseau gave credence to the suspicion, already planted by Locke, that civil society chains men, making them less free-spirited than their more "natural" predecessors, the dubious beneficiaries of mere civil liberty rather than the unfettered, natural, free men of the state of nature. Social and political institutions were mere encrustations devised to curtail human freedom. By the following century, Marx agreed. Property and in time capital were instruments of oppression: they open the door to alienation and estrangement, exploitation and injustice. In the future they must yield to a rebirth in which property, once used to enlarge the human storehouse and to reward the individual who initiated cultivation of previously empty land, would be reconstituted. The feeding, sheltering, and improvement of human life would continue. But the inequities and injustices built into the reward system, the estrangement of men from one another, would disappear along with the State, now portrayed as a repressive institution that did the bidding of those who were propertied or in control of society. The State, which had appeared to Locke as a necessary if somewhat belated afterthought amidst society's other, spontaneously developed institutions, would no longer be necessary or desirable, since the protection of individual title to property of the propertied classes, and therefore the class system, would disappear.

In various forms, this same imagery is at the heart of most political notions held sacred in the United States for the past two hundred years, and it has been important in one form or another throughout the West. Thanks to Western territorial and cultural imperialism and technological innovation, it has been and still is shaping the rest of the world. It produced notions that serve humanity well, in particular images of political contracts (among men, between men and God, between nations) and rights (natural or inherent, civil or contractual)—each of these highlighted by the logical or "historical" transition from pre-civil to civil society. But today this imagery sounds pertinent only to those who believe repetition of an untruth produces a truth. It bears little or no relation to everyday understanding of events. No one believes any longer that humans sign ongoing political contracts. Government, on the contrary, is perceived as a hired hand or occasional partner, a house- and order-keeper whose primary function is to settle problems it is assigned, a servant who cleans up unsightly messes and otherwise keeps out of the way—though its hugeness in America has again and again shown that it is not easy, even by repeating slogans, to restrain an institution that visibly towers over all others.

Notions of natural rights, particularly as they are conceived as the birthright of individuals, have fared better. But as conflicts have repeatedly surfaced respecting the rights of those who are "different"—Indians, African Americans, Latinos as well as various ethnic groups, women, and so forth—natural rights imagery has not always been accepted. And to the extent we now wish to extend rights not only to those who live within our own polity but also globally, natural rights talk has not been very effective. The effort, mentioned earlier, to appeal to "common humanity" as the basis for granting equivalent status to every human being has also encountered difficulties. Among human beings, the word "we" inevitably suggests the existence of some "they," of those who are separable and separated, perhaps really different, maybe, after all, "less human" and consequently less entitled to rights. Many of the agonies of the twentieth century, particularly those that gave rise to horrifying genocidal episodes, give one pause as to whether terms like "common humanity," "common language," or "common culture" are potent enough to prevent hostility or indifference to the fate of others. Persistent, murderous ethnic, racial, and religious hatreds—and their heightened intensity in eastern Europe since the collapse of Soviet hegemony and political union in Yugoslavia and Czechoslovakia—raise still more doubts about holding things together with that kind of talk.

SEARCHING FOR PERTINENT IMAGERY

Richard Rorty has argued that "human solidarity" is not achieved by clearing away prejudice but only as a persistently advanced goal to which one clings and toward which one insistently moves, however slowly. He further maintains that what makes possible humaneness and decent consideration of "the needs of strangers" is not some universal essence or quality in human beings—common humanness, general or universal rights, or that humans share rationality as a characteristic and therefore are bound together—but the development of mutually comprehensible hopes and vocabularies. A broadened understanding of the word "we," he argues, depends upon "enough overlap [in human vocabularies] so that everybody has some words to express the desirability of entering into other people's fantasies as well as into one's own."[1] Nor is this a matter of decency or kindness or claims about human dignity. Rather, it demands know-how regarding the prevention of humiliation and of cruelty to one's fellows, graspable, he believes, in literary forms (including films) rather than political tracts. "It is to be achieved not by inquiry but by imagination, the imaginative ability to see strange people as fellow sufferers."[2] In other words, we must enlarge our grasp of the human situation and better sensitize ourselves to the conditions of those outside of our immediate field of vision. Until that happens, we can neither understand changes in our own situation nor compare them to the condition of others. We will remain locked into imagery that does not account for the changes technical advances have instituted. To control events rather than be controlled by them, we need new metaphors, new ways of talking about and understanding politics—or whatever we wish to call it—so that within feasible limits, and recognizing that the human experience always produces the unexpected, we control rather than merely stumble upon our destinies.

The ever-present possibility of change creates difficulties for those who wish for regularity and predictability. They chafe when they realize that sometimes even consistency has to be abandoned and opposite principles employed in varying situations. For example, in politics both equality and inequality are accepted and applauded. Without the concession that humans are unequal in some respects, leadership cannot be comprehended. In the absence of an insistence that all citizens are equal in standing and rights, free and voluntary associations cannot be constructed or maintained. Ideas associated with political and social relations are attuned to purposes, not truths, because a human truth employed in one context becomes a misleading and false claim in another. Politics is driven by selectivity, not the demands of logic.

This means that in politics we constantly create and choose images that incorporate truths as they are then understood, spoken about, and acted upon by particular individuals and groups. In what follows, I offer examples of "truths" in force for centuries that, insofar as they have little relevance to our situation, ought to be set aside or abandoned.

Plato, for example, thought human beings naturally lived in clusters or groups; that each person was identical in needs—among these was a need for self-sufficiency—but different in abilities. Therefore, since no person could be self-sufficient, people clustered together to ensure that their most fundamental needs might be met.[3] And so human life entails anomalies: differences in talent versus sameness of needs; individuality and separateness versus the constant presence and impact of others; the certainty that people do different things ably versus the search for self-sufficiency. These genetic and economic "facts" require the existence of a properly constructed polity. Conveniently, nature provides a foundational formula: "genetic difference = functional differentiation." In other words, the "nature" of humans is such that some are destined to make shoes, to become craftsmen, while others are better equipped to make war or to rule. Some are born to rule, others to be ruled; some naturally belong to the elite, others belong with the herd.

That may be a happy conclusion for those who believe that a handful are destined to lead while everyone else follows, who see the polity as the plaything of rulers. They apparently regard inequality as the logical first principle of political life and usually imagine themselves as the rulers or managers. But this raises the question of whether or not the polity actually exists for the well-being of all members. Plato's answer, as we have seen, relies on his Theory of Ideas, which claims that a series of eternal, fixed "Ideas" (the Good, sameness and difference, Justice, Beauty) "really" exist, that they are arranged in a hierarchy with the Idea of Good sitting above and ruling the others. According to him, an elite group ought to rule the polity as the trained servants of these eternal Ideas. He thereby checks unrestrained elite rulers by means of fixed truths. This linkage between the world of humans, politics, and the eternal sky of Ideas, eternally valid truths, presumably answers those who object to elites, but as the twentieth century has demonstrated, elite rulers acquainted with so-called unchanging verities are disastrous rulers. Plato would reply that ideological rigidity was not what he had in mind and that the Ideas, when grasped by philosopher-kings, produce a moral and just polity. Unfortunately, in the over two thousand years since he wrote, no one has figured out exactly how to grasp them, or if fully understood, how to put them to use in the daily affairs of mere men and women.

This is not, however, a call for the burning of Plato's works. The richness of his thought makes him indispensable in education. But his political prescription, that rulers can and ought to be an elite governed by fixed truths, which has been influential throughout Western history, deserves a rest.

With it should go the idea that polity reflects the makeup or "nature" of men, which implies that a collective impulse drives them inexorably to come together. This Aristotelian construct portrays men as forming families, villages, and "States" naturally—in other words, views humans as if they were servants who function together as a single organism or akin to acorns (in which one can presumably see the potential to become a tree). It deemphasizes choice, suggests that humans cannot control their destinies, and tends to undermine the exciting notion that human beings invent or concoct institutions and constantly transform their inheritance into something never before seen on earth. This "naturalism" or "essentialism" also lies behind the view that we can understand psychology and political life by uncovering unvarying truths about "human nature," that humans are good or aggressive, grasping, selfish. To the extent that we accept such portraits, we rob political life of something men and women have struggled to bring about throughout history, particularly in the past five centuries: that they in fact can make a better world. For how is a better world possible if human nature is fixed and never to be changed by circumstance and time? It is well and good to be awed by genetic codes, but it is important to recognize that they do not lay down prescriptions for the good society.

A third candidate for shelving is Hobbes' hypothetical "natural condition of mankind," which portrays humans as free-floating, aggressive, amoral particles who desire the same objects, use cunning and violence to get what they want, and therefore are in constant combat with and at continuous risk relative to one another. Hobbes' individualistic credo and his observation that men might learn the significance of speech and reasoning by a demonstration of what life would be like in their absence are invaluable. So is the notion, rooted in the inexorable logic operating in the hypothetical "natural condition" Hobbes constructed, that men discover a law that commands them to seek peace, that confined together in a relatively small place while operating on the principle of free movement toward and away from objects of desire and fear, they will be driven to war against one another in the name of personal safety. But Hobbes meant this to be hypothetical. It is not a sociology or description of actual human conduct nor an ideological blueprint to be taken seriously. To the extent we treat humans as if they were replicas of Hobbes' imagined natural beings, we distort his view, downplay his emphasis on artificing, treat human nature as fixed and combative and humans as mutually hostile—and we do so not as students of Hobbes but as contemporary ideologues.

A fourth candidate for retirement is Locke's political theory, still beloved by Americans. Locke neutralizes the State and government and converts them into narrowly empowered, interest-driven machines. Government's real purpose is to protect propertied persons from the non-propertied who are said by Locke to be lazy and contentious. Palmed off as an impartial, judge-like interpreter of "natural law," the government is treated as agent for those with antecedent and present property claims. Property holders' disagreements with one another are to be settled by a "neutral" magistrate, and established claims always take precedence over new ones. The empowered commonwealth mirrors established societal (propertied) interests. No wonder Karl Marx labeled the State "the executive committee of the bourgeoisie," an instrument of the dominant propertied class, and claimed that it would disappear. Likewise, law, no longer simply the will of the sovereign in this portrait, is the enforcer of property rights that antedate its own operational existence. This view helps justify a situation in which elites and special interests capture both government and the law, bending them to the selfish purposes they disguise as "the good of all."

The much-admired Lockean contract theory has too many deficiencies. It pretends that government comes to exist at a time when all men are equal but after property has been privatized, thereby making men unequal. This is not simply a romance posing as theory; it also eliminates the notion that there are public affairs or needs—aside from the convenient presence of law enforcers. In the absence of a viable alternative, and Marxism clearly is not that, this political perspective increasingly paralyzes us. Locke's reduction of political life to mere magistracy, enthusiastically echoed in the United States, has produced that singularly American mix: too many governments; indifference to the meaning of public affairs and public business; a disinclination to come to grips with public problems except in crisis; the pretense (thanks to propaganda spread by publicists, politicians, and academicians) that the public good is a by-product of close combat among selfish, self-seeking interest groups; and the conviction that the major business of the United States is the health of the economy—incongruously topped off by the ludicrous claim that we believe in and practice limited government.

In suggesting that these ideas be set aside, I do not intend to slight their originators, who could never have imagined the purposes for which their analyses have been employed. Their views have simply been worn out by time. Rather, the aim here is to reiterate the need to weigh inherited truths carefully and to recognize that they are not equivalent to laws governing the universe. In the world that humans make and unmake, contingency and variability are the fundamental laws. What is required is imagery that fits our circumstances, not endless reiteration of the decayed remains of ideas that once perceptively addressed human affairs.

IGNORING "GAMES OF RULES"

By "games" I mean those transactions and activities that involve us with others. They are all governed by rules, whether written down or generally understood and resulting from socialization, thus the term "games of rules." They operate and govern all situations in which humans deal with one another—in the family, community, religion, law, corporate entity, economy, or polity at large. Before beginning the search for new metaphors for what is being described as "a new age," or in a hateful phrase reminiscent of Adolf Hitler, a "new world order," instances of the shambles we are making of these games ought to be noted.

First, despite constant talk of returning government to the people, which I take to mean to the communities and states, which allegedly are "closer to the people" than the national government, there is little evidence that this is taking place; nor does the population appear to appreciate this supposed connection, except in ritualistic rhetoric, on automobile stickers and licenses, or in response to pollsters. State and local elections usually bring out abysmally low turnouts of voters, as if a majority of citizens do not care who governs or believe that public policies are of little importance except to the extent they directly affect them or their family and friends. Among the poor there is very little involvement except when frustration reaches a peak. Of course, whether people know it or not, the political system intrudes on every layer of American society. But a strong sense of connectedness is not visible in this society other than during disasters, wars, or problems of overwhelming magnitude. Americans appear to be minimally, and even then erratically, involved in or aware of their communities. Meanwhile, minimally supported and seemingly incapable of sorting out or acting upon priorities, U.S. governments pile up unimaginable debts and turn to self-defeating budget-balancing acts to cover the trail of unsolved problems.

Second, our family structures are being radically altered by what are seen as economic necessities, particularly the need for an income level that can only be sustained by both parents holding jobs or by a breakdown in stability that has produced the one-parent family. In both instances, the old order and rules appear to be irrelevant.

Third, our capacity to empower and then support leaders has been seriously eroded by the conduct of those who have held or been entrusted with offices. I refer not only to the continuing savings and loan bailout, the result of possibly the greatest examples of fraud, chicanery, private corruption, and unforgivable lapses in public responsibility in the nation's history, but also to a general cynicism about other professionals, including teachers, physicians, law enforcement officials, lawyers, and politicians.[4] Unprofessional conduct has been exposed repeatedly, and the result is lack of confidence.

Fourth, loss of confidence in politics grew following a sequence of events that began with the Vietnam War, included the first resignation of a U.S. president, and continued with episodes of covert and possibly illegal conduct "authorized" by the president of the United States. The war exposed government willingness to lie and deceive in order to pursue aims it was unable or unwilling to explain or justify and in time damaged confidence in the trustworthiness of political leaders and U.S. politicking. The unseating of a president did the same. More recently, business and political leaders, in incident after incident of dubious conduct and indifference to the well-being of the community at large, have contributed to further erosion of faith in the system and its politicians.

Perhaps new "truths" can be substituted for these much-abused games of rules. Science, we might think, ought to be helpful—but that has not turned out to be so. For example, the observation that human beings are similar, that they exemplify something called "human nature" or behave in a manner consistent with fixed behavioral laws, does not reinforce and often contradicts our stated political ideas. Scientifically reliable observations may be worthless environmentally, historically, or circumstantially speaking. If for purposes of biological or genetic study we discover likenesses and probabilities that help explain those areas and adapt them for the study of politics, it does not follow that the isolated constants have any bearing on human relationships. Human blood groups are classified according to a simple system, but it does not follow that humans with A-negative blood are replicas of one another other than in that one respect. "A-negative humans" gathered in a political unit turn out to be as diverse as any other collection of people. Politically speaking, blood type can become relevant only because humans decide to make it so.

Likewise, discoveries about human aggressiveness do not prove that in political arrangements this single characteristic is especially significant. That humans can be "aggressive" we well know; that they are alike we acknowledge. But that they are identical or that aggressiveness is their outstanding characteristic is no more certain than Rousseau's claim that they are moved by empathy or pity for others. What we believe valid respecting human beings is drawn from a mixed bag of behaviors differentially displayed by individuals. Furthermore, efforts to adapt observations drawn from religious norms, philosophy, metaphysics, or psychological studies, however logical or coherent, have little to do with behavior of people as "political beings." These borrowings focus on problems that may indeed impact on polities but are not definitively political because political "truths" are created, made, rather than discovered in or derived from natural laws or regularities. To learn what "people in politics" are like, study politics, not chemistry; discover politics' virtues, values, and dangers, rather than draw lessons from areas whose truths derive from other circumstances, constants, and variables. Politics is not merely derivative; the word, as these comments have attempted to show, has its own substantiality, references, and meanings.

So neither the Hobbesian-Lockean-American formula that "plenty" = "orderliness" nor truths of behavioral or physical sciences can serve as metaphors for political life. They lead to the conclusion that basic behaviors are embedded in human nature, which eliminates human responsibility for reorienting ourselves as the world changes. Worse yet, they suggest that we can no more account for change than we can change our ways, and they read the future and present as mere repetitions of the past. But to assess political life demands an awareness of contingency, of the impact of time, moment, and circumstance as well as inheritance and, ultimately, recognition that politics is something we generate, we sustain, we turn off. But since we have been taught that politics is derivative rather than valuable in its own right, we are unable to breathe life into inherited analogies and metaphors. Our political rhetoric is, accordingly, lifeless, and willingness to participate fades out correspondingly. Old stories are always worth hearing, but when political imagery consists entirely of tales drawn from other times, we are not in position to say with certainty why politics is important now. At the height of American influence, Americans no longer can attest to contemporary political power's significance or potential value. They understand violence much better. And that is why we have confounded the two and confused as well as deceived ourselves.

This is not, however, to say that stale images, defunct ideologies, and worthless metaphors directly cause breakdowns in civility. They contribute to such breakdowns, but their real significance is that they incorrectly tell us how to look at the world. When they are relevant, we better understand the world; when irrelevant, they are stale residues of the past. By insisting that the world is as it is not, they raise the frustration level of huge numbers of people who have to contend daily with the imaginings of newspaper columnists, dead writers, philosophers, analysts, and academicians, whose errors prove too costly to be borne any further. In the case of the former communist nations, the old ideology governed the way things were done, and the breakdown was total. In our case, the problem is not yet as extreme because our economic and political arrangements have been—and in many respects remain—successful.

When we falter, our situation bears more resemblance to that of the communists than we like to admit. If people are told, on the one hand, that individual effort will improve their lot and, on the other, that the world's bedrock is fixed, if evidence assaults their eyes that improvements are few and far between, then when things no longer work as they perhaps once did or are supposed to, the invocation of these "explanations" and justifications for selfishness will engender in some a sense of helplessness and in others rage. To cling to tales that once inspired lessons said to be true for all time but that now explain little is to admit that change, novelty, and, for that matter, failure cannot be explained. If we keep "taking care of Number One," as we have been taught to do, and lose track entirely of connectedness, we will be disappointed repeatedly. In other words, we will be unable to deal with the world realistically, and that can only generate increasing disillusionment among those for whom the system does not seem to work and a consequent urge to shatter the rules whenever that promises some relief or success. The rules become expendable, disillusionment grows exponentially, and trust is all but forgotten. For acceptance of the rules is nothing other than an expression of our trust in one another and what we are doing.

In a time of rapid change, when the rules are broken repeatedly and trust is on the wane, we must seek better ways to look at the world. Again we may turn to Richard Rorty for help. He points out that many believe that language either represents or expresses an underlying reality correspondent with the "actual" self or world at large. I take that to mean that when we speak about something, we are trying to describe it exactly as it "really" is. If this is so, if language clarifies "reality," we should always reject statements that appear to be inaccurate with respect to this "reality," that do not speak the truth as we understand it. But language is less a matter of "hard" realities than is often assumed; it can be filled with "stumbles, mumbles, malapropisms, metaphors" and is as likely as not to send signals that are not scientific probabilities or certainties. Language often consists of *sharable* rather than *correct* references to the world. This sharing suggests that agreement is important to language, which means that language itself is "political" to the extent that it requires generalized support or agreement, and that this is as true of scientific and philosophic talk as of everyday speech. Otherwise, "my" language is necessarily a mystery to anyone who hasn't agreed to it, a condition that means the abandonment of all communication. In this sense, language is, to use a word prominent here, empowered; it creates, rather than transparently describes, reality.

I think this view of language is extremely valuable for talk about politics. Language does not indisputably pin down reality but "constructs" either by employing previously shared understandings, which we call "literal" talk, or by using meanings that are taken from or transferred from other settings or contexts, which we call "metaphorical" talk or metaphor. For example, the phrases "state of nature" and "civil society" were metaphors for the historical notion that in human development there had been an earlier "primitive" or "natural" time that was then followed by a "civilized" or "artificial" time. Eventually, the metaphor achieved a kind of literalness because people accepted it as an actual stage of human development. This, despite its original user's (Locke) denial of its reality and his predecessor's (Hobbes) clear statement that an earlier version, "the natural condition of mankind," was a hypothetical, not a real, time. Literal and metaphorical allusion, Rorty argues, differ from each other because they represent the "distinction between familiar and unfamiliar uses of noises and marks. The literal uses . . . are [those] we can handle by our old theories about what people will say under various conditions. Their metaphorical use is the sort that makes us get busy developing a new theory."[5] Insofar as this discussion is concerned, Rorty is saying that literal talk presents us with familiar images and stories, while metaphor makes us look at something in a way we never contemplated before. It is not the words as such nor their proximity or correspondence to "reality" that makes them literal or metaphoric but the familiarity or freshness of the imagery they engender. When the "metaphorical use" becomes commonplace, it is understood literally. The language or words used are so familiar or stale that they conjure up old explanations that may no longer explain anything.

Indeed, language neither exclusively reveals "a hidden reality outside us . . . [nor] expresses a hidden reality within us."[6] There is, according to Rorty, "no deep sense of how things are which it is the duty of philosophers to spell out in language."[7] Again, to put that into a more familiar kind of talk, Rorty is saying that philosophers are not the officially designated sources of underlying, deep, permanent truths. But he is also suggesting that whenever we talk about the world in our own time, it may be impossible to uncover the "deep sense of how things are," possibly because language itself, whether "literal" or "metaphoric," creates "how things are." Language, indeed, everything, insofar as metaphorical reference is employed, *may be seen* as a product of time and chance. And that means, I suggest, that when we employ metaphor, we are looking for a fresh way of facing up to the contingent—the accidental and circumstantial—specialness of present conditions and trying to clarify novelties so that what we say has meaning for and impact upon our contemporaries, who will understand these "transfers" of meaning, whereas they would have been gibberish to their ancestors. To state that differently, concern with metaphoric allusion, rather than literalness, reflects the desire to use imagery more meaningful than what has been inherited. If it no longer means anything to say that we are joined together because we are, explicitly or implicitly, signatories of a social contract; or that necessity teaches us to work together; or that God orders us to do so, then we have to speculate about what images or metaphors address "coming together." Telling people that they are parties to a social contract, something that has less to do with their experience than landings on the moon, is to waste time on images that no longer are persuasive and may dim our vision with respect to joining together. The people on the Mayflower signed a compact because they recognized that they were entering into a new world, the exact nature of which was still a mystery to them. They had to tie themselves together in order to face the dangers and possibilities this new experience would bring. It is foolhardy, however, to persist in using that tale to instruct anyone or to give a "feel" for what politics is about. The more we rely on past and dead images to explain the present, the less likely are we to take them seriously except as items that show up on examinations or quiz shows. We certainly cannot rely on the Mayflower Compact, the establishment of trading companies to settle the New World, or the Puritans' conviction that they constituted a New Zion to persuade late-twentieth-century folks of the need to join together. The conditions that once made that imagery fresh and pertinent are gone. Indeed, the likely consequence of continued insistence on the relevance of lessons drawn from those experiences and the imagery they left in their wake is to make that imagery appear quaint and antiquated. The image of "new" or "open" physical space or founding a new religious colony, a city on the hill, is remote from either our situation or our perspective. For us it is a boast, not a religious goal toward which we strive. Indeed, insistence that this past imagery is now pertinent is likely to produce an opposite reaction. The obvious answer to lectures that declare us bound to one another because "that's the way it has always been" is that "things are different now." An alternative, calculated to infuriate parents lecturing children or teachers preaching to students, is to reply that each of us is a particle disconnected from all others, that we have to be perpetually at the ready to defend ourselves against incursions into "our" space. For we do not have vast territories to conquer, only our small turf to protect against indifferent neighbors and an occasionally hostile world. That message, indeed, is the one now regularly being delivered to us by those we have failed to persuade of the necessity of coming together.

That suggests another implication in what Rorty says. We are often confronted today with talk about generational gaps and misunderstandings. Older folks hear what younger people call music and throw up their hands in despair. "That isn't what I listened to when I was your age." Exactly. What one generation doesn't understand or appreciate or approve of may be, indeed is, regarded as meaningful by others. In a diverse society like America, we can see without much effort that there are different sorts of films that appeal to distinct groups as well as music that has "meaning" for one group and sounds like noise to another. Each of these "genres" speaks in a different language to one or another collection of human beings, and the way in which each speaks is not always through the use of different words, although that happens regularly, particularly in a society with languages differentiated by racial groups, regions, classes, generations, and more, but through different signals and meanings that are delivered metaphorically. To persist in believing that the only communication that makes sense is the school language we were taught twenty, thirty, or forty years ago is to overlook the potential for, if I may ape the tendency to sloganeer, a "metaphor gap." Rorty, though he is hardly responsible for and might not approve of a single word I have written, is not only telling us something about contemporary life but issuing a warning, namely, that meanings are not necessarily carried by the sciences, humanities, and literary traditions we teach in our schools. The "miracle" of communication has put people in touch with the world in endlessly evolving ways, and we have to face up to the possibility not only that we can expect the unexpected but that we necessarily always deal with contingency and accident.

We search, then, for fresh images. But disclaimers are necessary. The likeliest creators of new metaphors are poets, writers of fictions, and storytellers, those whose art and craft illuminate our lives and stimulate our imaginations. My search for new imagery is reflexive rather than original. I don't wish to create images to alter the way people look at the world but am trying to understand the way they currently look at the world. What I hope to see is what Americans now regard as significant, meaningful, telling, inspiring, lesson-giving; and in particular, what they see insofar as their perceptions have something to do with our uses and abuses of power, violence, and politics. In doing so, I recognize that outside the daily rounds of job and home, what they see and hear, in large part, are messages carried by the media. Despite the hype of market researchers, the degree to which they pay attention can only be guessed at. But we do know that some read newspapers and see films in cinemas or at home. We know as well that among television viewers, a reasonable percentage watch sports programs. Many listen to music in a bewildering variety of formats, all available through television and film as well as audio and video devices installed at home and in cars or carried around, which reproduce the fidelity if not (yet) the full effects of the live performance, though these, too, are now electronically reproducible. Human imagery, given this near riot of possible sense impressions, has been enlarged in ways undreamed of in the past.

The second disclaimer has to do with the use of the word "metaphor" in the contemporary world of scholars. It would seem that in their eagerness to suggest that general language is not as clear as scientific terminology, some have implied that we cannot rely upon any kind of factual clarity in our search for meanings. The metaphor, with its transferral of meanings from one arena to another, thereby provides a way to uncover symbolic, general, meaningful truths. Dependence on the world's "facticity" is thereby put aside. Given my stress on ambiguity and on the flatness or irrelevance of our symbols and metaphors, the same accusation might well be hurled at me. However, my concerns are not those of literary scholars or philosophers. I am trying to treat metaphors as modes of expression that attempt to give fresh meaning where older talk has failed or broken down, or where the acts that are by-products of that talk increasingly seem to be futile and frustrating. I am, accordingly, not engaged in scholarly debate about metaphors and facts, but simply struggling with a way to get at our imagery and to restore our ability to act together, which I take to be the reason for and basis of political decision making.

NOTES

1. Richard Rorty, *Contingency, Irony, and Solidarity* (New York: Cambridge University Press, 1989); see pp. 83–86.

2. Ibid., pp. xv–xvi; see also p. 93.

3. Plato, *Republic*, Francis MacDonald Cornford, translator (New York: Oxford University Press, 1977), Part 2, Book 2, Chapter 6, 367E–372A.

4. For an "appreciation" of the savings and loan scandal, see L. J. Davis, "Chronicle of a Debacle Foretold: How Deregulation Begat the S&L Scandal," *Harper's*, vol. 281, no. 1684, September 1990, pp. 50–66; Michael M. Thomas, "The Greatest American Shambles," *New York Review*, vol. 38, no. 3, 31 January 1991, pp. 30–35; Robert Sherrill, "The Looting Decade: S&Ls, Big Banks and Other Triumphs of Capitalism," *The Nation*, vol. 251, no. 17, 12 November 1990, pp. 589–623. These in turn quote or rely upon recent books as well as articles in the *New York Times* and *Wall Street Journal*.

5. Rorty, *Contingency, Irony, and Solidarity*, p. 17.

6. Ibid., p. 19.

7. Ibid., p. 21.

11

Searching for Political Life's Appropriate Imagery

TRADITIONAL POLITICAL METAPHORS

"All philosophical terms are metaphors," Hannah Arendt wrote in the posthumously published *Life of the Mind*, "frozen analogies, as it were, whose true meaning discloses itself when we dissolve the term into the original context, which must have been vividly in the mind of the first philosopher to use it."[1] Plato's Theory of Ideas, for example, can be expressed metaphorically by uncovering its underlying "frozen analogy," which I would express as follows: the gods themselves or God alone crafted the universe. To do so, He (or they) first drew up a plan much as the architect and builder make blueprints before a building is constructed. But God's plan is unknown to humans, other than to those—called by Plato "philosopher-rulers"—who come to comprehend or grasp it, for it is invisible, to quote Arendt again, "localized in the sky of ideas." That is, the Ideas are not literally visible in the sky—like clouds or stars—but are invisible to those who have neither the talent nor training to see them. Talented individuals must be trained to "see" what is invisible. In other words, most of us see only what our senses inform us is there. But it is possible, according to Plato, that the fixed and eternal invisible Ideas that govern the universe may be seen by a properly educated elite, who as a result will be able to create a just society. The "frozen analogy" in this instance is akin to the blueprint that envisions a house before it is built and that can later be consulted to study its original, permanent, underlying pattern. The problem, of course, is to know how to read blueprints. In Plato's philosophy, accordingly, the analogy means that the measure of "justice" in human affairs is the degree that the polity's arrangements correspond to the Ideas, above all the Idea of the Good. That correspondence can occur only if philosophy and philosophers rule.

The underlying analogue in Jean-Jacques Rousseau stresses the contrast between freedom and fetters. In his most mature political work, *The Social Contract*, the metaphor is stated literally: "Man is born free; and everywhere he is in chains."[2] Human beings are naturally unfettered; when men engage themselves with others—in the family, in title to property, in society—they change dramatically. They had been innocent, direct, happy creatures, but once bonded to one another, men find it important, the young Rousseau writes, to "appear what they really [are] not. To be and to seem to be became two totally different things."[3] Civil life gives us men "in chains," but the pre-civil world was a luxuriant Garden of Eden, where men loved without family responsibilities and lived without obligation to or responsibility for one another. Unless the chains can be justified, civil life is no match for the pastoral past.

In *Leviathan* and *De Corpore* Thomas Hobbes "froze" two analogies. He portrays the human body as a machine ("for what is the heart but a spring?"), treats God as a super clockmaker who sets the universe in motion and grants men the capacity to imitate His creativity by artificing a commonwealth. The imagery is drawn from Euclidean geometry's implied "motions"—"lines" without "width" are extended from "points" without dimensions toward other similarly defined points—and from a combination of Galileo's constructions of the universe's laws of motion and inertia and William Harvey's analysis of the circulation of the blood. This mixture, transferred to the thoughts, actions, and life patterns of humans, produces, Hobbes believes, a science of politics that combines the "motions" of geometry with the principles that control the beating of the heart and the heating and cooling of the emotions (emotions are high-speed "internal" motions). Hobbes' metaphor mixes mechanics and physiology, pulling them together in what he apparently thought of as a new language that drew upon seventeenth-century science as well as Euclidean geometry.

Arendt's work lends itself to similar treatment. Her analogues are biological and topological: being unique, each human brings novelty and newness into the world. Being part of a plurality, a collection of similar but non-identical beings who share a space, each is born into a humanly constructed world that sets up boundaries that, at least to a degree, encourage conformity. Characteristically, this world reflects the tension between self-concern (uniqueness) and shared concerns (plurality). Neither usually prevails—the shape of things is not totally determined by individual inclinations or inherited institutions. Humans initiate activities and alter the world, but some older patterns persist. However, unlike other animals, they "politick," thereby changing the quality of life and the topological layout into which they were born. "Natality," the birth of unique new humans, and "plurality," the presence of similar others, mean that each new "somebody" has significant potential for novelty but is bounded by a previously constructed, though malleable, political life. When subjected to excesses, human affairs swing, pendulum-like, between one extreme, continuous novelty and change, and its opposite, complete petrification.

The context into which Arendt's metaphor "dissolves" is the world that bred totalitarianism and bureaucracy, each of which displaces political life. Totalitarianism abandons historically accepted limitations on public action—for example, the distinction between the private and public worlds—and thereby creates chaos with respect to what is mine alone and what is of concern to "the powers that be." Bureaucracy reduces human decisions to repetitious rigidities and attempts to encase society in rules that eliminate contingency, personal decision making, and responsibility.

Under totalitarianism, and to an extent bureaucracy, the life processes, which require *labor*,[4] become entirely futile. Nature still requires that humans eat to live and labor to eat; therefore life's "normal" futilities persist—after laboring one eats and sleeps but must labor again; yesterday's meal cannot satisfy today's hunger; last night's sleep cannot ameliorate tonight's weariness. But in the totalitarian and bureaucratic worlds, futility becomes all-embracing. Under totalitarianism everyone's "place" becomes uncertain, a condition underscored by death camps, mass murders, and paranoid leadership. The composition and placement of the population, the non-public activities of citizens, and the character of the culture are subjected to the whims of the leadership. Bureaucracy has an opposite but equally devastating effect, regulations set down by routine-worshipping "managers." In either instance, the sense of meaninglessness—through perpetual motion or paralysis—grows. The satisfactions of work vanish along with political dialogue and action. The "hazardous flux to which all things human are subject"[5]—by which Arendt means the constant propensity to initiate, to act, to innovate—is altered either by the dizzying, arbitrary changes enforced by totalitarian regimes or by the endless obstacles to change that are the hallmark of mindless bureaucracy.[6]

Arendt's image of a world whose "normal" boundaries are obliterated fits the rise and brief triumph of Nazism, Stalinism, and bureaucratized society. But the technological revolution was even more overwhelming than she imagined, and the anti-political revolutions of the twentieth century have been equally overwhelming. The old empires broke up—first the worldwide imperialist model, then the Soviet-style contiguous-land monolith. New states appeared in the "underdeveloped" or "third" world. Materialism and economic success, not political or anti-political innovation, seized the human imagination. Global economics achieved priority over nationalism. Rulership was increasingly tied to economic success, and the collapse of communism reflected its singular economic ineptness. All of this was instantly visible worldwide by way of television. As a result the sense of spatial relations, time, or boundaries could not remain unaffected. New ways of seeing are inevitable.

Arendt looked back to older categories and the possibility of a new imagery for political life—particularly given the havoc wreaked by totalitarianism—did not engage her. New mixtures of social, economic, and political categories did not suggest a new topology to her, and that is well illustrated by a glance at one of her favorite distinctions, that between the private and the public. Films and television literally bring into every household representations of styles of life, intimacies, and issues previously available to the literate alone, if to anyone. Much of the information Arendt thought of as basic, fundamental, or foundational has been nudged aside by communications systems and ways of thinking unthinkable a generation or two ago. Furthermore, she did not live to witness the Persian Gulf War and therefore never saw instantaneous news management and presentation—the horrors of wartime killing made "palatable" somewhat in the style of a televised football game. These images, coupled with the worldwide conviction that material well-being was possible for everyone, created a situation in which old verities and values no longer seemed to mean much. While her outlook did not parallel that of academic elitists who look upon all "modernity" as hostile to the truths they find in Plato and Aristotle, her work does analyze twentieth-century political tragedies in the light of imagery drawn from the past. But when patterns change and new information develops at previously unthinkable rates of speed, and when tradition itself has been challenged and undermined, it seems futile to call upon a past that has been rejected to rescue us from the present; and it is possibly irrelevant to insist that once meaningful values be restored so the world might be civil once again—as if it had ever achieved that blissful condition in an entirely satisfactory way. This does not diminish the fecundity of her spatial and topological images, particularly as they anticipated present-day global and environmental concerns. She was among the first to understand that there were "new things under the sun," and her attempt to describe them anticipates the contemporary need, so well expressed by Richard Rorty, for fresh metaphors. Her instinctual reliance on the linkage between civility and topology—placement of people and things in a world they construct—seems to me to be eminently sensible.

GLOBALISM, A PREMATURELY USED CONTEMPORARY METAPHOR

The sense of "place"—where I am now, where I locate myself with reference to things and other persons—precedes notions of larger spaces, of the earth itself, of outer space or the heavens. The infant, ejected from a warm, cozy, confined casing becomes aware—we can only guess at what "awareness" consists of in such a context, but the behavior suggests extreme discomfort or alarm—that he or she has been pushed out into an emptier something, that the shield and envelope are gone.

This jolt and accompanying sense of placelessness or displacement has to produce a reaction, an effort to locate oneself. To go from warmth to chilly air, fixed boundaries to free space and movement, interior darkness to outer light, muffled sounds to a noisy environment—others' voices, one's own—and automatic feeding to bouts of hunger and awareness of an exterior source of food, this is obviously a profound experience. The question "where am I?" must surface into consciousness—although I do not intend to suggest that the "question" takes the form of later linguistic habits.

The point is that locations are "measured" by immediate surroundings. Time and adjustments are needed, including better eyesight and improved "sorting" faculties, before more distant spaces become real and enter the consciousness. Is there, then, some natural sequence, some place before space—my immediate place, the world as a larger space—discovered perhaps in that order? Possibly. But we have to remember that in earlier times a human's vision might reach to the heavens without benefit of telescopes, while awareness of the earth was necessarily limited by "travel"—on foot or horseback, by small boat or large sailing vessel, and so on. Vista was limited by horizon, and awareness of sky as "space" was variable. At one point some thought the earth and other heavenly bodies were surrounded by a moving canopy with a "hole" behind which lay a fire (the sun). If the earth was flat—and that too was not always and in all places a conviction—then it was self-evident that there were at least four planes on which people might live; inhabitants of one could hardly reach the others without "falling off the edge." Each place on earth had a built-in isolation; each other place was and apparently always would remain a mystery.

In sum, at an early moment in life awareness of place comes, with a consequent sense of "my" place, namely, where I am, where I live, my home, and so on. Consciousness of the general space occupied by others grows as dependency on parents fades. Family, neighborhood, friends, city, area, region, "the whole wide world," all become manifest as circumstance, situation, education, and sophistication permit.

What, then, of the modern phenomenon *global awareness* or *globalism*? Obviously, awareness of the entire globe's existence is not automatic, but mundane concerns contribute. Trade stimulates interest in what lies beyond the horizon. The possibility of sailing to "the other half" or around the world was probably entangled with economic motives and convictions, particularly among western Europeans, who for a long time knew that "falling off the edge" was unlikely. Understanding of the rest of the world rose and fell in accord with adventurousness, equipment, and desire, including the dream of discovering treasures and jewels, but the discovery of the New World speeded things up. Extended travel over the surface of the globe made possible a conception of it as a unit or single entity. Global talk began to make sense. First came a distinct notion of the earth as a large spherical entity with variable land masses that subdivide both naturally and artificially into "places" and "place names": rivers, mountains, borders, customs, languages. Different languages inevitably produced different images; for example, to Arabs the "Arab nation" refers to all Arabs, and what Westerners call nations (Iraq, Egypt, and so on) are regarded as "regions." In time, attention divided between the issue of global domination—contributing, for example, to the sixteenth-century clash between England and Spain—and the narrower questions associated with internal or domestic political entities, known increasingly, after Machiavelli's use of the word, as "states." The growing consciousness that humanity was scattered around the globe did not eliminate attachment to "nation," "state," or "polity." But authentic global relationships had to have been well underway before anyone could dream up the geopolitical slogan, "Who rules the World Island [the land masses of Europe, Asia, and Africa] commands the World" (Halford Mackinder, 1861–1947).

Globalism has since advanced rapidly with technological compression of distance. Penetrations into outer space increased awareness of the relative smallness of the earth and the brevity of human history. Technology magnifies as well as diminishes the significance of distance. We are becoming increasingly literate with respect to global ecology. That is, our imagery is increasingly governed by perception of the planet as a single, though complex, ecosystem. Intervention at any spot on the globe has distant as well as local effects. We can reach inside our own turf, do damage, and affect the entire globe. Or we can fly out into the heavens, only to leave debris in space that affects the entire planet. The term "local pollution problem" is an oxymoron. Every problem, *ipso facto*, has worldwide import.

Strange things happen if one uses this skeletal portrait of place-space awareness—of my concern with my immediate surroundings and my larger concerns with dispersed places like New Hampshire, the United States, the Western Hemisphere, the globe—and gives it a specific American context. The first non-Native Americans abandoned familiar, established places and homes and set out across a gigantic ocean seeking better circumstances. They did so for three sometimes simultaneously held reasons: religious freedom, political separation, and economic opportunity. These first Americans radically transformed their personal and group situations. They dreamed of new places, new colonies, a New Zion in a New World—the word "new" is a constant in the American lexicography. From the beginning, Americans have searched for new, better homes; they not only were to build "a city on the hill," for they also needed a place to worship the Lord and warm hearths for themselves and their families. This creates an ambiguity—the sense of being homeless and in need of a new home coupled with the excitement and thrill of having the opportunity to seek one out—which is also very much a part of the American context. We are aware of the dangers of not having a base from which to operate, but it's also thrilling to be on the road. As one writer has pointed out, the theme appears and reappears in American culture whether "high," "middle," or "lowbrow."[7] It is as important to the *Wizard of Oz* and *Gone with the Wind* as to the *Grapes of Wrath* and *Invisible Man* (the first three, important films and books; the last, the great American novel of invisibility) as well as Mark Twain's classic, *The Adventures of Huckleberry Finn*. The homeless and parentless Huck, Jim—the escaping slave whom Huck "steals" from his "rightful owners"—and Jim's "sold" and displaced family make up an American mosaic. The same imagery is borrowed repeatedly by Hollywood in road pictures, particularly the intense films of the past two decades. The question "where do I belong?" again and again shapes and divides the American imagination and polity: What place do the poor have in a society where economic success is the measure? Where do "fatherless," "motherless," or "parentless" children belong? Where do I belong when my loyalty to this immediate locale clashes with a wider loyalty to the United States or its perceived well-being as enunciated by those in charge? Are African Americans the perpetually homeless Americans? Is American life a tale of westward wanderlust and ultimately of a perpetual, restless search for "upward" mobility?

Political life, in other words, is a reference not merely to place but also to belonging. Initially, blacks were carted off from Africa, bringing short-term profits to a few in the North and the South, long-term disaster to the slaves and their descendents, a social, political, and economic system to the South that made it economically backward compared to the rest of the young country, and an as-yet-unresolved racial problem to the society. Where do African Americans belong? Well, obviously here, but . . . In contrast, immigrants and migrants, like the first settlers, displaced themselves. Movement to America became a way of life and a major factor in nineteenth-century Western history, while in the United States relocation itself evolved into a synonym for seeking one's fortune. And it has meant the right to pack up and move—as slaves and most Europeans could not. Although no right to resettle is mentioned in the Constitution, it became part of our political and social practice. Of course, there is a down side. The conviction that the grass is always greener elsewhere became a national fetish and increased the tendency to resolve problems by moving on. Restlessness became indigenous to our way of life.

The federal system, with its insistence that each state is sovereign and different, exaggerates these tendencies. For Americans it became axiomatic that if you have a problem, you should move on. These days if you don't like the tax system in Massachusetts, you move across the border to the tax haven known as New Hampshire, returning only for whatever advantages still come with a highly urbanized life style. But a move to another state exchanges one sovereign for another, while the distant, ubiquitous federal government remains a fixture, to some Americans apparently a distasteful one except when their state or business needs federal dollars. This arrangement has generated overlapping jurisdictions, variable remedies for national problems, and a tedious competition for tax revenues. To the question "where do I belong?" the American answer has been and remains "in at least two jurisdictions, a state and the nation, even though you can only hang your hat in one place at a time." For some Americans, unwelcome in either jurisdiction and with no hooks on which to hang hats—or no hats—the answer is "neither here nor there."

Political life supposedly provides a place within which I and others coexist peacefully. The American arena, however, is heavily beset with violence, often growing out of a sense of placelessness, which means that an individual doesn't fit or belong, doesn't have a territory that he or she shares with others. It is not simply a matter of owning a home or a ranch or being able to rent a spot to call "one's own," about which Americans speak so much, but a matter of being with others in a situation in which a mutual or shared sense of belonging exists, a sense we often describe by words like neighborhood or community. Even "ghetto" would do, provided it didn't come to mean being walled in with dangers. That lack of mutually shared spaces—or appreciation of mutuality—makes us apolitical; our lives are surprisingly untouched by what political power is supposed to bring into existence. Furthermore, answers to "location" questions are obfuscated by the nation's idealism with respect to civil rights, that is, by an insistence on universal equality that further complicates the problem of "belonging." Every identifiable ethnic, racial, or religious group, after settling here or moving to a particular region of the country, has been put on trial. The ancestry and race of Japanese Americans, the skin color and race of African Americans, the religion and ethnicity of Irish or Italian Americans, and the religious persistence and cultural identity of Jews have variously produced efforts to hamper the group in question and thereby raised doubts in response to whether they can, do, or ought to fit into a single polity. Immigrants, because of the need for lingual and cultural security, have clustered together in miniature polities within an already-complicated federal system, captured control of their immediate environs, and driven others off, an oft-repeated group-driven scenario. Our cities have been nets of tightly knit enclaves until the recent diaspora to suburbia, and what remains is an increasingly divided entity, with the comfortable and poor unhappily living side by side. There have also been, and occasionally still are, ethnic, racial, and religious struggles for control of the community or streets, often involving not only "power" but also violence. In some places those struggles continue, as in confrontations in New York City and during the 1992 Los Angeles riots involving, among others, African and Asian Americans. Finding a way to exist within the polity at large rather than in single-group strongholds has been surprisingly difficult. The breakup of many older city neighborhoods, the growth of suburbs, and the dispersal of families and their conversion into contact units that depend on telephones and airplanes have brought in their wake unneighborly neighborhoods, places, apparently, where no one belongs, trailer parks where people plug in temporarily then pull out. The retirees now wandering the highways in so-called recreational vehicles, miniature homes on wheels, are an unintended commentary on what has become an American way of life. These older folks knew what it was to live in relatively tightly knit communities; now they imitate the life style of the young, who shuffle from one locale to another. Disconnecting is an important American activity, but like every generalization about a country this huge, it is not inevitable and exceptions can be found.

Territorial and racial conflicts resurface regularly. The 1991 elections in Louisiana made visible the widespread belief among white voters that African Americans, in conspiracy with white liberals, were intent on "taking away" or "taking over" their world—that is, jobs, neighborhoods, communities, towns, cities, Louisiana, the United States itself, and even the value system. This means that one of political life's important qualities—maintenance of the sense of connectedness—is continuously hampered by underlying group hostilities. This groupism is anti-political because it is unable to measure any issue from a point of view larger than the group's. For African Americans, government, which at the national level in the last half-century has been their strongest ally, is a justifiable object of suspicion because it is still "white." Whites preoccupied with the contrasting black and white faces of the society see every government as a potential ally of African Americans, the more so given twentieth-century interpretations of the Fourteenth Amendment. As a result, to many Americans the general purposes and broad connections that empower a government in the first place are as mysterious as speculations about heaven and hell and potentially as lethal as the latter. In many instances, Americans have developed traditions of self-identity in which their roots and "hyphenated" nationalities (German Americans, Polish Americans, and so forth) as well as their economic positions take precedence over any generalizing "togetherness" symbolized by the nation. Of course, I'm not speaking about Fourth of July rituals or "easy" wars but about daily tensions and more than occasional violence when "groups" (individuals of one ethnic or racial background) move into an area or claim an equal status that locals are unwilling to concede. At that point the patriotism—or, more accurately, its supposed linkage with equality—is quickly put aside. Then the real convictions surface. The government is perceived as an ostensibly neutral, disinterested entity whose value is realized only when it is prevented from enforcing the presumably central American notions of equality and civil rights. Securing those rights is often treated as a zero-sum game in which the grant of equality to one group is considered a loss for others whose rights are presumably not at issue, although without doubt advocacy of broadened human rights is more acceptable now than in earlier times.

The phenomenal success of groups and elites in achieving selfish goals—think of moments in American history when, variously, governments have taken up the causes of farmers, workers, industrialists, large corporations, small businesses, minorities, or bankers—has discouraged serious attention to the public interest. A pattern has developed, reminiscent of marketing and advertising, whereby every selfish concern is hypocritically advocated as "good for everyone."

I suspect, therefore, that although Americans now talk about a global environment and a new era of worldwide partnership and pacificity, and many sincerely believe what they say, they understand neither its meaning nor its implications. They feign world citizenship and global environmental concern but refuse to act as citizens in their neighborhoods, towns, cities, states, and nation. They express contempt for politics or government but want global harmony, seeing no apparent connection between internal concordance and global responsibility. They have no apparent notion of what their responsibilities would be when expanded to include, in addition to local, county, state, and national political life, a "government" or at least "political power" for the entire globe. They equate their particular group's selfish desires and well-being with the general good, but they ask that everyone consider the globe as primary.

Without a sense of local place within the worldwide global village, globalism is little more than sloganeering. Without linkage to a place or portion of the globe, of connectedness to those who are fellow inhabitants of that sector, what is the source of understanding with respect to fellow citizens of the world? If there is little awareness that healthy parts of the globe are necessary to the survival of a planet that accepts the idea of "humanity's" general interest, how can anyone speak with certainty of global connectedness? If Americans cannot accept the costs, pains, problems, and failures of citizenship and membership in the relatively small world of a single municipality or neighborhood but want only "triumphs," if they fail to care for this portion of the globe, how can they possibly develop world consciousness? How can a nation that selfishly gobbles up the world's resources—the United States, with 5 percent of the population, uses 25 percent of the world's oil production—be counted upon to act with due regard for others' needs? How can those who can't manage to keep their neighborhoods clean and safe speak so casually about cleaning up the world or pulling together the peoples of the entire globe? The truth is that we have not yet figured out how to compact or deal with our own garbage.

I fear that the sense of place has not been enlarged by present-day talk of global responsibilities and connections. Until globalism is coupled with awareness of the significance of localities and regions, we will remain as far away from achieving harmony globally as we are from managing it on many city streets. We must understand that it is possible to "operate" only in the immediate presence of others—not only where but also with whom we belong, the context and framework, the shapes and patterns, within which our individual lives unfold. The extent to which life can be artificed and altered depends on the existence of an authorized place within which patterns can be duly and dutifully made, that is, a polity— call it what you will—that provides an arena and institutional envelope. Although globalism sounds new and hip and is a welcome invitation to think in terms of humanity's general interest—putting aside those who use it as cover for one nation's or civilization's dreams of world domination—it can be meaningful only when we understand the elemental problem of living in a confined place within the larger space we call the planet Earth.

NOTES

1. Hannah Arendt, *The Life of the Mind*, vol. 1, *Thinking* (New York: Harcourt, Brace, Jovanovich, 1977), p. 104. The phrase "localized in the sky of ideas" is from the same page of Arendt's text.

2. Jean-Jacques Rousseau, *The Social Contract or Principles of Political Right* (1762), in *The Social Contact and Discourses*, translated by G. D. H. Cole (New York: E. P. Dutton, 1950), p. 3.

3. Jean-Jacques Rousseau, *A Discourse on the Origin and Foundation of Inequality among Men* (1755), Cole translation (New York: E. P. Dutton, 1950), p. 247.

4. The distinctions among labor, work, and action are discussed at length in Arendt's *Human Condition* (Chicago: University of Chicago Press, 1958) and are the three aspects of the *vita activa*, the life of activity, as distinguished from the *vita contemplativa*, the life of contemplation, she discusses in the book. *Labor*— unlike work, which produces a world of objects and therefore a sense of closure, completion, permanence, and accomplishment—demands the continuous expenditure of energy that requires rapid replenishment and replacement. Work and action, however, traditionally rescue human beings from futility. *Work* refers to our making of the world around us, the humanly fabricated things that surround us and give shape to our existences. *Action*, which involves initiation and

beginnings, makes possible the space or realm that attempts to deal with "everybody's business" (*res publica*) and brings into being what she calls the "space of appearance," the arrangement or arena within which we deal with one another and through which we recall the past and will in the future recall the present. The world of things (the result of work) and the space of appearance, including the realm of politics (both the result of action), are, she believes, the means whereby the sense of futility associated with mere laboring may be overcome and humans may achieve a sense of meaningfulness. But human constructs—the world of things and the "space of appearance" within which humans relate to one another—also generate boundaries in moral codes, in principles of aesthetics regulating craftsmanship and art and, generally speaking, in rules governing living together. For humans to exist meaningfully, she is saying, they are required to respect and adapt themselves to those boundaries, even while they change the details and quality of their lives and thereby alter the boundaries, reshape the rules.

5. "Death not merely ends life, it also bestows upon it a silent completeness, snatched from the hazardous flux to which all things human are subject" (Arendt, *The Life of the Mind*, vol. 1, *Thinking*, p. 164).

6. Appendix B contains a detailed discussion of Arendt's metaphor.

7. Mimi Kramer, in a theater-movie review in *The New Yorker* of 2 April 1990.

12

Metaphors for a New Age

PROFESSIONAL SPORTS AS METAPHORS FOR VIOLENCE AND POWER

Treated as metaphors, professional baseball and football provide insights into our political life—but there are pitfalls.[1] A baseball field may well be, as George Will claims, a "circumscribed area of controlled striving." However, it is not—to continue his sentence—even "in a limited sense . . . a model of a good society, where rules are respected and excellence rewarded."[2] Will is suggesting that life ought to imitate baseball. That's doubtful. American ball parks are part of, not alternatives to, the society: the franchises are privately owned, but public support and involvement are extensive and necessary; television coverage brings the games to millions; enormous sums of money change hands for media sponsorship; towns, cities, and even states subsidize and protect teams' locations by building or financing stadia and providing access roads; and the locals regard the teams as theirs—the Cubs and Bears are Chicago's; the Eagles and Phillies are Philadelphia's; the football Giants and Jets, suburban New York's, that is, northern New Jersey's, and Manhattan's. Professional sports is the creation of, not a model for, American society. No stadium quite measures up to good old Fenway Park, but there is no reason to believe that its green grass, manicured infield, and uniformed players symbolize the good life or society at large.

Nothing makes this clearer than a glance at the record of both professional baseball and football with respect to commercialism and racism. The greed with which owners, agents, and players now approach the playing fields speaks for itself. As for racism, professional baseball first acknowledged the existence of African Americans during the past half century as football did a bit earlier, at a time when the game was a commercial pygmy compared to baseball. In both, racial barriers have been more stubborn at the managerial, coaching, and administrative levels. Again, these games and the complex structures and relationships they have developed over the years reflect or are perhaps an analogue of some aspects of society, but they give us only a peek at a part of American life.

The attempt to make them symbolic of something beyond their scope hooks the unwary reader or television watcher by converting a truism—society is better off when every person does his or her best—into an ideological formula. But the formula in this case is irrelevant: this is no longer a society or economy that particularly values craft or, for that matter, "Men at Work."

Actually, sports have been important for the opposite reason; they provide, not lessons for, but a respite from daily life. Professional baseball, football, basketball, and so forth, are a relief from the daily "busyness" of a stressful society. A crowd of rabid fans at a football game played at home by the Chicago Bears, Cleveland Browns, or New York Giants let go; they relate the team's victory to themselves, to their realization that at the game ordinary people can be part of the action and that elsewhere they often simply go through the motions. They get high on the games, not their jobs. The ball park gives them the chance to shout and groan, to feel part of something, to say, "we're number one" or "wait 'til next year," to make their individual presences felt within a constituency that, in turn, is part of a "league."

Will, on the other hand, though he says we can learn from the game, tries to use it for his brand of politicking. "Because baseball is a game of failure, and hence a constantly humbling experience," he writes, "it is good that the national government is well stocked with students of the national pastime."[3] Perhaps he is right; he is expert in both arenas and may in one short sentence have provided an explanation, however trivial, of the ineptitude of our government. I object less to the sentiment than to the literalness, the way he treats "government" and "baseball" as if they are interchangeable because both are games of rules and direct carriers of identical messages about everyday American life, when what he wants to do is both express his love of the game and his belief that it is a ready-made vehicle for his ideological message.

My concerns are metaphorical, *not* literal. I speculate about the extent to which baseball and football give us imagery that "speaks" to Americans as well as talk we can use to revitalize understanding of political life. And under no circumstance do I see either game as a "model" for political life.

Football is treated here—with apologies—as a metaphor for violence and therefore as opposite to power. Baseball is portrayed as a metaphor for politics itself; specifically, for the productive or positive uses of power.

That this exaggerates I readily admit. Football in fact involves teamwork. Baseball admits of force and violence in the hurling of a lethal, hard ball close to the heads of opposing players—a classic example of the "one against all" that Hannah Arendt equates with violence. But I set football's exemplifications of "power" and baseball's "violence" aside precisely because I'm looking for fresh metaphoric insight into political life and not trying to describe these games as an expert might.

Football

"Baseball is what life should be. . . . Football is what life is," Naomi Fein writes.[4] The statement is literal but suggests metaphor. Football makes giants of mere humans. Padded, protected by plastic helmets, faces behind masks that hide individual features, players appear robot-like and larger than life. In fact, they are bigger and tougher than the rest of us.[5]

Like other sports, football is played on bounded fields, once grass, now often artificial turf, whose hard surfaces inflict physical damage on the players. The object of the game is to push a peculiarly shaped ball, an "oblong spheroid," down the field and over a goal line, to "break the plane" of that line physically. The other team "submits" to superior strength or guile and gives up territory until the ball crosses the line, is thrown over the heads of defenders, or is kicked over and through goal posts. The primary means of scoring is with the ball. The strategies and tactics for moving it seem limitless, particularly for teams with a good coach and quarterback, the team's field general. In fact, the quarterback and those who specialize in kicking the football are partial exceptions to the general metaphor I want to suggest here. They also use the instruments of violence but, along with the coaches, rely on head and heart rather than sheer strength and, being more vulnerable than others, are fiercely protected by teammates from attacks (the words "blitz" and "sack," both of which refer to attempts to get at the quarterback, are in tune with the war imagery); the rules are stringent in protecting kickers, who are also vulnerable when they are kicking. Nothing, however, prevents a quarterback from being shoved about violently if an opposing player can get to him, though there is always the danger of a penalty for "unnecessary roughness" (now often euphemistically retitled "personal foul"). What the opposite phrase "necessary roughness" actually means is unclear. In another time, the heart of the matter was to push and shove the other team down the field, yard by yard, clutching the ball desperately every inch of the way. But the forward pass speeded up progress toward the goal line and created ingenious new ways of penetrating enemy territory. Football, like the warfare from which much of its vocabulary is drawn, is always in search of better weaponry and more imaginative forms of deception.

The division of the playing field into two territories guarded by opposing teams promotes the imagery and language of battlefields and violence. In the forward positions, the game involves pushing the other line back, "opening holes" in their solid walls and formations, in order to permit the ball and its carrier to penetrate deeper into the other side's territory. The clash of opposing lines is often referred to as a "battle in the trenches." Blocking for a runner is analogous to development of a spearhead in a land battle where tanks followed by infantry break through enemy lines. Ball carriers are tackled, taken off their feet, to stop them. To slow them down for the rest of the game, tackling cannot be gentlemanly or effete. Neither are the runners. They stick their arms out and shove would-be tacklers away if they can, although it is better to elude them, make them miss their tackles. A common phrase is "to break a tackle," that is, to break through the arms of a would-be tackler. Defenders are equally violent. Since the installation of passing, quarterbacks and specialists in penetrating the defenses and catching the ball have become more prominent and defensive players have become more aggressive. Their object is to "sack" the quarterback, shove him to the ground before he lets go of the ball—the surest defense against the pass is to prevent the quarterback from throwing. Receivers are hit hard, so that they shy away in fear of either what *might* happen when they are in a particularly vulnerable position or what *will* happen, whatever their stance, after they catch the ball. If they catch the ball and do not escape at once, they are hit hard. The development of plastic equipment, helmets in particular, and artificial turf, gives the game bone-breaking, ligamenttearing, rib-cracking sounds that can be heard by spectators and the television audience. The aim is to get the ball over the goal line, but the equipment, no less than a gun, stick, or bomb, amplifies individual strength. Rules forbid direct physical assaults, but there is violence enough to go around. Helmets are used to spear opponents in the ribs; players are thrown to the ground; tackles are made while individuals are in the air and therefore most vulnerable to injury. Referees attempt to control excesses, but they never succeed entirely because of the game's necessary body contact and the increased use of dangerous "protective" gear. Fans complain when a key player is injured and forced to miss games, but they expect to see hard hitting, just as they expect body checks at hockey games.

Football, if one chooses to look at it this way, meets the tests for violence previously discussed. Its rules distinguish justified from unjustified violence. "That's a legitimate hit," says the fan or sportscaster, suggesting the presence of agreed-upon limitations that require judgments by referees as to the legitimacy of the act. Some acts draw "penalties," usually the loss of territory. Throwing ball carriers to the ground is justified; indeed, that is the prescribed way of stopping them; but extreme measures are forbidden. The grill-like protective mask may not be grabbed to put someone down ("face-masking"), but the rules penalize offenders differentially. Deliberate face-masking and accidental face-masking draw different penalties, as if an official can actually distinguish motives in connection with a little head and neck twisting. There are legitimate ways to knock someone down even if his leg breaks and career ends as a result. (Players, of course, know that the risks are high; the game has built-in expectations of injury.) In other words, a thin line separates justified from unjustified violence; referees decide which is which, consistent with the rule book.

If all this is true—and I have purposely stressed the violence—why should we consider football as a possible metaphor that gives us a fresh way to speculate about political life? The beginnings of an answer lie in what has already been suggested, that power and violence *per se* are theoretical opposites. They are indubitably related to one another: When one is completely absent, the other is bound to be present. Power provides an antidote to violence; violence provides a solution to the failure of power and politics to resolve pressing questions. Violence is a way for an individual or group to take matters into his or their own hands and impose outcomes. Football takes matters to another level. It is organized. It is organized violence bounded by rules, a game that authorizes the use of violence; that sets violence that generates chaos and unpredictability within a planned, orderly procedure; that expects the unpredictable within a setting in which predictability seems to be the order of the day. The size of the field is specified, the number of players preset, the offensive patterns limited by the rules (number of linemen, number of "backs"), and rules of procedure put in place. Yet in spite of its apparent predictability, the unpredictable is bound to occur, if by no other route than the peculiar bounces that a peculiarly shaped "ball" takes. That unpredictability, parallel to life's, makes the game exciting. And so football, a game of rules that simulates warfare, appeals to many Americans.

Football—setting aside the virtues of teamwork, athleticism, and the brotherhood of man that have been claimed for it by exponents and successful practitioners—exemplifies the truism that the world is not always in consonance. Agreement often eludes us. Partisanship is a fact of life. In some instances violence replaces calmly worked-out compromises. Psychologically, it may well be that the visibility of this game as a weekend phenomenon for about twenty weeks a year gives those who watch or participate an outlet for their own feelings of dissonance. I'm not certain. What ought to be clear, however, is that we have to regard the fascination with violence seriously before we can appreciate—or teach others to accept—the virtues of its opposite. And to do that it is instructive to examine people's approval of confined playing fields on which the violence, compared to warfare and the hundreds of ways men have suffered cruel deprivations, is comparatively harmless. In any case, football's or any other game's violence may help us open our minds to the prospect that political life, which we have regarded incorrectly as an inferior or unnecessary activity equivalent to control and domination, therefore violence, may have important metaphoric lessons that we ignore at our peril. But this time we should understand that merely "saying no" to something that is violent and destructive has no particular impact in a context in which there are neither palpable nor desirable alternatives to its "pleasures" and "satisfactions."

Baseball

The difference in equipment between baseball and football is striking. The catcher's paraphernalia reminds us, vaguely, of football. He wears a mask, padding, and shin guards; batters use helmets, and plate umpires wear protective gear. But no player in the field wears "armor." Baseball equipment protects the wearer—the catcher and umpire from being struck, the batter from being hit in the head by the ball—and, generally, may not be used to hurt another player. In baseball, body contact, although relatively rare, may take place as many as four or five times in a game at home plate, and something akin to it may occur in base running. Hitting people with equipment—a baseball or bat is potentially a lethal weapon—is not part of the game, although on occasion an angry player, bat in hand, may stalk someone. Persistent behavior of that kind is tantamount to a request to be barred from the game.

The equipment is also there to maintain order. The gloves are to help catch or manage the baseball, whether in flight or skipping along the ground. The bat has the opposite purpose—to see that the ball is not controlled either by the pitcher who throws the ball or the fielder who handles it. The ball is attacked or placed; it "breaks through" or goes "into the hole" (between infielders); it is caught or stopped from escaping. But it, not the players' bodies, is the object of "violence," disorder, and control.

A baseball, which is extremely hard and thrown by pitchers at speeds that sometimes reach upwards of ninety or even one hundred miles an hour, can be lethal. But although throwing the ball toward home plate at high speed and "brushing back" the hitter is permissible, excesses are not tolerated. And hitting a batter with the ball, whether or not he tries to dodge or escape, automatically places him on base and thereby endangers the defending team.

Baseball is keyed to orderliness and control: the fielding team's purpose is to pick up the ball and throw out batters, catch it on the fly, and prevent it from being hit "fairly" beyond the playing field or from being hit at all. The team at bat attempts to create disorder by forcing the fielding team to lose control of the ball, that is, permit runners to reach base and to score runs. The difficulty in doing so may be understood by considering what is regarded as a good batting average, namely, .300, which means that a player has successfully hit the ball three out of every ten times at bat. That may be what prompts George Will to say that baseball is a game of failure—a good hitter fails to get a hit approximately seven out of ten times or in a season possibly 350 times out of 500 turns at bat. In short, he "fails" far more than he succeeds. But the key to failure and success is where the ball lands and falls, and the defensive object is to prevent the ball from hitting the ground, that is, to catch it on the fly; or to pick it up from the ground and throw the runner out before he reaches base safely. Order is preserved by not letting the ball get out of hand or out of bounds. A pitcher "fails" when the batter hits the ball beyond the confines of the field out of the reach of a defensive outfielder or when he loses control of the ball and walks batters and puts them on base. The winning team succeeds best in preventing the ball from bouncing around loosely or sailing out of the park.

The more successful the defensive team is in keeping the ball controlled, the fewer hits and "runs" the opposition gets. In baseball, a very dull but perfect game would be played if for nine innings no batter gets on base—all are struck out or whatever they hit is fielded properly or caught on the fly. To some, this is boring because "nothing happens," but it confirms the game's stress on control and order; the combined defensive efforts of an entire team have managed to stifle the opposition, and if both teams manage this during the same game, something special has taken place. Baseball is a slow, quiet game compared to football, hockey, or basketball.[6] Since one team tries to make something happen and the other tries to prevent it, the game consists of much talk and chatter on the field and in the stands and only intermittent action. Some writers see it as twenty minutes of action and two and a half hours of standing or sitting around and watching the ball land in the catcher's mitt. But that is an exaggeration; every pitch is in itself a complex defensive action, as is every signal preceding it and every rearrangement of fielders in anticipation of possible results. Not inaction, but extremely cerebral action to prevent something untoward from happening or, conversely, to figure out the pitch in advance and hit it safely, is what is going on; most of this is unseen by many fans, though there are millions who understand the nuances. But, of course, baseball, like every other game, demands closure, and the rules require action to continue past the ninth inning until a winner can be determined; that is, runs must be scored.

No one catches the sense of baseball, I believe, as well as Roger Angell:

The ball rarely escapes the control of the players. It is released . . . but almost always, almost instantly recaptured and returned to control and safety and harmlessness. Nothing is altered, nothing has been allowed to happen. This orderliness and constraint are part of the attractions of the sport; a handful of men can police a great green country, forestalling unimaginable disasters. . . . Too much civilization, however, is deadly—in this game, a deadly bore. A deeper need is stifled. The ball . . . lives in a slow, guarded world of order, vigilance and rules. Nothing can ever happen here. . . . [But] suddenly we see the ball streaking wild through the air and then bounding along distant and untouched in the sweet green grass. We leap up, thousands of us, and shout for its joyful flight—free, set free, free at last.[7]

The term "foul ball" also suggests the orientation of the game, since it refers to the field's legitimate ("fair") lanes, which radiate from home plate at a ninety-degree angle. The bases, viewed from above and behind home plate, reinforce the sense of order. They point like a diamond toward center field and are set around a square at identical distances (ninety feet) from one another. The pitcher's mound is always an identical distance from home plate (sixty feet plus). Only the length of the field at its extremities is variable, depending on the location of the fence and the shape resulting from the contouring of the stands. Some parks are easier to hit in for right-handed than left-handed batters or vice versa. The old Polo Grounds in New York, with an extremely close overhanging ledge between the right field's upper and lower decks, gave left-handed batters an opportunity to hit home runs that on other fields would have been simple fly balls easily handled by fielders. The game and the rules governing it are complicated by these man-made and variable factors, so that the shape and contours of a field will determine how a pitcher chooses to aim the ball, namely, on the inside or outside corner of a plate and how fielders will play in relation to the idiosyncrasies of the field, the wind factor, the sun angle peculiar to that setting, and so on.

Some of the finest baseball books and stories treat the game as a metaphor for American life itself, seeing even the greed and money making that have been escalating over the past fifty years as reflective of similar excesses in the society. They see baseball as a "field of dreams," a place that, to the extent that it shakes off or resists those excesses, is a relief from and exception to everyday disappointments. It is not at all surprising to read a sports writer who believes that baseball may yet save America, that the purer and finer values of life and work may survive on the baseball field and that in the long run lessons will be applied to everyday societal activities.

Perhaps that is why in recent years books and movies about baseball have been popular. Consider one of the more successful recent films, *Field of Dreams* (1988), based on W. P. Kinsella's *Shoeless Joe*.[8] The movie has been pilloried by film critics. Some complained about careless research. *Field of Dreams* doesn't bother, for example, to make certain that Shoeless

Joe Jackson, who is central to the movie's heroics, bats from the correct side of the plate. Others complained that the movie is a sentimental tear-jerker, forgetting that it is consistent with the book's perspective, which is that the society has come to love disorder and villainy, that it is being taught to look with contempt on good, pure, or noble characters and to believe that life, at least where the action is, is about the bad guys.

From my point of view, these criticisms are irrelevant. In Kinsella's book, a baseball field, be it the field of dreams built by the book's hero in his Iowa cornfield or Boston's Fenway Park, is a pure, unsullied place, unlike the streets and surroundings that provide the setting. Even Iowa's cornfields are commercial properties, impure when compared to the un-touched woods of Vermont or the baseball field the hero, Kinsella, con-structs when urged to do so by a voice that initially only he hears. Building the field brings to it the ghosts of the Chicago White Sox, the eight who had been barred from the game for life for violating the sacred rules that forbid players to gamble. In time, with more urging from the voice, others are involved: his family, who in time see what he sees in the field; a famous writer (J. D. Salinger in the book, but not the movie) who has been hiding for years from the public and whose involvement in the story promises to bring him back into active engagement with the world; an old, kindly physician who appears in the story as both an elderly ghost and as a youngster who once actually played a single inning with the New York Giants; the hero's dead father, with whom he had never made peace; and, in the book, a twin brother whom he hasn't seen for years. This field contrasts sharply with society's "fields," on which everyone struggles to survive and withstand the pains of life. Each and every baseball field shares that purity and is a contrast to Cleveland, or Chicago, or Boston, or the world of commercial activity as depicted in the book.

I park the car and walk in the sun along the sleazy street outside Fenway Park, where winos, unkempt as groundhogs, sun themselves and half-heartedly cadge quarters, supposedly for food.[9] . . . Baseball can soothe even [the] pains [of growing up], for it is stable and permanent.[10] . . . The year might be 1900 or 1929 or 1978 for all the field itself has changed. Here the sense of urgency that governs most lives is pushed to one side like junk mail shoved to the back of a desk.[11]

Insofar as baseball is a field of dreams, it may indeed well represent the American ethic of success. The best players rise to the top, make it to the majors, and perform feats indelibly recorded in the mountains of statistics gathered over the years covering every aspect of the game—not only the best and worst, but also every detail of what has happened, preserved on score cards and in encyclopedic record books that memorialize batters, pitchers, fielders, and so on. The game of rules called baseball does what every political entity does—it develops processes and institutions, remembers its past, and plans for an even better future. And every spring, summer, and fall it reawakens the skills, craft, concentration, devotion, and hard work that bring victory to the best teams or in life itself, ideally conceived. Thus the seeming accuracy of the analogy or metaphor. But this imagery may safely be left to those who over the years have written with such elegance about achievements in a bounded world largely untouched by the hard necessities of everyday living.

The view here, since we are concerned with something else that ought to be a commonplace in the United States, an understanding and appreciation of political life, is that baseball, like football, provides us with an opportunity to transfer meanings from one setting to another. But the message is not purity and individuality triumphant. Baseball involves a rule structure far more complex than most other games, and the character of that rule structure makes it the game of rules par excellence. Games of rules teach us how rules come to be, how they may be utilized to advantage, how they may be applied to prevent individuals from violating them and "spoiling" the game. In other words, everyone who plays baseball follows rules that, if disobeyed, mean removal from the game and understands that the rules make the game possible and allow it to be played out. Players learn that an individual encased in rules is not entangled as in a spider's web but has been set free to display himself, to demonstrate his skills, to become a major leaguer, to be seen and noticed, to be visible. And the spectators understand the game no less clearly.

Baseball as metaphor can reinforce our understanding that political life itself is also a game of rules that works when similarly bounded. When there is an agreed-upon set of rules whose existence sets human beings free to conduct their business and get on with their lives, and when these can be readily enforced and penalties assessed for violations, their existence frees men and women to conduct their business and get on with their lives. All games of rules carry similar lessons.

In baseball, the rules of the game are physical or "natural" as well as man-made. The flight and movement of the ball, whether it be the velocity of a pitch, the ability to make the ball curve or sink, the force with which the bat strikes the ball, the angle at which the ball is met, the upward, downward, or straight motion of the bat—all have to do with forces that work with enormous consistency time after time. But there are equally important man-made rules that are as consistent or regular as scientific laws. These are religiously compiled for every player who makes his way to the big leagues, then studied until a profile emerges. In other words, there are "rules" that have to do with the particular makeup of individuals, their idiosyncrasies, whether they bat from the left or right side or switch, the effectiveness of left- or right-handed pitchers against batters who bat from the right or left, and so on. The effect of this data is that the individual's ball-playing idiosyncrasies emerge as more or less public information set within a context of relationships with others and contribute to the cerebral character of the game. All professional sports require these detailed studies, but in baseball they are most highly evolved and give the game an aura of "history" and "order"—both transcending any single game taking place at a particular time.

This transcendence of time and place—which we are or were more likely to associate with nations—parallels the effort of every political entity, namely, to establish order-maintaining rules rooted in or vindicated by experience so that appropriate action may be initiated as new problems surface. On the playing field itself, the problems seem simple enough— to score or prevent runs from scoring. But the fascination with order and history implies a more serious concern, namely, sustaining and nurturing existence itself. To quote the hero of *Shoeless Joe*: "If only life were so simple, I have often thought, *if only there was a framework to life, rules to live by.*"[12] There is indeed such a framework, though hardly available to solve the entire range of life's problems. It depends on power and ensures orderly relations as an alternative to violence.

Then there are loyalty, affiliation, and partisanship, always essential in games of rules, including baseball, football, and political life. Partisanship means attachment to one team, or in politics, a point of view, a particular "player" or locale or principle or proposition or ideology. The inevitable response to this partisanship is to assume that it divides people from one another, socialists from other ideologues, Yankees fans from Red Sox fans, New York Giants fans from Washington Redskins fans. But in order to be a partisan an individual has to be part of a group connected in some way to "the game," someone who sits on one side of the stands or "roots" at home or votes for one particular set of candidates. "Taking sides" assumes the existence of others with whom we are connected because they, too, are partisans within the framework of the same game. The act of choosing sides is automatically a concession that there are sides, that there are other partisans, that some will root against my team because they are bound to their team. Partisanship viewed this way, is very different from warfare, in which the enemy sits before me and is to be killed or captured. *Partisanship in sports and politics, along with loyalty and affiliation, means being connected.*

What sense does it make for an adult to become so attached to a group of strangers decked out regularly in uniforms bearing team colors? It makes the same sense, as Roger Angell points out, as caring.[13] It means involvement and is a recognition and endorsement of the system, a form of feeling about what is going on that is tantamount to ever-reinforcing support for the system. The lesson can be read out for any game of rules, and therefore the images suggested by baseball affiliation, loyalty and rooting—football is no different—are the means by which millions declare that they are part of something bigger than themselves, that they are connected to one another by a willingness to display the joys and heartaches of loyalty. Is it possible that the escalation in attendance at and interest in sporting events somehow reflects the simultaneous weakening of concern about our political institutions, though not necessarily "the nation" when we are told it is threatened? I do not know. But rooting for a team links together all partisans, whoever their favorites may be, just as their distinctive loyalties divide them, more or less peaceably, when the game is in play. Fans of the Giants and Dodgers respond to different teams but care about the same game. Together, they make up the "power" of the system, and in this respect they may well suggest what is necessary to a political system that by definition is made up of people who are individuals with different points of view. Differences of opinion, insofar as they remain expressions of perspective and occasions for dialogue and conversation, are not occasions for violence, killing, and destructiveness. Indifference, not partisanship, means that a professional team can no longer operate. Indifference and ignorance, not partisanship, sound the death knell of power, of a political system that depends on support. They open the way to the use of violence as the only perceivable means of getting things done. Partisanship, though it appears to divide, actually represents recognition of mutuality, of the persistent presence of others who see things differently but who share similar concerns in a setting in which exchanges of views, not of bullets, are fundamental.

I am hesitant to explain these loyalties and connections. I believe they grow out of the need to connect and the degree to which everyday societal practices now close off opportunities to feel deeply about other than family attachments. Who can explain the behavior of Robert Polhill? Kidnapped on the twenty-fourth day of January 1987, the day before the New York Giants won Super Bowl XXI, he was deprived for eighteen months of the news that "his" team had won. Released by his captors on 22 April 1990 suffering from cancer of the larynx, Polhill could be found on Sunday, 15 October 1990, at the Redskins-Giants game in Washington, on a one-day leave from Walter Reed Hospital. Hearing of his condition and his attachment, the Giants had sent a former player to visit him in the hospital and show him a tape of the 1987 Super Bowl victory, then invited him to the game. He had previously turned down a Redskins jacket offered by that team's owner. Still waiting for the artificial larynx, he was silent throughout the game though he waved his arm repeatedly as the Giants won. He was the "Giant Fan Who Can't Yell," according to the headline, whose behavior spoke eloquently of these strange linkages that have become so important to many Americans. This sense of connection to those who don't know you but share your concerns in some way involves not only football but also the mutuality of political life.[14]

Compare the behavior of "citizens" with the intense commitments of "fans." We support policies that serve our interests but do not participate as voters or party "faithful." We no longer reform government; instead, we revile it and politicians. The decline of broadly partisan party politics does not demonstrate, as some think, the independence of the voter, but growing indifference and a responsiveness only to narrowly conceived self-interest. And what we need, in contrast, what baseball, football, and the other professional sports still generate, is partisanship, involvement, and mutual support for the game. These show us the ways of power, while our politics increasingly fails to do so, thereby becoming increasingly vulnerable to bouts of violence. Indeed, our political life is most alive when we are showing our support for war, which insofar as it is a contest "resembles" these games.

We can push the metaphor further. Certain situations in sports, the weakening of a baseball pitcher or the use of a pinch or substitute hitter, are responses to situations that have gotten out of hand. In baseball, relief pitchers are called upon; in football, substitute players, plays, and tactics are invoked to pull victory out at the last minute. Relief pitchers face a world they never made and are asked to restore that world to order, to do what is necessary to save the game.[15] That is also what political life is about. Every human being is born into circumstances and situations replete with problems. The job is to transform the world—to save or improve it. The games we watch and enjoy as a relief from life's everyday stresses offer us meanings that transfer to our nation's or state's or city's game of rules, its political life.

Seeing politics as a game of rules also provides us with insight into the notion of judging. Participants in political systems are judges. They observe or watch "representatives"—in sports their chosen teams—and judge their performance even while supporting them. Participation takes the form of expressing opinions rather than actually getting on the field. The analogue in politics is voting and joining in public discussion as distinct from running for, seeking, and accepting office. And judgment is important to politics because it provides an opportunity to look back, reexamine past events, and reach conclusions, even if tentative, about the value of what is done and therefore the potential value of what might be done in the future. But what is tricky and special about judging is that it demands, simultaneously, partisanship and involvement, in the absence of which we grow indifferent, plus enough balance and detachment for thoughtful consideration of past, present, and future. We know how to do this with respect to our teams; we have either forgotten how or totally lost interest in doing it reasonably and responsibly with respect to the affairs that govern the basic conditions under which we live.

There are other images that the sports metaphor supplies. Games of rules confirm the importance of results, even when we are not entirely enthralled by them. In life, as in sports, for events to proceed such outcomes are necessary; closure is required. The game begins and ends, customarily in nine innings or four quarters, and has a result. Tomorrow or next weekend or next year another opportunity will come. In politics, the policy is decided upon until we find reasons to do it over. Accepting outcomes means that we understand legitimacy; being unable to do so, as so often seems to be the case in contemporary political affairs, suggests an inability to accept the game itself and, when widespread, the character of games of rules so vital to political and social life. The loss of that understanding means that consensus, support, and order become elusive and violence becomes commonplace. Political life, power in all of its aspects, expects the game to continue. It seeks new strategies and deeper understanding, looks for other resources, evolves, and resensitizes itself to limitations not previously understood. This is a slow process, often likely to irritate but antipathetic to violence, which is speedy, incident creating, and without any procedure for moving predictably on to the next step. In political life there is always a next step, another time, another opportunity, and, potentially, a different and "better" outcome. Indeed, when that sense is absent, then it is likely that the polity is collapsing and that violence may replace power. At that point, every group and on occasion many individuals believe that their "rights" include the right to refuse to accept outcomes.

Games of rules make for predictability. The outcome may be unknown—it always is in human affairs—but the way we get there is laid out carefully and binds everyone identically. In football and baseball, the complex of rules is all that stands between the orderly and more or less peaceful (more in baseball, less in football) settlement and completion of the game. In political life, the existence of rules creates the foundation and framework that make it possible for activities to proceed without mayhem and disorder taking over. Games of rules make it clear to people that there are indeed orderly ways to pursue goals provided the goal that the game be played is shared. Perhaps—who knows?—understanding of orderliness is enhanced on—or by watching—the playing field; perhaps the meaning of '"games of rules" is tranferrable to issues that shape political life itself.

MUSIC

Music is among the art forms most affected by recent technological transformations. I'm not talking about music substantively, though that, particularly in the presentation and selling of popular music, has been greatly affected by technology, but about accessibility, which has grown steadily during the last three centuries and in quantum leaps during the twentieth. In America, "popular" music came out of the fields and churches, into theaters, cabarets, and places where it achieved a new popularity. Paralleling the emergence of enlightened and increasingly democratic rule, formal Western music, once the apparent property of a small upper class, increasingly spread socially "downward." Mozart (1756–1791), who achieved his greatest successes in Prague rather than in hostile Salzburg or among the aristocrats and patrons of Vienna, not only wrote operas that mocked, however obliquely, the privileges of the few but achieved his greatest success at the end of his short life with *The Magic Flute*, written for a popular theater and replete with references not only to delightful fantasies and magical characters and instruments but also to humanism and enlightenment. Later composers would be less and less beholden to the aristocracy, though the wealthy would remain patrons of their art, than to salability, publication, and popularity.

In America, meanwhile, music initially had little impact and, indeed, was frowned upon as a distraction by the Puritans. It would grow from other roots, among them folk music carried from overseas as well as the "native" and original music of the slaves. In time, American music became a mixture of European "classical" borrowings (making their greatest impact in the building of concert halls and the founding of philharmonic and symphonic societies during the nineteenth century), the spirituals and original music of African Americans that give rise to jazz, and a stream of popular music constantly borrowing from black originators. By the 1920s, sophisticated popular music had emerged, represented by a separate, undersupported but artistically vital black music, by Tin Pan Alley, the commercial fountainhead of American popular music, and then by the emergence of the Broadway musical comedy—at first a cross between European light classical and American popular music. By the 1920s, Tin Pan Alley had produced a group of original composers, a number of them the sons of immigrants, who captured the nation's imagination; among them was Irving Berlin, whose "popularity" was a by-product of a natural gift for melody and simple and direct expressiveness in lyrics, and George Gershwin, who authored remarkable, "jazzy" popular music and simultaneously wrote "serious" pieces and the first regularly performed American opera, whose story leaned heavily on and was built around one phase of African American experience in the South. Gershwin, in turn, as was often the case with Americans, had an enormous impact on the European composers with whom he studied during his brief lifetime.

Twentieth-century technology made a remarkable contribution to music's popular impact. The invention of mechanical techniques for recording and reproducing sound—cylinders, followed by short- and then long-playing records, and wire, tape, and compact discs, in other words, a technology evolving from mechanical to electric to electronic recording and reproducing techniques—made music as ubiquitous as the airwaves. By the mid- to late-twentieth century, Americans listened, almost universally, to the radio, watched television, and bought and played records, tapes, cassettes, and compact discs. They walked the streets holding boomboxes or they jogged with small sound reproducers and miniature headsets. The music "industry" had become a giant with worldwide influence, and the so-called serious music part of it, though accounting for anywhere from 5 percent to 8 percent of the sales of recorded music, had a much greater influence than this percentage would suggest through its impact on popular music and on Broadway and, above all, by the remarkable attendance of Americans at concerts and operas as well as the presentation of every kind of music on television and film.

I cannot discuss this penetration of music into culture over a short period of time on the basis of its musical substance or meaning from the point of view of musical scholarship. That should be left to musicians and musicologists. I am interested, however, in the possibility that musical "language" presents yet another "new" metaphor helpful in looking at the human world and therefore at political life.

I am *not* concerned with the literal political meanings of specific musical texts. It takes little effort to notice that a number of Mozart's operas, particularly with texts by Lorenzo Da Ponte, directly mock the aristocracy and their effort to manipulate and regulate the lives of "plainer" folk. Nor is it difficult to hear the political message in the blues or to find the "politics" in much of the music of the 1960s. But I think something more significant, political in the broader sense I have discussed in connection with "power," is inevitably entailed in music itself, and I will try to illustrate.

Bernice Johnson Reagon's discussion with Bill Moyers, televised by the Public Broadcasting System, makes my point.[16] Reagon maintains that blacks cannot sing African American music "without changing [their] condition." Singing together in harmony was and is a way for black Americans to announce their existence, to make themselves visible, to become in each instance an "I" because the group singing, the harmony, and the songs themselves (for instance, "I Ain't Gonna Slave No More") pull us together, "run through our bodies," and "change our condition." Songs, black American songs, are a way "to get to singing" and the circle of people singing in church "announce [their] existence" and presence to a world that otherwise treats them as if they are not there and tries to persuade them that their existence is of no consequence, as per the earlier discussion of "invisibility." In the long struggle to emancipate black Americans from slavery and semi-slavery, congregational singing, group singing, both in manner and substance, is a way of making their existence or, perhaps more accurately, their presence known, first to themselves, then to anyone who hears them. It is simultaneously a way of establishing the community, in our terms of polity, and each participant's individuality.

"Running songs through our bodies" is at the heart of black culture in a society that consigned blacks to slavery, near slavery, humiliations, and degradation. Jointly developed and performed texts establish or reinforce connectedness. The black infant, severed from mother as are all infants, then literally dragged away from home, hearth, and parents and sold on the block, was cut off from the primary circle of connectedness. Cut off as well, from general political life, indeed, expressly denied that possibility, blacks establish connectedness by raising voices jointly in announcement and recall of their jointly endured and ongoing deprivations. Each "I" song is a way of achieving visibility not within the wider cultural context but within the more confined circle made up of black people. When blacks sang and sing "I gotta right to the tree of life," it is the failure of the outer culture to permit blacks their individuality that stimulates the "I" phrasing. The metaphoric meaning or impact is to establish a substitute for land or turf or territory and to keep emphasizing that "we, the plural word" reinforces the American habit of constantly lumping blacks into a group, thereby confirming their invisibility. Their use of "I" in the songs confirms the existence of the group but affirms that within African American culture they clearly stand out as individuals who use the "I" proudly and meaningfully. "I" is the "communal expression" for blacks; in other words, "I" means that an individual's life is joined to the group's or community's, for group connectedness makes individual visibility possible.

"The Songs Are Free." They empower; they create a circle or arena, a space, a place in the world. Meanwhile, Reagon says, meaning is "placed" in the songs by the singers. Voices jointly raised—historically in a church and during the 1960s in marches and demonstrations—are means of overcoming the tensions inherent in their societal position or that surface when blacks attempt to establish their presence and to declare, in effect, that their rights are as significant as anyone else's. The protestors "take control of the space" or "establish the air" not simply by occupying a lunch counter, a bus station, a street, or the square outside a courtroom but through song, by setting a tone, by displaying themselves as individuals who are part of a distinctive culture. This habit, of course, grows out of a time and circumstance in which slavery meant no territory, no right to one's own body, and no control over the destiny of one's family nor any acknowledged, formal connection to that family; it grows also out of the later time when blacks were required to sit in the back section of the bus, step down from the curb when a white person was passing by, ride in separate railroad cars, and play all the identity games of Jim Crow. The singing, that is, the jointly made music, creates what Arendt called "a space of appearance."

At the same time, the words carry meanings that are wonderfully ambiguous and further strengthen the sense of connectedness. Reagon claims that the message in the old slave songs refers to yesterday's, today's, or tomorrow's actions. The songs' references are quite clear to the participants or congregation but, if overheard, fall safely within the bounds of what white folks thought were the naive and simplistic religious notions of the blacks. For instance, reference to "rising" or "crossing the Jordan" might refer to the imminence of death and the hoped-for trip to a better world, but it also might be a signal about escaping servitude later in the day or tomorrow. Black culture, accordingly, was and is bound by the singular lingual signals it employs within a musical context and is thereby bonded in a community even in the absence of independence, visible political life, apparent freedom, or official hierarchies (as distinct from unofficial hierarchies that exist both in political and non-political settings). "Power" is generated by coming together in song and in the songs cementing bonds through their emotional and their rhythmic character as well as words that potentially, depending on the situation, have ambiguous or coded meanings. Empowerment, the sense of coming together, is achieved in or through music. This seems to me to be as true today of "black" music, which as before remains the most distinctive and innovative American music. And this empowerment's foundations remain intact without formal instruments of governance, since efforts to construct them would be (and were) put down by overseers and masters. Instead, the church is the originating place and the preacher is the person who symbolizes the instrument and foundation building, the rule making that arrives in disguise. Here invisibility is stood on its head, turned into an "advantage" in that the complicated carryings-on, meanings, bondings, and connections are invisible to the outsider. Power and politics become a matter of code, giving the word "public" a special, cultural meaning. The third aspect of power, politicking, like the second, is undoubtedly there in the internal, but still more or less "secret," attitudes toward policy, possible stances toward uprisings, rebellions, or demands on masters that might be contemplated, and hierarchical struggles carried on out of sight of whites. For instance, there had to be vastly disparate attitudes between those slaves who were given the higher status of domestics and erstwhile close contact with "owners" and those who remained at hard labor in the field. The same is as true of the current divisions between middle-class blacks and the black masses who remain impoverished and ghettoized.

Sound, that is, vocalizing, becomes the culture's way of claiming territory. It says, "we're here," we can "control the space" even though being harried by police during demonstrations. Song establishes the territory and is the vehicle for message passing. "Steal away" or "crossing over" are likely to be secular messages. The phrase Reagon uses, "the songs are free," means that the singer gives them the particular or appropriate meaning. Canaan may be a biblical reference, but it could just as well refer to an escape to Canada. "If you don't go, go anyway," is a way of saying that you can control your own story, every precious moment of your life, even if you are enslaved or destitute. When Moyers asks how they could sing of the preciousness of life, or control of their destiny, Reagon's answer is simple. Blacks have not always had the goods or material possessions or freedom that are supposed to ensure happiness, but they are placed together in the universe through the culture, thus empowered, thus able to redeem their existences. And that, of course, is the foundational meaning of power that is not understood or grasped by most Americans, who equate power with control, influence, position, and domination. For black Americans, a different perspective on political power, which resurfaced momentarily in the 1960s, sees specialness and place, a cultural territory, as derivative from connections that have been reinforced by conditions and made more bearable by joint vocalizing. As Reagon indicates, black people created a world in America, that is, a "territory," that "could take care of the business of making a people." Not a land necessarily, but a culture. The full range of my power as a human being, she suggests, is exposed, made visible, when people are together. "The power is in this circle." And this happened in the face of conditions that were calculated to deny this very assertion or feeling. Thus the "galvanizing power of music."

In these linkages between music and identity, visibility and empowerment, a metaphor for political life is easy to see. Although nothing is more singular than the creation or authorship of formal or even individual music, and nothing symbolizes individuality as well as the spontaneity and virtuosic character of authentic jazz, music is from first to last a phenomenon of togetherness. It connects audience to performer. It ties performer to performer. We may go to hear the diva, but she cannot perform without accompaniment. The structure of what she sings fits in a complex format that demands cooperating elements, therefore jointness. Even in the seemingly freer world of jazz, music is dependent on framework and foundation. The system of notation alone is an example of an elaborate game of rules. But all basic elements in music are of this kind. Music is patterned sound that produces tonality and melody. It requires a rhythmic framework that may indeed be the most basic of its elements, as it emphasizes or deemphasizes, speeds up or delays beats and pulses, and thus gives it a living, evolving pattern. Music inevitably reflects organization. But what this organization permits, indeed, requires, is the assembly of voices of varying tonal qualities to give it fullness, richness, and depth. Likewise, it requires direction, proceeding from "point" to "point," which is what a melodic line does for it, as well as harmony, the combining of reinforcing and contrasting sound tones.

Humans need rules to make sense out of their lives, from simple communication to the building of complex instruments of destruction, but though nature furnishes some of them—mortality, for instance—humans are special in that they are aware of and can deal with and attempt to overcome nature's givens. This is what "power" attempts to do, and like all human phenomena that become institutionalized, it engenders games of rules.

I have discussed two. First, I focused on imagery that can be drawn from the world of sports that highlights the distinction between power and violence. From it, we can learn about the need to be scrupulous in our regard for the rules if we wish to play the game and keep the agreement to agree alive. Second, I used imagery drawn from music, concentrating on a single example that instructs us that identity depends to a degree on connectedness and that connectedness is not necessarily territorial. Given the communications revolution and the spread of American music throughout Western civilization, it is even conceivable that in music we find yet another ally to the globalism and mutual awareness of environmental concerns that so many reformers think necessary to the survival of the planet. Taken together—and putting aside the commercialism that infects both in an era that permits so much time to be spent on entertainment—they are examples of what we find, if we but look, in the world around us respecting human connectedness and its maintenance. Making clear the importance of that connectedness is an enormous educational task for schools, for the communications and information technologies now in existence, and for a political life that presently seems moribund and incapable of action.

These images are not intended to be conclusive or definitive. There are new forms of linkage or bonding, stimulated by the electronics revolution, that bring people together into "networks" that could not have existed in earlier times. These may prove to be new forms of mutuality within which shared orders are generated that, in turn, produce new games of rules. Perhaps what I'm speaking of is a mere extension of the old Aristotelian insight that different types of "cities" (states, polities, communities) elicit different "virtues" from citizens. However, with these newer formats the problem that cannot be resolved readily is that they abandon the traditional foundations for mutuality—that people share a space (the common link for "community" or nation) and order (rules) for that space and that they be in a condition that links them even if they are, so to speak, denied full title to their own destinies, as were the African Americans whose music became a kind of "territory" embracing participants and excluding outsiders. But even in that instance, the participants shared a specific place as well as a common condition. I do not for a moment, however, doubt that other forms of linking are possible. As for the United States, it seems to me possible to envision changes in the system that will reverse the sense that things are not working as well as they might.

NOTES

1. I stress professional sports because in the last century amateur athletics, playing the game for rewards other than financial, have all but vanished as a public phenomenon. No college or university in the United States "serious" about a sport like football or basketball stresses amateurism; winning titles and the celebrity and money that go with them now counts for all. Although exponents of professionalized collegiate athletics claim that like amateur sports their teams play for the sake of the game itself, their claims are suspect.

2. See Barbara Grizzuti Harrison's review of George Will, *Men at Work: The Craft of Baseball, New York Times Book Review*, 1 April 1990, pp. 1, 17.

3. George F. Will, *Men at Work: The Craft of Baseball* (New York: Macmillan Publishing Company, 1990), pp. 1–2.

4. Naomi Fein, "Confessions of a Gentlewoman Fanatic," *New York Sunday Times*, Sports of the Week, 9 September 1990, p. 9. An article that stresses football's violence and proximity to warfare ("War imagery dominates football") crossed my desk just as this manuscript was being packed up for shipment. The article is literal and quite telling with reference to the well-known fact that the game is marked by serious and often debilitating violence. Jacob Weisman, "Pro Football—The Maiming Game," *The Nation*, vol. 253, no. 3, 27 January 1992, pp. 84–87. The quotation can be found on p. 87.

5. I do not speak contemptuously but as a fan who has "suffered" with a team, the New York Giants, and on rare occasions been heartened by them ever since the good old days at the Polo Grounds, when kids were admitted to watch the Giants from the end zone for a quarter—a lot of money then but not an amount beyond reach even for the poor, particularly since the subway was only a nickel, as was the ride under the Hudson River. Like Fein, I too lost interest in baseball when greed removed the New York Giants from the Polo Grounds into a windy and near-frigid imitation ball park in San Francisco. But my interest in the New York [Football] Giants has never flagged, not even during the days when they too, like so many Americans, wandered hopelessly about, without a home field or a permanent site in which to play.

6. Some of the antics and delays, particularly by pitchers, add to what some regard as the game's boredom. See Roger Angell, *Five Seasons* (New York: Simon & Schuster, 1988), pp. 294–96, which describes the elaborate repertoire of carryings-on typical of Luis Tiant of the Boston Red Sox.

7. Ibid., pp. 22–23.

8. W. P. Kinsella, *Shoeless Joe* (New York: Ballantine Books, 1982).

9. Ibid., p. 46.

10. Ibid., p. 72.

11. Ibid., p. 73.

12. Ibid., p. 78.

13. Ibid., p. 306.

14. See David Anderson, "The Giant Fan Who Can't Yell," *New York Times*, Sports of the Times, 15 October 1990, p. C4.

15. See Angell, *Five Seasons*, p. 211.

16. "The Songs Are Free," Bernice Johnson Reagon interviewed by Bill Moyers, Wednesday, 6 February 1991, WGBH-TV, Boston (Channel 2). Reagon is a scholar holding a doctorate, a writer, songwriter, lecturer, performer of inordinate "power," founder of the powerful singing group Sweet Honey in the Rock, and interpreter of the history and character of African American music. In using the tape of the interview, I decided not to transcribe it—the tape's impact lies in the combination of sight and sound. In citing it, I've placed in quotation marks both directly quoted phrases and one or two paraphrases that closely follow Reagon's responses to Moyer's questionings or her observations to audiences (which were part of the presentation).

13

The Political Imperative

THE SPECIALNESS OF THE AMERICAN POLITY

I've given short shrift to justly praised American productivity, passion for freedom, capacity for work, and affection for law, due process, constitutional order, free speech, diversity, and limited government. No one can doubt their importance, but without derogating any of them, I suspect that this nation's obsession with a balancing act in political economy, an attempt to achieve equilibrium between economic development and political openness and to use the polity as an enforcer of economic priorities, has been the primary strength of our political life. This blend has produced many a business, technological, and engineering wizard—Fulton, Whitney, Carnegie, Edison, Rockefeller, Ford, and others—but also, despite the anti-political rhetoric so common today, many political geniuses—Franklin, Washington, Paine, Hamilton, Adams, Jefferson, Madison, the mysterious, melancholy, and brilliant Lincoln, and the two Roosevelts among them.

The attempt to treat political life and economic affairs separately while harnessing them together is as old as the nation. It can be seen in the Constitution of 1787, which freed individuals from government by protecting them against certain kinds of statutes—*ex post facto* laws or bills of attainders, for example. Once the Bill of Rights was appended (1791), individual rights were guaranteed. The founders were very far, however, from endorsing a free market economy. The document supports business and other economic interests positively: the obligations of contract are shielded; slaveholders are protected and the slave trade is left intact for twenty years; and though the grant is not spelled out clearly, the government is permitted to subsidize and ally itself with enterprise. Indirect subsidy, however, is explicitly made part of the Union's obligations. A highway and post road system is envisioned. A postal service, vital for business communications—and still subsidizing them—is established. Patents are protected. Regulation of commerce among the states, with foreign nations, and with Native American tribes is written into the fundamental law, however imprecisely. Unclear but palpable reference to the general welfare is included. The national government is given the right to tax imports but not exports, an effort to protect domestic agriculture and manufacture. Property rights are loosely referred to, then shielded under the contract clause, and later by a so-called liberty of contract that the Supreme Court interpolated into the document—by which combination business activities were given constitutional standing. The coinage system and Treasury were established to ensure governmental revenues as well as the flow of credit and exchanges that constitute the lifeblood of business. In affirmation of the document's intent, the newly installed authorities immediately took it upon themselves during George Washington's administration to make clear to investors that the credit of the new United States was a sacred national responsibility and that wartime debts would be assumed—a windfall for those shrewd enough to buy up what appeared to be worthless notes. Sidney Fine writes:

In practice the federal and state governments of the era before the Civil War did not confine their activities. . . . The federal government became the promoter of a variety of economic enterprises. It constructed the National Road and military roads on the frontiers, purchased stock in four canal companies, provided surveys and land grants for wagon roads, canals, and railroads, assigned land to the states for the general purpose of internal improvements, and itself improved rivers and harbors. It appropriated the money for the first magnetic telegraph line in the United States. It sought to aid manufacturers by enacting a protective tariff and to aid manufacturers of small arms by advancing them funds without interest on government contracts. It promoted the nation's merchant marine by imposing duties and tonnage taxes that discriminated in favor of United States shipping engaged in foreign commerce, by excluding foreign vessels from coastwise trade, and by providing subsidies for steamships. To the codfishery it offered bounties on exports and a cash subsidy to owners and crews of vessels engaged in the industry. Also, it provided the states with land for both common schools and state universities.[1]

Of course, protection had been extended to property in slaves or chattel from the beginning, and the national government's purchase or seizure of land, its westward expansion, made the national government a partner in economic development. Only the struggle over whether to proceed as a slave or "free" economy threatened the alliance, and that dispute was settled by the Civil War.

The countless activities of the federal government to assist, develop, support, aid, encourage, promote, and kowtow to the wishes of business interests have persisted since that time. The rail system is heavily a result of a federal land giveaway. Trade was assisted by the expensive building of the Panama Canal and followed up foreign and military policies. Tax policy encourages write-offs of losses. Bank deposits are insured. Banking interests have been given special dispensation and support by the government whereby profits are retained by surviving banks while losses are absorbed by the public. Agriculture has been supported and subsidized. A public highway system has been built and is the foundation for a "private" transportation industry and once profitable automobile industry; similar though less visible airline subsidies have long been in place. The national government's credit and financial manipulations assist businesses to maintain profitability and prop up consumer expenditures. Although we are now outspent by the Japanese and Germans, it is long-standing U.S. policy to mix "free enterprise" with public expenditure and to interlock the economy and political life.

This interlocking provides an important clue to a major tension that has persisted throughout American history. The eminent political economist Robert Heilbronner has written of the existence of two authorities in this nation, "one built on the verticality of wealth, the other on the horizontality of democracy."[2] Heilbronner appears to claim that in addition to the obvious complexities of the federal system, there is yet another division in final political authority—between a leading class of businessmen and financiers and the political order or institutions. I think his suggestion is largely correct, but I'm not at all certain he would or could endorse my usage of it.

The vertical or economic order is ladder-like and pyramidal, with place or position being determined by wealth or access to the instruments of wealth. This order, while subject to consumption and demand pressures, is heavily influenced and controlled by those in the highest positions. Loyalties and "support" are therefore exacted by position in the economic hierarchy—the higher the position, the greater the support that must be given. The horizontal or political order, on the other hand, is equalizing, a regime wherein, ostensibly at least, everyone has equivalent priority. The horizontal order legitimately speaks for everyone—it is empowered by political machinery rather than economic position; loyalty is not a vertical phenomenon going merely to those who are highly placed but, typical of political life, is a by-product of empowerment and the "equal standing" of citizens. Since the polity speaks for everyone—all being on a horizontal plane—its avowed purpose is to represent the largest possible number of citizens, irrespective of social or economic position. Support, in turn, rests on this presumed indifference to special interest. In contrast, the vertical order is driven by special interest and by the drive for profit, while it seeks political as well as economic leverage at every level of government or access points in the horizontal order. Meanwhile, the horizontal order attempts to contain and balance these economic pressures "in the public interest." The distinctive purposes of the economy and polity parallel in some ways the age-old difference, if one insists on their separation, between self-interest and public interest. But the customary situation is to find them woven together. For example, it is in the public interest that "private" corporations be profitable because the success of the economy is necessary to public togetherness. If there is not enough food available, if consumption falters, talk about common purposes is an empty rhetorical flourish—hunger and want reduce everyone to a primitive or primal self-interest. Given the widespread conviction that somehow or other our system mixes "free enterprise" with governmental responsibility for seeing to everyone's well-being, economic breakdowns are always seen as governmental lapses, even though, with wonderful illogic, economic success is always credited to entrepreneurial genius or the ability to overcome or sidestep political or governmental obstacles.

American policy, from the beginning, has presided over this shotgun wedding between the economic and political orders, but the two orders have repeatedly clashed. The economy answers the call of special or self-interest, of competition, of differential economic success. Political life, whether or not it ever achieves total disinterestedness, searches for the good of all, the good of the community, the general interest. Political life is grounded in a political imperative—*that each individual act as if the general interest is identical to his or her self-interest*. To state that differently, healthy political relationships require each individual to act in certain situations in such a way that he or she could and would live contentedly and safely if every other person were to adopt or choose the same action. The political game is played together by the mutual acceptance of one another's activities as if they were guided by identical interests, namely, outcomes that are good for the public.

Every soldier who has offered his life in defense of homeland, who demonstrates in deeds that the well-being of all is identical to his self-interest, even at the cost of his own life, is in this regard a true "politician" and at one with the political imperative. In contrast, by dint of what it is, a vertical economic regime, devoted to profits as well as economic advantage and growth, can never pass itself off as a political regime even if it captures control of every government agency at every level; it can never be authoritative for all citizens because it must respond to its reason for being and foundation, its place among the diverse, competing interests that make up the marketplace. To the extent that such an economic regime is collaborative or mutually supportive—and it must be if everyone is to play by the same rules—it is no longer being guided by economic imperatives, but by the political imperative.

Much of American history is and has been a balancing act between these two. It has been America's particular political genius, some might say foolishness, to insist on this. Breakdowns have been common—the Civil War resulted from the impossibility of welding together the political imperative, with its emphasis on equal standing under the law, and the economic imperative of slaveholding, with its emphasis on master-slave relationships, though there was an additional and significant division between the wage and slave systems as modes of organizing the economy. In the post–Civil War era, the tension between the needs of the economy and the political imperative again produced skirmishes that ultimately enlarged governmental roles both in the states and throughout the nation; governments became mediators or moderators, as well as supporters of, economic activity. During the last twenty years, however, economic concerns have been given increasing priority, sometimes to the detriment of political life.

I believe the time has come to turn the balance wheel again, to recall and reinvent our mutual political responsibilities and deemphasize unfettered economic "rights." That process will begin when we revitalize connectedness, refresh our understanding of political life, and thereby restore it along with its initiator, power. To contribute to that, I have attempted both to question old images out of which we have woven our inherited political belief system and suggest possible "new'" metaphors to reinvigorate our thinking about politics and to make possible active engagement in the resolution of public problems.

But doesn't the adoption of so-called new metaphors and the abandonment of older ones rooted in contract theories and natural rights also mean the loss of all standards? The answer is that humans have never in fact literally been bound by "nature's" or "science's" or even "God's" games of rules, even if they have used such talk metaphorically to suggest that there were rigid or fixed standards that prevented life from deteriorating into a free-for-all or that were a bulwark against arbitrary rulership. I believe that political life, though a humanly constructed "game," also entails standards, but there is a difference. "Nature," "science," and God presumably prescribe fixed standards against which humans measure their actions; they provide "eternally" valid rules of the game. But the simple truth is that humans have regularly manipulated this imagery to suit their purposes, and policies supposedly guided by fixed standards have always been malleable, that is, dependent on interpretation. Acknowledgment that political life is a contingent human construct ties it to a political imperative demanding that I conduct myself in a way that would make my actions consistent with the general interest; that would content and protect me if others behave the same way, thereby providing as consistent, coherent, and reliable a standard as the contract theory and natural rights imagery we have inherited. It maintains that the ever-present standard and governing motif of political life is the safety and well-being of the entire populace. That is the one rule that must be operative and present if the game of life and its accompanying games of rules are to continue peaceably and beneficially.

Finally, I have suggested as well—though no detail has been attempted, since these are *res publica*, matters that cannot be attended to without extensive and public dialogue—the need for both structural changes in our political institutions and action to resolve substantive social problems.

A FURTHER LOOK AT THE SPORTS AND MUSIC METAPHORS

I have stressed "games of rules" and used football and baseball as metaphors for violence and power (see Chapter 12). That usage is open to the criticism that sports partisanship is based on an "us-against-all-comers" attitude more akin to violence than power. I have also used black "church" music, whose power was forged in the shared experiences of slavery and, later, second-class citizenship. Both the partisanship that "unites" people in response to professional sports and the linking of blacks through church music appear, therefore, to originate in division and separation.

But it does not follow that a thing's origin explains its current appeal or meaningfulness, and I suspect that the criticism itself is rooted in a tendency in both the society and academic disciplines to regard differences, rather than commonalities, as significant. Furthermore, as the workaday world increases our "busyness," and consequently our isolation, a need for shared experiences, once satisfied by everyday community and family life, is met in stadia, theaters, and churches. These spaces serve, as they always have, as places of human contact and sharing, but they also suggest how important "agora," the public square, is to us and how we are drawn back to it and feel the need to join with others there, and at least share something.

Music, thanks to the electronic revolution, has now captured almost everyone's attention and imagination. Its "patrons," those who respond to it, are part of an "audience" and thereby share an "identity" tied to the music itself. Music moves people as individuals, of course, but it can make each one aware of the extent to which he or she is in sync with and related to others. This is another sense in which it offers us an apt metaphor for political life. But music provides a bonding experience not simply because of the words used to describe it, or the feelings it generates in an audience, or the commonality of the listeners' backgrounds and circumstances, or even the similarity of individual reactions, but because it "speaks" and carries "meanings." Its potential or power, therefore, is enormous. Through music it is possible to bring people together, whatever their differences, and a linking often takes place in spite of cultural separateness or incompatibility of condition. Though black church music is rooted in the suffering of slaves, that music—all music—can rise above its own origin and pull people into a recognition that a particular musical combination of sound, harmony, and rhythm connects them. Its potential in that respect is as yet unmeasured—and the same is undoubtedly true of other art forms. The point is not that music eliminates divisions, but that it today serves as a mass vehicle for connectedness, as do sports events. Both give us a glimpse of what we might achieve together politically.

Those with little feeling for sports, football in particular, often see the latter as a "dressed-up" version of street violence, and they see partisanship as a forerunner of disorder. Therefore, my claim that partisanship is participation, that it is preferable to indifference and a possible key to understanding power and political life, seems shocking. Football *is* violent. People get hurt playing it. The same is true of other sports—including more "gentle" games such as tennis. But football, baseball, hockey, and so forth are not forms of disorderly conduct. For athletes, these games are challenges to hone their skills, refine their self-discipline, and increase their earnings. For fans they provide—as does music—a stimulating opportunity to participate and judge. For those who choose to see this way, professional sports are "games of rules," therefore possible metaphors for other games of rules such as political life. While these games—and political life—depend on "sides," on "us-against-them," they are not Hobbes' war of each against all, nor combat, nor akin to the disorder now rampant in American society. Yes, people get hurt playing or attending sports events—at European soccer games, for instance, and some rock concerts in this country. But the casualty lists cannot match those produced by society's street violence, pervasive extralegal conduct, or indifference to others' suffering. Comparatively speaking, a Super Bowl or a Sunday at Giants Stadium, on the field, in the stands, and in the parking lot is a tea party—and those who go expecting to see rowdyism and disorder are in for a great disappointment. The players struggle, the fans eat and shout, but the real warfare in this society takes place elsewhere.

I argue, accordingly, that to some extent professional sports and musical performances currently serve as repositories for our need to be connected to others. How we apply this need to the actual business of pulling ourselves together politically is a different question. My guess is that it will not be a matter of banners waving and bands playing, but a far slower and more difficult effort in civic re-education and reform.

RESTORING THE SENSE OF PUBLIC SPACE

We tend to think of the United States as a three-tiered layer cake of governance: local, state, national. But as Morton Grodzins points out, that description has never, not even before the Constitution was adopted, accurately described the American way of government. A better image is that of a swirled marble cake with functions criss-crossing and inter-mingling in thousands of permutations and combinations.[3] Grodzins describes this pattern by listing the salary and functions of a single health officer or sanitarian appointed in a particular border state:

Salary: *joint federal-state funding*

Office: *supplied by county*

Added salary: *appointed by one city in county as plumbing inspector*

Pure foods standards: *federal government*

Non-interstate commodities: *state laws*

Interstate milk products: *state laws*

Impure drug impoundment: *acts as federal officer*

Typhoid immunization: *joint federal-state official*

Industrial hygiene standards: *state laws*

Water supply: *state-city officer*

Garbage disposal by butchers: *city officer*

Federalism, a concoction mixed together to cope with colonial differences and state "sovereignty," was attuned to the needs of a small population united in their opposition to British rule but otherwise isolated from one another, unique in history, and distinctive, though not entirely disparate, in culture. Union was achieved by a series of ingenious compromises. But our problem is not to unite thirteen different governments but to make sense out of what we have now. And neither the original two-level federal system—states and nation—nor the three tiers of government—local, state, national—are currently working very well. We have to make some alterations.

At the local level, we have to think in strictly political terms and stop trying to imitate the rules that are supposed to govern businesses. Local governance is not supposed to be a profit-making activity; operating local services is not a profit-making activity, it is simply a matter of making available whatever is necessary to make daily activities possible and to do that as well as can be managed. The notion that service comes first, and that it is a necessity, not a luxury, can be understood by looking at what appears to be a totally absurd idea but is an attempt, which certainly makes no claim of being definitive, to think outside the usual economic categories and to invest energy and money in a political solution to what is clearly a municipal service problem.

Suppose the citizens of New York City decide to ignore past economic priorities with respect to their subway and bus system. They conclude that public transit is a public right and benefit as well as a tourist attraction and that it should be treated as a public asset. They insist that turnstiles and change booths be removed, that the trains and buses be open to all who choose to use them. They also close the system down after 2:00 AM and more or less silence the city until 6:00 AM—and use the time for cleaning equipment and stations. Being responsible, they will not hurt the people who currently work in the system; their incomes are protected. The public, being aware of new tax burdens this would impose, recognizes that the lost revenue would have to be recouped through taxation— although money will be saved by eliminating the need to chase after the many who now don't pay and from sales of scrap metal like gates, turnstiles, and coin boxes. In sum, they adopt a public policy that revolutionizes public transit.

Should anyone actually offer such a plan, the inevitable outcry would be "impossible!" even though, of all the cities in the United States, New York has been among those that collect a minimal percentage of revenues from service income generally and more in percentage terms (over 50 percent) specifically through transit fares.[4]

Public benefits or needs, however, cannot always be measured by profit-and-loss statements. Where would New York City be without its publicly supported collegiate system, presumably still the producer of an enormous number of contributors to American life? What would the Midwestern states or California or the Southwest be like without their state university traditions? Public transit can be managed—if we choose to do so—in a manner consistent with the well-being and benefit of the pubic at large rather than on the basis of "business" principles that don't necessarily work in that setting any more than they do in the operations of a library. And surely if we can subsidize private banks, farmers, and hospitals, we might do the same for public transportation. In political life, decisions made for the benefit of the public at large extend the beginning that is made when humans first acknowledge the fundamental importance of joining together. Each decision refines and reshapes the original initiation of "power" and thereby reenergizes it. Strictly speaking, the benefit is not economic, though there are economic benefits. It is horizontal; that is, it spreads across the entire polity and therefore is equal in significance to economic benefits though different in character. Public activity properly understood, is undertaken and supported by the population at large and reminds each of us of opportunities, conveniences, and problems shared. It enlarges our awareness of and therefore our sensibilities with respect to one another while resolving everyday problems that are common, so that we can get on with other business.

This brings us to the states. Although many differences remain and individual states are still distinguishable, it is nonsense to speak of them as sovereign entities. For decades they have needed federal grants-in-aid and directives to resolve problems and generate enough money to handle their responsibilities. Highway, airport, and hospital building, as well as water-pollution control programs and welfare programs have depended on federal funds. Cities have increasingly bypassed the states and been linked to federal initiative and finance. The states have been and are incapable of keeping themselves fiscally sound, unless they abandon or refuse to engage in activities that are now considered a normal part of their responsibilities. Nor is "business" an in-state activity; the majority cross state boundaries. And as government projects have multiplied to meet assorted demands, overlapping as well as cooperative efforts have also increased. The United States, as a result, is a sea of governmental jurisdictions, joint activities, separate legal codes, and complicated variable tax laws that differ not only from state to state but from city to city and even county to county. Indeed, the states have been forced to become master complicators of tax statutes. And there is no telling where the citizen or analyst of the system is going to bump into excessive complications—the attorney general of the United States recently spoke of seventeen thousand (!) police jursdictions in the country. If there were Martians and should they choose to land in this country, could they make sense out of the complications—and with them the added expenses—we have concocted? Could James Madison, the father of the Constitution, make head or tail out of the maze we have constructed?

A new look at how we have divided the governmental pie is needed to untangle confusions and overlaps in the system. The point is to get on with fundamental change to achieve equity and sense. Fortunately, state officials and administrators know more about widespread problems—though these cross state borders—than other officials. State legislators know problems within their states far better than their opposites in Congress do; as a group, governors may be our outstanding public servants. My purpose here, accordingly, is not to eliminate state officials or the states but to recognize that the present system is fossilized and often paralyzed.

The political structure ought to reflect the actual layout of the nation, which is a Union of localities, municipalities, rural areas, and regions as well as states and a federal government, the current "sovereigns." States and counties are important not only for historical reasons but also because they constitute, with a handful of possible exceptions, units of a reasonable size. And they are at the heart of an ingenious arrangement whereby even the smaller states have equal representation in one branch of the national legislature. Regions also deserve recognition—six, seven, or eight of them. Rural and municipal entities ought to be given constitutional guarantees and integrity. The spectacle of the leading commercial and artistic center of the United States regularly begging the State of New York for rescue missions—and similar hassles elsewhere—is appalling and usually turns out to be less kindly responded to than requests for help from overseas. The constitutional recognition and governmental use of regions—New England, the Middle Atlantic states, and the like—would in the long run be a blessing provided that we simultaneously reassert the priority of "home," of the place where each of us lives, be it town or city, metropolitan or rural area. If the nation's present organizations could be assured that the constitutional sanctity of civil rights would remain untouched, then an overhaul of major proportions, one that preserves what is good, valuable, and necessary, and that safeguards freedom and clarifies and upgrades minority rights, is certainly in order.

The tax system reflects problems at the three levels and is now in desperate need of reform. More taxes could be collected by the federal government and distributed, using fair formulas, to regions, cities, and states. But the cities are currently creatures of the states without independent legal standing, even though they receive direct monies from the federal government. The system needs a fairness doctrine providing for equitable distribution of money to resolve similar problems in different locales. Without destroying incentive, the tax burden should be equalized across the nation in a reasonably progressive way. Once the system is coordinated effectively, the net effect should be a reduction in taxes, although that will take years. To begin, federal income tax laws and state taxing policies need to be better coordinated. One possible route is to convert the current deduction system—whereby certain state and local taxes are treated as deductions to gross income on federal returns—and give them equal standing by subtracting them from net federal taxes. That, however, would require a major overhaul of tax policies; otherwise states could in effect use their taxing authority to all but eliminate federal taxes, obviously an impossible arrangement. But my point is not to offer a solution—experts are needed—but to urge an end to tax-raising anarchy and in conjunction with an allocation of monies to the states that takes into account the diversity in their populations and problems. In the long run, if undertaken systematically and carried out with scrupulous regard for fair play, such a reform would help restore confidence in government and politics—although pressure groups and elites can be counted upon to fight change.

But why go through the nightmare of argumentation and discussion that such reconstructions would require? The answer is simple. We have reached the point where many substantive policy questions cannot be resolved, and in many instances the United States' complicated political structure adds yet another obstacle to resolution of differences. It was clearly the intent of the founders to slow down or minimalize governmental action, to confine it to collective security, basic protections, and maintenance of a favorable climate for economic activities. But this is not 1787. We no longer have four million people living in thirteen states. We have two hundred fifty million in fifty states, two of them non-contiguous. And we have problems that constantly run into the many obstacles created by our governmental maze and enhanced by the breakdown of connectedness that has characterized the society for some time. These problems have been mentioned intermittently throughout the book: a deteriorating infrastructure, the death of inner cities, persistent racism, entrenched poverty, major alterations in family life and the ubiquity of working parents or single-parent families, and escalating health costs coupled with increasing differentials in ability to pay. Taken together they tell us that our neighborhoods no longer are neighborly, that our sense of being tied together or connected is constantly unraveling, that we have scattered ourselves in suburbia and allowed many resources that once were the glories of our cities to be threatened with neglect and abandonment, that the automobile has encouraged neglect of public transit and increasing indifference to shared problems, and that even our businesses and stores have abandoned neighborliness in favor of superstores and international bureaucratic management systems. If this continues much longer, our capacity to deal with one another and to resolve problems will be paralyzed. And as that happens, people grow angry, even enraged, and begin to believe that since cooperation and politicking accomplishes nothing, then violence might. They disconnect, withdraw, concentrate on individual and family problems. No thoughtful consideration of those possibilities would allow them to develop further without considering alternatives.

Several substantive problems ought to be mentioned, though clearly we need to bring expertise to bear in each instance and engage in widespread and informed airing out of issues. All these issues cross through the various sectors of the "marble cake" Morton Grodzins described and reflect the degree to which our local, state, and national problems now melt into one another in ways that the drafters of the Constitution could not have imagined. They also demonstrate the degree to which Americans have been insensitive to the care of their political life and their apparent intent—or the unwillingness of their leadership to propose alternatives—to enter the twenty-first century with the Union's structure still in place. This, in spite of conditions and problems that bear little resemblance to those of the 1780s. Apparently, we have forgotten Jefferson's warning—hardly original, since every child and adult can figure this out—that you cannot make a man wear the same clothes he wore as a boy. If the clothes still fit, they look wrong. But since they don't fit, he looks ridiculous. We are willing, however, to permit our political life to look equally ridiculous.

The first of these concerns is the dream that Thomas Jefferson almost succeeded in having adopted as national policy: providing an education for everyone. He failed, and the current system is in trouble.

Universal education too often fails to train students in history and literature, mathematics and geography. But that is not all. Schools are not merely purveyors of "knowledge" but also models for the community and therefore of citizenship. They are not the source of plurality, which is a given in this or any other society, but places within which youngsters learn to live with the facts of plurality. From the beginning they have been mixing or melting pots where children learned to deal with people who are "different." That fundamental civics lesson has been allowed to lapse. The high schools, originally designed to acculturate immigrant children, have become a nightmare of stopgap measures to keep youngsters busy and, in some instances, to prepare them for college or university.

The college and university scene is little better. Differences between the majority of colleges and universities and the smaller percentage of prestigious schools are rarely acknowledged. "Higher education" is discussed as a single unit, and curriculum coherence, mission, and cultural literacy are seen as universals indistinguishable from place to place with few allowances made for the singularities and differences among them and the varying populations they serve. Faculties at schools that admit virtually non-literate students are hard-pressed to live up to the demands made on them. The large college and university systems such as California's—the California State University alone registers 360 thousand students on twenty campuses, and this excludes the more prestigious university system and junior and community college systems, which are enormous—spend considerable time on general education requirements, partly because of the failings of high schools, and they refuse to acknowledge that they are training grounds for those who are going to do the bulk of the skilled technological work of the future. Faculties seem uninspired by a remarkable mission—offering a college education to minority students whose parents barely speak English—and look for inspiration to the institutions from which they received doctorates. This produces conflict between those obsessed with Ivy League and university "higher learning" and those who stress training and skill development as the first order of business. A related struggle has to do with job preparation versus general education. Meanwhile, non-teaching positions multiply aimlessly while student-faculty ratios swell.

There is almost complete indifference to the political role of colleges, using "political" in its broadest sense. The nation's universities, independent or public, are themselves communities and "fit" the communities they serve. This is aside from their mission as training, teaching, and research institutions. The civic function of universities ought to be revived and the young converted from civic illiteracy to citizenship. If we have chosen democracy as the preferred system of governance, ought it not be self-evident that a bachelor's degree includes preparation for citizenship and community participation?

American political parties are an additional national problem with state and local implications. Though unmentioned in the Constitution, they have been the vehicles that energized the electoral and therefore the political system. They present candidates who reflect historical alliances and shifting points of view in the society. But contemporary celebration of voter independence and non-partisanship reinforces indifference to the general interest and in its place substitutes concentration on single issues attuned to self-interest. Without coherent political parties and their loyal supporters, the electorate becomes increasingly volatile, and politicians read opinion polls nightly to find out what they are supposed to believe in.

Electoral reform would also help. We spend too much time electing a president, and the excuse that this is a large country no longer has any meaning. We should allow no more than six weeks for primaries, conducting them regionally and seriatim, rotating the order in which regions vote every four years. Conventions should be confined to the two weeks following the conclusion of the regionals. The election itself should take place six weeks later. Both of our current parties and any third or fourth party that establishes itself should be given air time to present candidates and analyses of issues. Since television stations are publicly licensed, they should be required, during the last three weeks of the electoral period, to surrender prime-time segments to the parties—identical segments so that potential voters will either watch or be forced to rent tapes to pass the evening away. Citizens need to be educated as to the importance of these processes. National funding would be relatively inexpensive, once television stations are forced to live up to their public responsibilities, at which time control over party treasuries becomes possible. PACs, an inadvertent creation of Congress, ought to be driven out of business. What we need is discussion and dialogue, not a variation on the old saw that "money talks." Finally, efforts of television stations and networks to turn elections into circuses and manipulate them should be squashed. Political life is *res publica*, not entertainment. Precious civil rights will be better preserved by incorruptible parties, non-commercial exposure of candidates, and time given over for free-ranging criticism of what candidates are proposing—a function, one would have thought, that would already have been seized by television executives—than by outcries that broadcasters' rights to do as they will are protected by the Constitution. Television stations are licensees of the national government. It would not be a national disaster if licenses granted "in the public interest" were more often used in that spirit.

The revival of political life, of course, is not merely a quadrennial problem. As long as it, in the words of Nicholas Lemman, "is not a presence except on television[,] [p]olicemen don't walk the beat, most schools don't teach, fathers don't live at home, crime goes unpunished, ward and precinct bosses who once offered a link to the political system are disappearing, and old fashioned settlement house and social training functions [continue to wither away], then the problem cannot be surmounted.''[5] To resolve this, he suggests, we must bring together the segments of the black population, the relatively small middle class, and the huge lower class, which can only happen under conditions "successful" blacks can accept. But it will cost money, and there are other minority groups. What Lemman is saying, quite correctly, is that either we accept one another in a relationship of mutual responsibility, similar to that we have with our families, and as equals, or violence will regularly be substituted for power. People who come together resolve problems, but coming together requires a visible community. The alternatives are continued deterioration in the cities, ongoing struggles between groups, and domination of the society by unrestrained and uninformed selfishness.

In the twenty-first century, we are going to face a public realm or political life dramatically different from anything the world has ever seen. My argument all along has been that political life is constructed by human beings, that it is contingent to the extent that circumstances keep changing, which is the way it will always be among human beings, and that it has a degree of stability in that questions of "safety," "general welfare,""equity," and "equal standing" in the horizontal order called political life will remain central concerns no matter how many changes take place. But the world is changing, and the system we have developed in the United States is not capable—as I've tried to demonstrate—of dealing with the newer qualities that are clearly going to have an impact. For in the twenty-first century, we will achieve a degree of mobility never seen amongst human beings. This has to mean that the idea and fact of territoriality is going to alter. We've looked at one available metaphor—in musical language—that speaks to the creation of space and relationships without regard to territoriality. We are going to have to use it or something like it in order to grapple with the relationships that develop in a highly mobile world. Similarly, we will communicate not by direct face-to-face discourse but over the airwaves, using the astonishing electronic equipment already in hand and yet to come. Those communications are going to revolutionize many activities, including old-fashioned, hands-on medicine. We will have to develop ways of politicking consistent with this newer way of being together. Finally, we have to provide fundamental services as our technology makes possible a healthier and longer human existence and attempts to reverse the negative effects of the careless industrializing societies of the past and present. That will demand not less understanding and cooperation but still more. It will demand a greater understanding of power. And since everything in the horizontal order will be pulling us more firmly together, in the sense of equalizing our situations and prospects, we will have to be ever more vigilant in the face of those who, inevitably, will seek special advantages for themselves and who are constantly on the alert for opportunities to control others. And that again requires a deepened understanding of power and its opposite, violence. The twenty-first century, in sum, will not eliminate the need for the political imperative and for public space because the economic and technological order promises to grow ever more resourceful and inspired by novelty. On the contrary, more than ever we will need the security, the comfort, and mutuality it provides us.

But that should pose no problem if we put our minds to it, since, in truth, there is nothing new or surprising about people's awareness of public and civic responsibilities. "Ordinary" people in their daily rounds usually behave in a manner consistent with old-fashioned notions of civility provided they are not forced by unhappy circumstances or miseducation into a war of each against all. At times this everyday civility is no match for violence or disorder as "news." But it is always present, a resource available for tapping, a testimonial to the understanding that in addition to food, goods, housing, and affection, there is also a place for the political imperative and for the games of rules it entails. What we are now witnessing is people's loss of faith in the current system's execution and management of its responsibilities; they have not lost their capacity either to work together or to change.

Were this nation, while its strengths were still almost universally envied, to overhaul its "politics" and "political life," it would be as if a newborn child had simultaneously been delivered to every household. We would find ourselves bonded together by the process itself—initiators, cofounders, and creators of a transformation of the world that, according to democratic convictions, is ours to make and unmake. The belief that matters must and can be taken in hand would itself become a "new" metaphor, a metaphor for possibility. We would recall that those who rebuild a house are as much creators and founders as those who first conceived and constructed it and that in the life of every house there comes a time when creative reconstruction is necessary. In the public house called the United States of America, this is one of those times.

NOTES

1. Sidney Fine, *Laissez-Faire and the General Welfare State* (Ann Arbor, Mich.: University of Michigan Press, 1956), p. vii, quoted by Joel B. Grossman and Richard S. Wells, *Constitutional Law and Judicial Policy Making*, 2d edition (New York: Longman, 1980), p. 320.

2. Robert Heilbronner, "Reflections: The Triumph of Capitalism," *The New Yorker*, 23 January 1989.

3. See Morton Grodzins, ed., *Goals for Americans: The Report of the President's Commission on National Goals*, pp. 265–82. Also reprinted in Peter Woll, *American Government: Readings and Cases* (Glenview, Ill.: Scott/Foresman, 1990), pp. 110–16.

4. See Lawrence J. Herson and John M. Holland, *The Urban Web: Politics, Policy, and Theory* (Chicago: Nelson-Hall Publishers, 1990), pp. 332–33, who demonstrate that 65 percent of Northern cities have fee-to-tax ratios of less than .35; in other words, they tend to use taxes to provide general services rather than charge user fees. New York City's ratio in 1986 was .185, among the lowest in the nation. However, it is the case, as mentioned in the text, that New York City more than any other city currently depends on user revenue to pay for buses and subway trains. With the fare increase to $1.25, effective 1 January 1992, the percentage is in the neighborhood of 55, according to the *New York Times*, 31 December 1991, p. B1, compared to 31 percent in Boston, 51 in Washington, and 35 in Atlanta.

5. Nicholas Lemman, "Notes: Healing the Ghettoes," *The Atlantic*, vol. 267, no. 3, March 1991.

Appendix A
Interest Groups

My classification of interests groups need concern only those who think it useful for analysis of their role in the political process.

The general term "interest group" refers to a group linked together by characteristics and/or attitudes *and* who become active in the political process in response to issues and/or problems. Interest groups, however, are of different types. Some have a short life span; they appear temporarily in reaction to a particular issue or circumstance or problem, for example, an anti-tax group or a "right-to-life" network. Or they may be reasonably permanent, organized to deal with recurring issues or questions. Examples include the innumerable Tax Payers Associations in the United States or Reform Committees that once regularly appeared as part of our municipal and state politics. They may be permanent associations—the American Bar Association (ABA), the American Medical Association (AMA)—originally organized for professional purposes but often operating as pressure groups or lobbies that access courts, legislatures, executives, and governmental as well as non-governmental agencies in order to protect their "interests." The original activity that bound them together was professional, as in the cases of these lawyers' and doctors' associations. But they have become enmeshed in politicking and rule making: The ABA and AMA have won direct political control within their areas of specialty. The ABA sets up bar examinations and law school standards and "clears" judges for bench appointments, up to and including the U.S. Supreme Court. The AMA in effect controls hospitals—and through them the practices of doctors—and it has been the primary force controlling both medical schools and admission to practice.

It turns out, and this is a complication to which Arthur Bentley paid little attention in his *Process of Government*, that after a group organizes, the organization develops leaders, directors, managers, and bureaucrats, and in line with Roberto Michels' "iron law of oligarchy," a hierarchy, and the hierarchy develops interests distinct from those that first inspired the membership to form the organization. They have a full-time, vested interest in the group's organizational apparatus, where the membership's concern with the group's politicking is less pressing. A full study of any particular group's role in the political process would require some separate consideration of the officialdom or permanent cadre and the membership at large.

There are also interest groups that explode suddenly into the public arena, responding to and focusing attention on a particular political issue, and yet have no significant, certainly no permanent, organization. This has become a more likely phenomenon in the age of the communications network—a creation of modern technology. In California, for example, a group appeared that objected to a series of decisions by the State Supreme Judicial Court concerning individuals found guilty of murder—the court had in instance after instance found procedural reasons for setting aside the death penalty. Spurred on by newspaper reports of court decisions and by a handful of citizens, a group surfaced, rapidly became a statewide force, developed very informal organizational paraphernalia, and succeeded in removing from office three members of the state's highest court in an election campaign marked by heavy spending in the media. Groups of this kind have about them an air of urgency or crisis—in California an unknowing observer might have concluded that the state's highest court was embarked on a campaign to turn killers loose on an innocent and, until then, unsuspecting population. Although short-lived, these groups can have profound effects on political decision making.

These variations suggest that "types" of groups ought to be distinguished. The following attempts to do so.

1. *Interest group* (general definition): A group of persons linked together by characteristics and/or attitudes who, in response to issues or problems, become active in the political process.

2. *Potential interest group:* People linked together by a similar characteristic that they share, for example, "the group of Americans sixty-five years of age or older." The characteristic is measurable or discoverable and is here labeled "potential" because the identified "group" is not as such necessarily active in the political process. Thus, Americans who have blond hair could be called a potential interest group, inactive in the political process unless and until some crazy comes along and makes hair color an issue. (This example is not farfetched: the pages of American history are filled with instances in which people of dark skin color and hair have been regarded as less than worthy immigrants or even citizens.)

3. *Potential opinion group:* People who share an attitude respecting a particular issue, for example, supporting or opposing "the right to life"

or "choice." This group's size can be estimated by survey research or polling techniques, or its "members" may reveal themselves when votes are cast. In recent elections, narrowly won by African American candidates for office in Virginia and New York City and lost by an avowedly racist candidate in Louisiana, a large group of voters were guided by their conviction that they preferred white officeholders. Of course, once such people cast votes, they are no longer a "potential" group but have, however briefly, been activated and therefore involved in the political process.

4. *Pressure group:* A permanently organized interest group. Examples abound: National Association for the Advancement of Colored People (NAACP); National Association of Manufacturers (NAM); the American Federation of Labor–Congress of Industrial Organizations (AFL-CIO); the National Rifle Association (NRA); the American Farm Bureau Federation (AFBF), and so on, and so on. So-called public-interest groups such as Common Cause or the Clamshell Alliance also fall into this category. The word "permanent" is, of course, something of an exaggeration, but many of these organizations have a long history.

5. *Unorganized interest grouping:* Any interest group not formally organized but activated in the political process. In the past fifty years, large numbers of individuals have been involved or regard themselves as deeply concerned with issues without at the same time involving themselves in any formal organizations. Questions have included the right to an abortion, the rights of fetuses, the rights of women, the rights of minorities, the right to burn flags or to punish those who do so, the rights of homosexuals, the right to prevent building or use of nuclear power plants, the need to restore "the balance of nature," the presence of drugs in the schools and on the streets, the presence of communists in and out of the government, and the presence of objectionable books in the library. In any instance, there may well be pressure groups (organized interest groups) that concern themselves with the issue in question; indeed, in some instances pressure groups have appeared as a result of persistent and widespread concern about a perceived problem, whether "real" or not. Non-joiners may express opinions to friends, write letters to newspapers, and sign petitions and vote accordingly. The issues may have serious consequences for the society's quality of life or may appear silly to outside observers (a flap in Illinois over whether the University of Illinois' mascot will continue to be a Native American) but may have a major impact on the political process or politicians who wind up on the wrong side of the barricades.

Lack of formal organization or their ephemeral character appears to handicap unorganized interest groupings, but numbers often work to their advantage. They usually expose deeply felt concerns that sweep through the entire population—again, the communications revolution has speeded up and intensified these waves of opinion—and they usually produce some kind of response by political agencies and personalities. Whenever such groupings appear to be present, a governmental response is likely. The depression produced a grouping generally favorable to the presidency of Franklin Delano Roosevelt and even with erosion of support won him four terms in office and a unique place in American history. But the programmatic input is of greater consequence. Because of this deep and widespread "unorganized" support, Franklin Delano Roosevelt was able to exercise leadership in ways that have rarely been seen since his time. Other examples of such groupings include the political response to the alleged presence of subversives and communists in positions of importance—this occurring in the 1920s, 1940s, and 1950s; the anti-war groupings that helped produce a negative climate respecting U.S. involvement in Vietnam in the 1960s; the civil rights movements during the same time period, which ultimately produced strenuous efforts to change the status of African Americans and also encouraged founding of the women's and gay rights movements; and the wave of patriotism and pro-war sentiment during the Persian Gulf War against Iraq. Since electoral politics is important in a society such as the United States, lack of organization should not be automatically regarded as a guarantee that widely expressed sentiments will have no effect politically. In the age of communications, the prospects seem quite the opposite—instantaneous pressures for political action unchecked either by institutional barriers or the time delays that allow for reflection. Unorganized interest groupings may well be the instant replays of contemporary U.S. politics, as in the recent reversal of Congress' decision to raise its own salaries along with those of judges.

6. *Sponsored pressure group:* This is a new type of interest group that must be taken into account, possibly a sub-division of what we called a pressure group (a permanently organized interest group), yet a unique product of the last decade or so. These sponsored pressure groups are commonly known as political action committees (PACs). They differ from the historical pressure group in that they did not develop "naturally" in response to changing issues, that is, as the result of some interest that became organized, but are political arms of successful, ongoing economic organizations. For example, labor unions thrust themselves into political activity to establish and protect the right to organize and still later to pressure Congress, presidents, state governments, and so on, for support of what they had already won in labor wars and then shifted their attention to political action in direct support of selected issues and candidates. Such committees and groups had long since played a role in U.S. politics on behalf of professional groups (doctors, lawyers, educators, architects, writers, and so on). Doctors took up political action once their organizations stabilized and they realized the importance of the tight

connection between the political order (control of licensing, subsidies for education, hospital construction, and civil suits) and their economic well-being. In 1974, in an attempt to regulate the activities of groups associated with corporations, Congress, with the approval of the president, amended the Federal Campaign Election Act and inadvertently opened the door to an explosion in the number of pressure groups. As a result of the amendments, the Federal Election Commission ruled that corporations could solicit money from stockholders and employees to support PACs. By 1982 PACs were giving over $80 million a year, largely to incumbent congressmen and senators—which helps explain the increasing tendency of members of both parties to retain their seats.[1] There are PACs of every kind and description representing unions, corporations, what have you. Inevitably, some have names that prove our sense of humor is intact: NUTPAC represents the nutgrowers and packers, SIXPAC the beer distributors. Incumbents, as indicated, are the darlings of these groups; thus very conservative PACs have seen no inconsistency in supporting a liberal, Dan Rostenkowski, the long-time Democratic House Ways and Means Committee chairman, a position whose holder has much to say about who pays what taxes. And there are always instances of suspicious conduct. Senatorial connections to Lincoln Savings and Loan of California are an example; they produced understandable embarrassment over the relations between free-spending lobbyists and PACs and members of the U.S. Congress. The problem of controlling these organizations' tactics as well as the cooperation between them and holders of pubic offices results from a change in tactics: direct bribery and tinkering with the laws are largely a thing of the past. Now senators, congressmen, and high-ranking executive officials are asked, in exchange for "campaign contributions," to press governmental agencies to act or slow down. And the contributions are legal. The National Association of Automobile Dealers spent $1,035,000 in 1980, the fourth most generous PAC that year, and shortly thereafter legislation passed, signed by the president, permitting modifications in the then-new sticker requirements that were supposed to protect car buyers from sharp practices. The top five spenders in 1983–84 were the National Conservative Political Action Committee (more than $19 million), the Fund for a Conservative Majority (over $5 million), National Congressional Club (over $5 million), Realtors Political Action Committee (more than $3 million), and National Rifle Association Political Victory Fund (over $3 million). The top five corporate money raisers were Amoco PAC ($650,000), Bears Stearn & Company PAC ($585,000), Civic Involvement Program, General Motors ($556,000), Tenneco Employees Good Government Fund ($547,000), and Lockheed Political Action Committee ($511,000). Not to be outdone, the top five labor PAC money raisers were National Education Association PAC (over $2,498,000), UAW Voluntary Community Action Program ($2,136,000),

Machinists Non-Partisan Political League ($1,849,000), Democratic Republican Independent Voter Education Committee ($1,826,000), Active Ballot Club, United Food & Commercial Workers ($1,748,000). The top five trade/membership/health PAC money raisers: Realtors Political Action Committee ($4,291,572), AMA PAC ($4,032,000), National Rifle Association Political Victory Fund ($3,331,000), League of Conservation Voters ($1,768,000), BUILD PAC (National Association of Home Builders) ($1,767,000).[2] These groups, transparently, do not fit into Bentley's original model but are the direct result of what happens in politics after analysis reveals the way things work. In this case, the interest-group theory itself, having exposed part of the truth about the system, feeds back into the system; everyone gets the idea: in order to get what you want, you must have a lobbyist in Washington. When legislation seeking to curb some of these activities by registering them and making them public went awry, the result was the wholesale descent on Washington and the state capitals of lobbying buzzards who, by spreading election donations around irrespective of party, can make allies of congressmen, since these days congressmen and even some state legislators must spend a fortune to retain their seats.

NOTES

1. See Jeffrey M. Berry, *The Interest Group Society* (Boston: Little, Brown and Company, 1984), Chapter 8.

2. Source: Federal Election Commission Release, 19 May 1985.

Appendix B

Hannah Arendt's Metaphor: The "Normal" Field or Plain of Human Affairs

Hannah Arendt's works create a metaphor that can be interpreted as a kind of political topology. This "topology" envisions a human world laid out into bounded spaces or separations, for example, between "self" and "others" or "the public" and "the private." But "separation" does not mean to be totally apart from something else. Without others, there can be no self. Without a public space, there can be no privacy. Furthermore, the border between the self and others is the same line that divides the private from the public. Ultimately, each self may be seen as appearing among others in what she calls the "space of appearance." All such spaces are "political," and they are vital to the existence both of each "self" and of larger groupings of humans. The imagery she employs to describe this normal plain or field can be illustrated by the following three *samples* of her work.

THE "SELF" CAN BE MEANINGFULLY IDENTIFIED ONLY IN THE PRESENCE OF OTHERS

"Appearance . . . constitutes reality," Arendt asserts.[1] What does that mean? First of all, our senses operate in such a way that they register impressions that prompt us to say, "I hear X," "I see Y." But only the presence of others to bear witness to what we see and hear confirms the existence of that something and of ourselves. This is not an argument that when I feel something, it is "unreal" in the absence of witnesses; that would be silly as well as untrue. It is an argument that *from the point of view of the world* nothing intimate, no passion, thought, or delight can be fully validated without witnesses, even though common sense tells me that when I am alone and no one is present as witness, I can cut myself and even bleed to death. What Arendt means is that confirmation, insofar as I live in a world populated by others, is provided by those others who share sights and sounds with me. But, of course, such confirmations do not apply to everything. I cannot draw from anyone as certain a proof of the fierceness of my toothache, however much I moan in apparent pain, as I can of the fact "we" are sitting in a room or in a field gazing at something that has caught our attention. Even though the pain of a toothache is a common and therefore "shareable" experience, others' pain cannot be directly felt. We can empathize or sympathize, but we cannot literally feel others' pain or their experiences; we share in that "we" are present. Arendt's point is that only what appears, that is, what occupies what she calls a "space of appearance" with others, can be fully shared. (Perhaps art represents this indirectly shareable pain in such a way as to bring the viewer of, say, Picasso's *Guernica*, as close as possible to full empathy with the horror by "representing" the resulting complex of emotions so that the viewer "feels" the pain. And perhaps linguistic metaphors likewise induce "understanding" or similar feeling respecting a phenomenon about which direct expression otherwise seems ineffectual.)

Appearance, accordingly, makes my existence dependent not on some essence, some primary material that undergirds and accounts for my humanness, but on testimony. Self-awareness is insufficient: pinching myself will prove something, but not enough; others, in whose presence I appear, are crucial. Furthermore, this reality (appearance or being able to appear) depends on some means through which the "we" functions. This is the space of appearance or public space. "Our feeling for reality depends utterly upon appearance and therefore upon the existence of a public realm into which things can appear."[2] What if the public realm is weakened, as is apparently the case in the United States, or is radically altered, as in Stalinist or Nazi totalitarianism? Then, according to her, the boundaries between the private and the public change to the point where the basis for our understanding of the world is threatened. The private and the public are like sides of a coin or contiguous seasons—winter and spring, spring and summer, summer and fall, fall and winter. There is a rhythm and "rightness" in their contrasts and relationships; they appropriately or "correctly" succeed one another. Likewise, an individual *appears* in public from a private place that shielded him or her from being seen or, conversely, *leaves* the public realm to return to privacy. The two—the hidden and the visible—fit together, make each other meaningful, seem to be necessary to one another, yet are distinctive and separate. Each is, with respect to the other, a boundary. Privacy ends when one appears in public; publicity ends when one "disappears" into the private sphere. But totalitarianism and bureaucracy blur this distinction.

Totalitarianism blends together the public and the private. Bureaucracy, concerned with regulations, rules, and precedents, tends to overlook the presence of persons; to appear before a bureau officer is to be in the presence of someone who sees humans as exemplifications of categories. In other words, private persons disappear. In totalitarianism there is no surviving private human being. In liberal democracy, in contrast, with its neglect of, indifference to, or hostility to things political, the well-being of individuals and their presumed right to pursue their goals with as little restraint as can be tolerated and still maintain some kind of order, the public or political realm becomes less and less consequential. The result is that the far preferable liberal democracy, if it permits "private man" to replace "public man," also threatens the balance between what is "legitimately" private and "legitimately" public.

There are other consequences. The sense of common humanness, if there can be such a thing, depends on the presence of others and the realization of the connections among humans. Looked at through Arendt's lenses, reality, which is to say, appearance, is primarily a "political" phenomenon because from the world's point of view it is dependent on the presence of others and the existence of relationships, however secondary, with them. It follows that the "self," an entity requiring confirmation of its place by others, cannot be certain of its identity or existence in the absence of polity or "space of appearance," by whatever name it is known. Furthermore, if the space of appearance no longer has the original meaning she ascribes to it, the boundary between the public and private realm has disappeared.

Arendt's final book retains this view. *"Being and Appearing coincide.* . . . Nothing and nobody exists in this world whose very being does not presuppose a *spectator*. In other words, nothing that is, insofar as it appears, exists in the singular; everything that is is meant to be perceived by somebody."[3] Furthermore, "no discourse . . . using established rules to draw conclusions from accepted premises . . . can ever match the simple unquestioned and unquestionable certainty of visible evidence. 'What is it that appears there? It is a man.'"[4]

The space of appearance is the common ground, that is, ground we create, upon which we make our appearance. It is our reality, not nature's construct like a beehive, but ours—though it may be in our "nature," since we require one another. We create a space of appearance or lose the possibility of being seen, of evidence respecting one another and even confirmation of our humanness. This space, like the institutions and organizations with which we fill it, are of our design. They are our handiwork and responsibility.

MEANINGLESS ACTIVITIES AND PROCESSES

Arendt suspects that humans caught up in highly energized economic and societal processes get swept up in them and lose control both of the capacity to choose and of events. Processes themselves, rather than the substantive changes they are supposed to bring about, become all-important. Discussing Cecil Rhodes' imperialistic dreams for Britain, she comments, "No matter what individual qualities or defects a man may have, once he entered the maelstrom of an unending process of expansion, he will, as it were, *cease to be what he was and obey the laws of the process.*"[5]

He has lost the individual and unique substantiality of his own contribution: he will think of himself as a mere function of the process.[6] He will also think himself, as Rhodes did, incapable of wrongdoing, since he merely serves the laws of expansion and the dynamics of history. He is no longer responsible for but merely the instrument of some "higher" historical purpose or market process. Years later she sees a similar tendency in the conduct of Adolf Eichmann. Eichmann quickly loses or puts aside his conscience and makes himself over into a functionary of the process through which Nazism is rearranging the population, namely, eliminating "undesirable" groups of humans. The formidable boundary that conscience draws across each individual's path, when it says, "you must not cross this line," when it engages us at critical times and forces a rethinking of what we are about to do, vanishes. When that happens, no internal restraint exists. The unthinkable becomes the doable, and Eichmann, with others, simply executes orders said to be consistent with the higher processes of history as interpreted by leaders.[7]

A similar image shapes her discussion of laboring. A man, considered as a laboring being, *animal laborans,* is entirely caught up in the biological process that keeps him fit to function; he "is ejected from [the world] insofar as he is imprisoned in the privacy of his own body, caught in the fulfillment of needs which nobody can share and which nobody can fully communicate."[8] Absent slaves, laborers are continuously subject to the process of expending energy and rejuvenating themselves—they labor, consume, and rest. No other activity, however, would be possible if humans were required to spend every minute laboring; to ward off that possibility the ancients and a number of antebellum Americans conceived of slavery as a means for preventing this "necessary" time-consuming cycle from interfering with their "more important" or significant activities.

Arendt argues that to eliminate or escape from the effort and pain of laboring is to threaten human vitality. The Boers, who "treated the natives as raw material and lived on them as one might live on the fruits of wild trees,"[9] became unproductive and parasitic, ultimately victims of the style of life and racism they concocted to justify the violence done to the native population. In her terms, by abandoning labor as an element in a human life, they lost a sense of the proper order and place of things. Furthermore, to sustain racial exploitation and enslavement of others, they were forced to make racism and apartheid the hallmarks of their society. In time that meant the substitution of race for nationality, and bureaucracy for government.[10] Productivity was shifted to others' backs; with it, Arendt believed, went judgment. When life becomes "easy" (as for a "master class"), vitality and the joy of living disappear; with them go attempts to overcome the futility that is inherent in the process of laboring.[11]

COLLAPSING BOUNDARIES AND POLITICS

Action, according to Arendt, is not possible in isolation. The word refers to the human capacity to unleash a chain of events—deeds and/or words themselves, reactions, counter-actions. To act means to initiate change, to do something in the presence of others, to cut or drive through and alter current arrangements or patterns. Since action takes place within an already-existent web of relationships, the chain of responses has both unpredictable and potentially boundaryless outcomes. By their deeds and words humans interrupt pre-existent patterns and relations and thereby disturb, redirect, and rearrange human affairs. To take action is *ipso facto* a mode of altering the human world; it is to begin something, to initiate, to transform. And since every action precipitates a response that stimulates another response, we can speak of action in and of itself as producing continuous, unpredictable consequences, and therefore as un-bounded, without a terminal point. Since action's outcomes are unpredictable—I initiate something, which in turn produces certain other actions, which produce still others, the process having no definite conclusion except possibly for individuals who when the first act was done were not present—action is the initiation of a string or sequence of events.

Boundaries—fences, border checkpoints, territorial demarcations, laws, rules, moral imperatives, consciences (if operating)—check, or dam up, or put a stop to, this flow of events. Without them, human affairs would be in a total flux. For example, the new beginnings Arendt celebrates in her use of the term "natality" would turn the world into an eerie nightmare of unrecognizable newness were the process not checked. Politics is one boundary, one effort to contain or bottle up action and keep what humans initiate from continuing forward endlessly in a perpetual series of reactions. While each action presumably has some purpose, the unintended consequences, indeed, the complications, appear to be limitless and unpredictable. The process set in motion seems unstoppable, and the web of relationships affected is potentially so enormous and complex that "he who acts never quite knows what he is doing, [and therefore] always becomes 'guilty' of consequences he never intended."[12] Authorship of action is therefore often, in effect if not in fact, anonymous.

Humans learn to cope with this boundlessness and lack of authorship in various ways (among them forgiving, forgetting, and promising or contracting).[13] Contracting, reinforced by the presence of a sovereign or governing entity as final arbiter, provides humans with the possibility of controlling unchecked chain reactions. The polity, which stands behind contracts and provides a more or less neutral authority to ensure their execution, protects human beings from the oppressiveness of too many unwanted consequences of actions. Humans make promises through contracts and that writes *finis* to certain kind of actions. Simultaneously, the polity is a more or less "safe" arena for the miraculous capacity to begin something new in that it exists to keep action from initiating a full-fledged chain reaction whose consequences cannot be controlled and whose origin, if reactions continue indefinitely, will be forgotten. That is, politics provides the space in which actions can be responsibly controlled even as it depends on the capacity to transform, to begin something new. It is therefore quite specifically a space designed for action, for "absorption" of and fulfillment of the consequences of natality. "Men, though they must die, are not born in order to die but in order to begin. . . . The miracle that saves the world, the realm of human affairs, from its normal 'natural' ruin is ultimately the fact of natality, in which the faculty of action is ontologically rooted."[14] That is, action is the means whereby humans transform their world, and the political realm is the place within which they attempt to work out those transformations. Furthermore, though politics does not encompass "the whole of man's and the world's existence," it provides the arena within which humans learn to work together, that is, where deeds and words are evaluated, where "we are free to alter and to change"—but only for as long as it can maintain its "integrity and [keep] its promises." This "integrity," however, requires the polity to stay within the terms of its agreed-upon assignments; it is an empowered, not a natural or divinely authored, entity and therefore is bounded by the terms of the empowerment. These days "the people" in Western or Western-influenced societies are usually regarded as empowerers, the source of support and of disapproval. When the polity extends beyond or fails to carry out its responsibilities, falling victim to special interests and the narrow concerns of elites, parties, or pressure groups, or into the hands of criminals who manipulate its enforcing rights for other than public or general purposes, then the polity is no longer as intended. It becomes capable of anything, including horrors such as the Holocaust or "unusual" covert or unauthorized wars, since it is not contained within designated boundaries and no longer represents the public space-making entity that Arendt thinks political entities have always been. It has evolved into something "new under the sun." So she regarded the totalitarian regimes of the twentieth century. So, one suspects, she would regard government by extra-legal means in any guise. Such governments become polities in name only, and they conduct their affairs so that those who hold positions of rulership no longer recognize previously agreed-upon limits. By that time, the polity may be said to have forsaken its proper sphere of control, which has to do with the public business and public affairs.[15] Hers is not, incidentally, an argument for a never-changing definition of politics nor a conservative call for a state that ought to abandon activities she regards as improper. It is, however, an insistent claim that there are proper and legitimate public activities but also activities that bypass the polity's legitimate, that is, previously assigned, turf. In such instances, she has become suspicious that the government is now acting not as public agent but as the representative of a special group, interest, elite, or maniacal ideology.

Given these three examples of her imagery, we can work out the general shape of the "field" or "plain" of human affairs as Arendt conceived it. It is marked, first of all, by the imperatives of labor, work, action, and thought as well as those entailed by "mental" activities, thinking, willing, and judging.[16] This plain or field is divided or sectored and constantly being rearranged by humans so that their activities (labor, work, action, and thought) each take place within sectors surrounded, metaphorically speaking, by limitations, which we may call canals, dikes, or ravines. These serve as boundaries as well as generously proportioned containers or moats that permit some spillage and alteration. No damage is done by "overflows," alterations in the current shapes or patterns, because it is understood that change in the landscape is consistent with the birth of new humans. The purpose of the canals, dikes, and ravines is to prevent not changes but excesses, and, of course, what is or is not excessive is a matter for discussion and judgment. The channels and ravines must be deep enough, the dikes strong enough, to prevent too much spillage lest the humanly constructed world lose all continuity and recognizability. Human activity, accordingly, should avoid too much or too little change, too flexible or too rigid boundaries. And so the boundaries—the retaining walls or channels—permit and encourage newness and preservation. If restrictions are too formidable, human affairs will be endlessly repetitive like the "affairs" or, more accurately, the behavior of insects. On the other hand, should constraints disappear altogether, placelessness and rootlessness will disorient human beings and confuse their affairs, making them entirely unpredictable and subject to whimsical shifts and changes.

These canals or boundaries also constitute a network. Each of the visible, relational activities—labor, work, action, "thought"—and "mental" activities—thinking, willing, judging—has consequences for the "health" or ongoing success of the others. Human works—buildings, paintings,

machines—though they may outlast their designers and builders, are subject to the ravages of nature. Labor is required to build them, not only
to construct them initially but also to protect them when complete. Here
the public realm is important and directs that energy be used to preserve
them; it also provides the arena within which they are remembered or
recalled, if they have been abandoned. To do that the political realm must
regard them as worth salvaging. When civilizations sink beneath the surface of the earth, what disappears along with the buildings, roads, and
aqueducts are the memories of the words and deeds important to that
entity, literally, the history of the civilization. As long as the polity exists, constituting the appropriate space, remembrance and "stories" (or
history) remain possible. Great deeds and significant words as well as
their meanings are entrusted to the common or public space. Without
that common and connecting entity, no shared need to remember can
survive. Similarly, the relational and mental activities interlock, and the
"mental" network has its own internal connections—for example, thinking is a precursor for willing and judging, although it is an uncontrolled
"normal" activity that exists in its own right.

This gestalt-like metaphoric field or plain, whether or not I have yet
found a way to describe it adequately, makes possible a better understanding of her work. The topology that serves as metaphor for the human
condition, the notion that the human world is a spatial manifold within
which boundaries are erected for the "proper" carrying on of human
affairs, seems to me to have been erected precisely in response to destructive novelties that had such an enormous impact during her lifetime.
Nazis, Stalinists, bureaucrats, and others, hacking mindlessly at the landscape, displacing, dominating, directing, and destroying people, suggested the possible or imminent collapse of civilization. Furthermore,
among intellectuals, a cultural relativism was pervasive that denied the
possibility of judging any of these actions by a fixed and permanent standard. To respond to this state of affairs, Arendt looked not to Plato's "sky
of Ideas," an ancient metaphor designed to emphasize the potential for
fixity even in a sensory world necessarily influenced by flux and uncer-
tainty, but literally to the ground and space where people appear and
learn to deal with one another. Did human arrangements depend upon
some principles or rules of existence that, while not fixed or eternal, as
older systems of metaphysics might insist, could, if understood, prevent
the destruction of civil society and its replacement by savage and ultimately self-destructive conduct and turbulence or repressions? Her answer
took the form of attempting to assess what she called "the space of appearance," the political setting, and link its existence to the topological
metaphor.

The metaphor also permitted her to question the widely held view,
rooted again in older systems of metaphysics, that "invisible" laws govern

the human universe and demand obedience. The danger in such beliefs is the implication that human judgment counts for little and that human responsibility may be waived away in the face of all-encompassing universals. And this has lessons for those who wish to avoid the realm of metaphysics. It may seem pretentious to take note of this critique of metaphysics, but the claims made in daily newspapers or by justices of the Supreme Court that natural laws govern the marketplace or constitute a viable category in legal interpretation ought to serve as warning that such ideas are not only available for use but also—so it seems—extremely malleable even though at first glance they seem as rigid or fixed as Plato's Ideas.

Against this view, Arendt argued that what was visible, what is on the surface, what I have called the topology laid out in her metaphor or "frozen analogy," is not a secondary phenomenon.[17] On her account, no underlying reality transcends in value or importance what appears to us in the constitution of a space of appearance.

The spatial, topological metaphor appears regularly in her writing. In a letter dated July 24, 1963, written privately in response to an attack on her book *Eichmann in Jerusalem,* she writes:

You are quite right: I changed my mind and do no longer speak of "radical evil." . . . Evil is never "radical," . . . it is only extreme, and . . . it possesses neither depth nor demonic dimension. It can overgrow and lay waste the whole world precisely because it spreads like a fungus on the surface. It is "thought defying" . . . because thought tries to go to the roots and the moment it concerns itself with evil, it is frustrated because there is nothing. That is its "banality." Only the good has depth and can be radical.[18]

Likewise, the metaphor provided Arendt with an answer to those who believed a nation's policies could never be judged except in terms of its own conception of self-interest. She insisted that we have the right and obligation to judge the conduct of nations as well as individual acts. Without judgment, without application of standards to what human beings do in the world of affairs, our very humanity will be threatened. Accordingly, in the epilogue of *Eichmann in Jerusalem* she offers a judgment against Eichmann that might have been written from the bench:

And just as you supported and carried out a policy of not wanting to share the earth with the Jewish people and the people of a number of other nations—as though you and your superiors had any right to determine who should and should not inhabit the world—we find that no one, that is, no member of the human race, can be expected to want to share the earth with you. This is the reason, and the only reason, you must hang.[19]

The idea of sharing the only earth humans have been given to build the world, their civilization, is at the heart of Arendt's topological metaphor. An aspect of that building effort that must be dealt with is the simple fact that humans are divided—because they see certain distinctions as consequential—into separate peoples based on categories such as race, tribe, ethnic group, and religion. These together with the given conditions on earth create three distinct but interrelated problems. First, a polity connects people by other than racial or ethnic linkages (although that was not true of the original Greek polities). Second, human ecology is exceedingly complicated and does not depend on simple or straightforward divisions—there are natural, physical boundaries and also those territorial borders humans have imposed on themselves based on appearances and accidents, that is, ethnicity, religion, race, particular territories that have been accepted as the basis for setting up national or state territories. Third, having walled themselves into units, usually regarded as ''political,'' they face another elementary human problem, getting along with one another within each polity. This interior, order-maintaining problem, also political, is serious enough to occasion repeated internal breakdowns. External relations have been even more difficult to pacify—possibly modern technology, which has made lengthy, full-scale war unacceptably costly, will at long last prevent global wars from taking place. But the underlying condition, she thought, for pacific internal or external relations is an understanding and acceptance of the boundaries that separate one ''state'' from another and that mark off the private space of each individual within each state—what is authentically private as distinct from what is public and what may represent a mixture of the two.

There is no way, according to Arendt, that either of these separations can be maintained in a world in which Eichmann and his leaders hold sway or, having carried out their deadly mission, are allowed to live. What they are guilty of is the most serious breach of an ecological truth, namely, that each person's space is sacred. ''Natality'' carries with it the right to exist free of the menace of genocide or group exterminations. The Nazis' ''crime against humanity'' consisted of actions they initiated based on the claim that they and not ''nature'' had the right to determine which persons or groups might live. That decision is permissible when the state deals with criminals. Even natural rights theory permits the state to exact a maximum penalty, life itself, for certain crimes. But no one person, no group, no nation, has the right to decide arbitrarily on the basis of culture, religion, or skin color who may not exist. To claim otherwise undermines the foundation of human co-existence. In this way, of course, Arendt does suggest that there is a natural order within the human universe.

The crime of crimes, however, is to eliminate the possibility of politics—that is, of people choosing to co-exist irrespective of cultural, racial, ethnic, or opinion differences, which amounts to destroying the spatial boundaries that make politics possible. Any group or state that refuses to permit mutuality to survive, literally the willingness to co-exist within or outside of particular man-made borders, has begun to pull down the structures that humans have determined they need in order to keep the planet habitable. To permit that is to help destroy the political understanding that makes the earth habitable. The alternative, attempted at various times in history by groups or states other than the Nazis, is the chaos that occurs when violence replaces political power.

Any person or gang that claims such rights and then carries out murderous schemes breaks through the boundaries that protect human affairs. No human anywhere on the planet is safe if agents of violence are permitted to continue, since they have destroyed barriers that, if left in place, make a civil existence both possible and bearable. In sum, no one is truly human in a situation in which the decision to eliminate groups, classes, or persons is permitted. To believe otherwise is to forfeit the capacity to act and to judge and what necessarily accompanies acting and judging, namely, the need to be judged.

NOTES

1. Hannah Arendt, *The Human Condition* (Chicago: University of Chicago Press, 1958), p. 50.

2. Ibid., p. 51.

3. Hannah Arendt, *The Life of the Mind*, vol. 1, *Thinking* (New York: Harcourt, Brace, Jovanovich, 1977), p. 19.

4. Ibid., p. 120.

5. Hannah Arendt, *The Origins of Totalitarianism* (New York: Harcourt, Brace, Jovanovich, 1966), p. 215 (emphasis added).

6. Ibid.

7. Hannah Arendt, *Eichmann in Jerusalem: A Report on the Banality of Evil* (New York: Viking Books, 1963; New York: Penguin Books, revised and enlarged edition, 1977).

8. *The Human Condition*, pp. 118-19.

9. *The Origins of Totalitarianism*, p. 197.

10. Ibid., p. 189.

11. See *The Human Condition*, p. 120.

12. Ibid., p. 233.

13. Ibid., pp. 243-44.

14. Ibid., pp. 246-47.

15. See Hannah Arendt, ''Truth and Politics,'' in *Between Past and Future: Eight Exercises in Political Thought* (New York: Viking Press, 1961), pp. 227-64.

16. Labor, work, and action are the concern of her book *The Human Condition*; thinking, willing, and judging are discussed in *The Life of the Mind*, volume one of which is entitled *Thinking*; volume two is entitled *Willing*.

17. *The Human Condition*, pp. 73–78.

18. Reprinted in Ron H. Feldman, ed., *The Jew as Pariah: Jewish Identity and Politics in the Modern Age* (New York: Grove Press, 1978), pp. 250–51, a collection consisting of letters and essays by Arendt published after her death.

19. *Eichmann in Jerusalem*, p. 279.

Selected Bibliography

BOOKS

Angell, Roger, *Five Seasons*. New York: Simon & Schuster, 1988.

Arendt, Hannah. *Between Past and Future: Eight Exercises in Political Thought*. New York: Viking Press, 1961.

Arendt, Hannah. *Eichmann in Jerusalem: A Report on the Banality of Evil*. New York: Penguin Books, 1977.

Arendt, Hannah. *On Violence*. New York: Harcourt, Brace and World, 1970.

Arendt, Hannah. *The Human Condition*. Chicago: University of Chicago Press, 1958.

Arendt, Hannah. *The Life of the Mind*. Volume 1, *Thinking*. Volume 2, *Willing*. New York: Harcourt, Brace, Jovanovich, 1977.

Arendt, Hannah. *The Origins of Totalitarianism*. New York: Harcourt, Brace, Jovanovich, 1966.

Aristotle. *Politics*. Translated by Ernest Barker. New York: Oxford University Press, 1962.

Beard, Charles. *An Economic Interpretation of the Constitution of the United States of America*. New York: Macmillan Company, 1962. (Original publication date: 1913).

Bentley, Arthur F. *The Process of Government*. New York: Harvard University Press, 1967. (Original publication date: 1908.)

Berry, Jeffrey M. *The Interest Group Society*. Boston: Little, Brown and Company, 1984.

Burch, Philip H., Jr. *Elites in American History*. 2 volumes. New York: Holmes and Meier, 1980.

Burch, Philip H., Jr. *The Managerial Revolution Reassessed: Family Control in America's Large Corporations*. Lexington, Mass.: D. C. Heath, 1972.

Culbertson, Gilbert Morris. *Political Myth and Epic*. Lansing, Mich.: Michigan State University Press, 1975.

Dewey, John, and Bentley, Arthur F. *Knowing and the Known*. Boston: Beacon Press, 1960. (Original publication date: 1949.)

DuBois, W. E. B. *The Souls of Black Folks*. New York: Signet, New American Library, 1969. (Original publication date: 1903.)

Easton, David. *A Systems Analysis of Political Life*. New York: John Wiley & Sons, 1965.

Ellison, Ralph. *Invisible Man*. New York: Vintage Books edition, 1972. (Original publication date: 1947.)

Feldman, Ron H. (ed.) *The Jew as Pariah: Jewish Identity and Politics in the Modern Age*. New York: Grove Press, 1978.

Finley, M. I. *Economy and Society in Ancient Greece*. Edited by B. D. Shaw and R. P. Saller. New York: Viking Press, 1982.

Garland, Robert. *The Greek Way of Life*. Ithaca, N.Y.: Cornell University Press, 1990.

Grossman, Joel B., and Wells, Richard S. *Constitutional Law and Judicial Policy Making*. New York: Longman, 1984.

Harman, Gabriel. *Ritualised Friendship and the Greek City*. Cambridge: Cambridge University Press, 1987.

Hayek, Frederich A. *The Constitution of Liberty*. Chicago: Henry Regnery Company, Gateway edition, 1972.

Herson, Lawrence J., and Holland, John M. *The Urban Web: Politics, Policy, and Theory*. Chicago: Nelson-Hall Publishers, 1990.

Hesse, Herman. *Demian: The Story of a Youth*. New York: Henry Holt and Company, 1948. (Original publication date: 1923.)

Hobbes, Thomas. *English Works*. Collected and Edited by Sir William Molesworth. Volume 1: *De Corpore*. Volume 2: *Philosophical Rudiments Concerning Government and Society (De Cive)*. Volume 3: *Leviathan*. Germany: Scientia Verlag Aalen, 1966. (First published in 1839: London, John Bohn.)

Ignatieff, Michael. *The Needs of Strangers*. New York: Viking Penguin "Elizabeth Sifton Books," 1986.

Kinsella, W. P. *Shoeless Joe*. New York: Ballantine Books, 1982.

Locke, John. *Second Treatise of Civil Government*. Indianapolis: Hackett Publishing Company, 1980. (Original publication date: 1690.)

Lowi, Theodore. *The End of Liberalism*. New York: W. W. Norton and Company, 1969.

MacIver, R. M. *The Web of Government*. New York: Macmillan Company, 1947.

Michels, Roberto. *Political Parties: A Sociological Study of the Oligarchical Tendencies of Modern Democracy*. New York: Dover Publications, 1959. (Original publication date: 1915.)

Miller, David (ed.) *The Blackwell Encyclopedia of Political Thought*. Oxford: Basil Blackwell, 1987.

Mills, C. Wright. *The Power Elite*. New York: Oxford University Press, Galaxy Books, 1959.

Mills, C. Wright. *The Sociological Imagination*. New York: Oxford University Press, 1959.

Minogue, Kenneth. *Alien Powers: The Pure Theory of Ideology*. New York: St. Martin's Press, 1985.

Perry, Garaint. *Political Elites*. New York: Praeger, 1969.

Plato. *Republic*. Translated by Francis MacDonald Cornford. New York: Oxford University Press, 1977.

Ritchie, David. *Natural Rights*. London: George Allen and Allen Unwin, 1894; 5th impression, 1952.

Rorty, Richard. *Contingency, Irony, and Solidarity*. New York: Cambridge University Press, 1989.

Ross, Bernhard H., Levine, Myron A., and Stedman, Murray, Jr. *Urban Politics: Power in Metropolitan Areas*. Itasca, Ill.: Peacock Publishers, 1991, 4th edition.

Rousseau, Jean-Jacques. *The Social Contract and Discourses*. Translated by G. D. H. Cole. New York: E. P. Dutton, 1950. *A Discourse on the Origin and Foundation of Inequality among Men*. (Original publication date: 1755.) *The Social Contract or Principles of Political Right*. (Original publication date: 1762.)

Smith, Adam. *The Theory of Moral Sentiments*. (Original publication date: 1755). Edited by Robert L. Heilbroner. *The Essential Adam Smith*. New York: W. W. Norton & Company, 1987.

Smith, J. Allen. *The Spirit of American Government: A Study of the Constitution: Its Origin, Influence and Relation to Democracy*. New York: Macmillan Company, 1907.

Will, George F. *Men at Work: The Craft of Baseball*. New York: Macmillan Company, 1990.

Woll, Peter. *American Government: Readings and Cases*. Glenview, Ill.: Scott/Foresman, 1990.

ARTICLES, PUBLIC DOCUMENTS, AND VIDEOTAPES

Anderson, David. "The Giant Fan Who Can't Yell," *New York Times*, Sports of the Times, 15 October 1990, p. C4.

Davis, L. J. "Chronicle of a Debacle Foretold: How Deregulation Begat the S&L Scandal," *Harper's*, vol. 281, no. 1684, September 1990, pp. 50–66.

Fein, Naomi. "Confessions of a Gentlewoman Fanatic," *New York Sunday Times*, Sports of the Week, 9 September 1990, p. 9.

Heilbronner, Robert. "Reflections: The Triumph of Capitalism," *The New Yorker*, 23 January 1989.

Harrison, Barbara Grizzuti. Review of George Will, *Men at Work: The Craft of Baseball, New York Times Book Review*, 1 April 1990, pp. 1, 17.

Kramer, Mimi. "Tender Grapes," *The Theatre, The New Yorker*, 2 April 1990, pp. 87–89.

Lemman, Nicholas. "Notes: Healing the Ghettoes," *The Atlantic*, vol. 267, no. 3, March 1991, pp. 20, 22, 24.

Reagon, Bernice Johnson (with Bill Moyers). "The Songs Are Free." (New York: Mystic Fire Video, Inc., No. 76204, 1991).

Sherrill, Robert. "The Looting Decade: S&Ls, Big Banks and Other Triumphs of Capitalism," *The Nation*, vol. 251, no. 17, 12 November 1990, pp. 589–623.

Thomas, Michael M. "The Greatest American Shambles," *New York Review*, vol. 38, no. 3, 31 January 1991, pp. 30–35.

Turner, Victor W. "Myth and Symbol," *International Encyclopedia of the Social Sciences*. Edited by David L. Sills. New York: Macmillan Company, 1968. Vol. 10, pp. 576–82.

United States Federal Election Commission. Release: 19 May 1985.
United States Supreme Court. *Dred Scott v. Sandford*, 19 Howard 393 (1857).
Weisman, Jacob. "Pro-Football—The Maiming Game," *The Nation*, vol. 253, no.
    3, 27 January 1992, pp. 84–87.

Index

About the Author

Prior to his retirement in 1988, Erwin A. Jaffe taught political science at Rutgers University, the University of New Hampshire, New England College, and California State University, Stanislaus. Currently, he lectures at the University of New Hampshire, Manchester.

DATE DUE

			Printed in USA